THE
PSALMS

VOL 3. PSALMS 73–106

JESUS'S PRAYER BOOK

DOUGLAS D. WEBSTER

KREGEL
ACADEMIC

The Psalms: Jesus's Prayer Book (Vol 3. Psalms 73–106)

© 2023 by Douglas D. Webster

Published by Kregel Academic, an imprint of Kregel Publications, 2450 Oak Industrial Dr. NE, Grand Rapids, MI 49505-6020.

The Greek font, GraecaU, is available from www.linguistsoftware.com/lgku.htm, +1-425-775-1130.

ISBN 978-0-8254-4755-6

Printed in the United States of America

23 24 25 26 27 / 5 4 3 2 1

Andrew and Jeanine

CONTENTS

Book 4

ACKNOWLEDGMENTS

I did not set out to write about 150 psalms. My original incentive was to encourage students at Beeson Divinity School to pray and preach the Psalms. However, it wasn't long before I was hooked on my meditative "hobby." My wife Virginia got into the project, reading, critiquing, and interacting with each psalm. These meditations became her morning devotions for several years. I brought her coffee and a psalm, and she contributed insights and edits. Virginia understood that there were times when the intensity of the Psalms matched a deep feeling of being "in the zone" for three or four hours a day.

I am indebted to excellent Old Testament scholars who have guided my preaching, prayer, and meditation on the Psalms over many years of pastoral ministry. My hope is that this work reflects the fruit of their labor and expertise. Their names and works are noted on nearly every page. For five years I met Monday morning with a group of mainly retirees from The Advent in Birmingham. We studied a psalm a week as I road-tested this work with the humblest, sincerest group of saints the Lord could have given me. They were a reminder of the value of the Psalms to shape and strengthen Christ's followers.

I am grateful to the Kregel team for embracing my pastoral approach to the Psalms and their Christ-centered focus. To publish a four-volume work like this is risky, but Laura Bartlett and Robert Hand became my advocates. Robert Hand shepherded this project with wisdom and patience along with Shawn Vander Lugt, Bethany Murphy, Deborah Helmers, and Kevin McKissick. They deserve my deepest gratitude and praise for their excellent work.

PREFACE

My father valued his tools. Back in his day he was a slide-rule–toting mathematician by vocation and a hammer-swinging carpenter by avocation. He loved his tools. He kept track of them, used them for their specific functions, and returned them to their designated places. Nothing made a job go better than having the right tool. My dad took special pride in his wood-turning lathe. A lathe is to a furniture maker what a potter's wheel is to the potter. With practice, my father became skilled in turning out matching table legs. Of all his tools, the lathe is the one that reminds me most of the Psalms: it locks a block of wood in place, rotates the wood at variable speeds by an electric motor, and allows the craftsman's blade to carve the wood into the desired shape. The Psalms are the right tool for shaping our spirituality and giving substance to our communion with God. They are *soul-carving tools*, to use Gregory of Nyssa's metaphor. Each psalm is its own unique instrument, "and these instruments are not alike in shape," but all share the common purpose of "carving our souls to the divine likeness."[1] We have plenty of tools for doing and getting, but as Eugene Peterson insists, we need "the primary technology of the Psalms, essential tools for being and becoming human."[2]

The Psalms are instrumental in the care of souls. John Calvin entitled the Psalms "An Anatomy of all the Parts of the Soul" because there is no emotion that is not represented in the Psalms.[3] Like an MRI, the Psalms are diagnostic. They see deep into the soul, mirror imaging our true condition, whether good or bad: "Though you probe my heart, though you examine me at night and test me, you will find that I have planned no evil; my mouth has not transgressed" (Ps. 17:3). Like a surgeon's scalpel they can cut to the bone in order to heal: "Though you have made me

---

1   Heine, *Gregory of Nyssa's Treatise*, 164–65.
2   Peterson, *Answering God*, 2.
3   Calvin, *Psalms*, 4.1:37.

see troubles, many and bitter, you will restore my life again" (Ps. 71:20). The Psalms render the soul transparent to God and ourselves. "The self is in sound health and free from despair," writes Kierkegaard, "only when, precisely by having been in despair, it is grounded transparently in God."[4]

The Psalms are necessary soul-carving tools in an age of distraction. They require deep thought and sustained commitment. They stand for everything our multitasking, distracted, buffered selves are wired to resist. They are the essential spiritual discipline for overcoming our indifference to communion with God. They call us out of our small worlds into the large world of God's making and redeeming. If we give them a chance, the Psalms will resonate with our souls. They are essential tools for Christian spirituality, but the learning curve can be steep.

If we're honest, praying the Psalms may feel more like speaking a foreign language than speaking our mother tongue. A missionary friend and his young family returned home from France for a summer sabbatical. Four years earlier, the entire family vowed to speak only French when they arrived in France. They were committed to learning the language; consequently, no one in the family spoke a word of their mother tongue, which was English. But when they returned home, after keeping their vow for four years, everyone in the family struggled. They felt awkward speaking their own language. English felt foreign to them. To neglect the Psalms is like refusing to speak our mother tongue. Deep down we have a sense that the Psalms ought to resonate with our souls, but we feel disconnected. We try to access the Psalms the way we look for a Hallmark greeting card. We want a verse that shows we care, a thought that expresses our feelings. We go to the Psalms the way we go to the medicine cabinet to get an aspirin. It is at such times that we wish the Psalms were better organized and indexed to somehow make them more accessible.

In *Deceived by God? A Journey through Suffering*, theologian John Feinberg honestly admits that his extensive study of the problem of evil did little to comfort him when his wife Patricia was diagnosed with Huntington's disease. This genetically transmitted disease involves the premature deterioration of the brain. During seminary, Feinberg wrote his master of divinity thesis on Job. Later, he devoted his master of

---

4   Kierkegaard, *Sickness unto Death*, 163.

theology thesis to God's sovereignty and human freedom. Still absorbed in the problem of evil, he focused his doctoral dissertation on the subject.

Yet after all the years of serious biblical and theological study, he felt as though he had no resource to help him deal with the devastating reality of his wife's life-threatening illness. All of his intellectual work had missed his soul. He was speaking a foreign language. "The truth is," Feinberg admits, "I couldn't figure it out. I had all the intellectual answers, but none of them made any difference in how I felt at the personal level. As a professor of theology, surely I should understand what God was doing in this situation. On the contrary, I began wondering if in fact I really understood anything at all about God. The emotional and psychological pain were unrelenting, and even devastating physical pain resulted from the stress. . . . I was experiencing a religious crisis, and none of this information I had stored away seemed to matter in the least."[5]

What makes Feinberg's book on pain especially worthwhile is his courage to contrast his own spiritual helplessness with his wife's deeply internalized faith. Patricia describes her initial reaction to the bad news:

> I was extremely shocked when this disease was diagnosed. I knew that when physical problems come, one should thank God for his presence and strength in the midst of those problems, rather than becoming bitter. And I knew that I should do that whether I felt like it or not; so that's what I did on the way home in the car. I also knew 1 Thessalonians 5:18, which says, "Give thanks in all circumstances, for this is God's will for you in Christ Jesus." No matter what the circumstances, God is still there, and he is in control of all that happens. He is faithful to his Word. That is reason for thanksgiving, and I continue to thank him each day.[6]

One of the first things that Patricia did was read through the Psalms. She wrote down every reference having to do with God's strength in times of trouble. Psalm 46:1 was especially comforting: "God is our refuge and strength, an ever-present help in trouble." Through prayer, Patricia was able to hear the Word of God in her pain. She wrote, "God made that verse true in my life. I have confidence in his presence, even in the

---

5 Feinberg, *Deceived by God?*, 33–34.
6 Feinberg, *Deceived by God?*, 135.

midst of this disease."[7] She found her voice in the Psalms. She was able to line up the Psalms with her life, finding in them a resource for living. Instead of being crushed by her terminal illness, she testified, "The Lord has given me such complete comfort that I wanted to find ways to share it with others."[8]

Patricia Feinberg's ability to process her experience through the Psalms started with a learned conviction. Her personal narrative was shaped by God's redemptive story. She had a history with God and the people of God before a tragic turn of events. Her practice of the spiritual disciplines did not happen automatically. They were nurtured over time. Patricia turned to the Psalms, as if it was her second nature to do so, only because over the years she was instructed and nurtured to think and act this way. She knew the Psalms the way she knew her mother tongue. The influence may have been subtle and indirect, but it grew out of her experience of the church. The body of Christ played a vital role in helping her embrace the Psalms personally.

We embrace the Psalms because they are God's answer to us and our answer to God. The Psalms hold up both sides of the conversation. We hear the voice of God in the Psalms and we discover our own voice—God's will and our will in dialogue. The Psalms are instruments of grace, tools of being and becoming, that guide us in true spirituality. By praying the Psalms, we learn what it is to be both human and holy in the presence of God. Their rhythmic arrangement, juxtaposing praise and pain, hate and love, saves us from shallow optimism and ornamental spirituality. Through the Psalms we gain a true understanding of ourselves, and we enter into solidarity with the body of Christ. In order to make the Psalms our own, we learn to pray the Psalms on behalf of others—the global church and the household of faith. We pray the Psalms in the light of Christ and in sync with our personal experience. Unselfish skill is required to line up the Psalms with life, to discover the deep correspondence between God's will and the human condition. Perhaps some courage is needed to become a psalm-driven person.

---

7   Feinberg, *Deceived by God?*, 137.
8   Feinberg, *Deceived by God?*, 137.

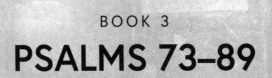

BOOK 3

PSALMS 73–89

PSALM 73

THE ARC OF DEVOTION

A saph and his sons were worship leaders from the tribe of Levi during the reigns of David and Solomon. Asaph was the chief musician in charge of musical accompaniment when they brought the ark of the covenant into Jerusalem (1 Chron. 6:39; 15:17; 16:5). In addition to being a conductor and instrumentalist, he was a poet credited with twelve psalms (Psalms 50, 73–83). "The style of Asaph is distinctive, forceful, and spiritual. He is referred to as a prophet and poet (2 Chron. 29:30; Neh. 12:46)."[1] Although Asaph led the people in worship when the ark was brought into Jerusalem (1 Chron. 15:16–19; 16:4–7, 37) and when the temple was dedicated under Solomon, most of his hymns focus on difficult times.

A CRISIS OF FAITH

> Surely God is good to Israel,
> to those who are pure in heart.
> But as for me, my feet had almost slipped;
> I had nearly lost my foothold.
> For I envied the arrogant
> when I saw the prosperity of the wicked.
> —Psalm 73:1–3

Asaph finds himself in a deep dilemma—a full-blown crisis of faith. His creedal sounding statement rolls off his tongue: "Surely God is good to Israel, to those who are pure in heart." He had said these words in

---

1   Feinberg, "Asaph," 345.

worship a thousand times before. He can say them in his sleep. But now this basic confession produces within him stomach-churning conflict. "Surely God is good to Israel" is in danger of becoming an empty cliché for a troubled soul. His feelings are in turmoil. Feelings pose a real danger when it comes to worshiping God, because "feelings lie. Feelings deceive. Feelings seduce." Peterson claims, "Feelings are the scourge of prayer. To pray by feelings is to be at the mercy of glands and weather and digestion. And there is no mercy in any of them."[2] Feelings are totally unreliable guides for true worship.

Asaph is disillusioned. He was ordained to lead a people in worship who did not know how to worship, nor did they care to learn. Their heart was not in it, and their daily lives opposed it. His conflict was not over liturgical form or musical genre or aesthetics, but over what it meant to worship God. Asaph believed that real worship, that is, worshiping God in spirit and in truth, was meant to produce the fruit of justice and righteousness. Asaph believed that a response to a personal, saving encounter with the living God was intuitively simple and inherently sacrificial. But when he looked around, that was not what he experienced. His creed was being challenged by his life experience.

Unless worship calls us "deeper into God's heart and deeper into the world for which Christ died,"[3] it is not very good worship. It may be safe and everybody in the congregation may be happy, but God, who is the primary audience of our worship, is not pleased. Religious people are capable of going to great lengths to perform high-energy, high-performance worship services, but if they neglect the widow and the orphan, take advantage of the poor, and turn a blind eye to the needy, their worship is a sham. Labberton writes, "That is the crux of the crisis. I and other Christians I know have been busy tithing the dill and cumin of worship forms while avoiding what Jesus calls the weightier matters of the Law: justice, mercy and faith."[4]

Worship can be dangerous *negatively* when we make it about ourselves, rather than about God; when we essentially lie about God and make our "worship" a platform for showcasing our talents or our passions.

---

2   Peterson, *Answering God*, 87.
3   Labberton, *Dangerous Act of Worship*, 35.
4   Labberton, *Called*, 39.

When worship doesn't change us or the world we serve, it is dangerous in a debilitating way. "Millions of American Christians spend hours in worship and yet lead lifestyles indistinguishable in priorities, values and practices from those in the broader culture."[5] Worship is dangerous *positively* when we encounter the living triune God; when it isn't safe, comfortable, or convenient; when it opens us up to the Word of God and lays us out in surrender to the will of God. Worship changes the way we see God, ourselves, and the world—dramatically so!

"But as for me . . .". Honesty prevails in Asaph's crisis of faith. He's in danger of "slip slidin' away" (in the words of the Paul Simon song). He cannot go through the motions. He envies the arrogant because of their prosperity. Evil begets evil. Asaph cannot in good conscience rise in front of his people and lead them in worship. He is tempted to internalize the aspirations of those around him. Evil triggers evil, resulting in bitterness, self-righteousness, and envy. We fall prey to the world's strategies for success. We envy the wealthy and powerful and aim for similar achievements at the expense of compassion, kindness, humility, gentleness, and patience. We lust after money, sex, and power, yet continue to show up for worship and sing hymns.

Asaph confronts his doubts in the best way possible, through prayer. Nineteenth-century Anglican bishop John Perowne said, "Unbelief does not doubt, faith doubts."[6] "The questions asked in this psalm are still asked today: Why do the righteous suffer? Why do the wicked prosper? Why doesn't God remove the wicked from the earth? Why does he look on as though he is unwilling or unable to deal with them the way they deserve? How is the Lord good to the godly?"[7]

THE BEAUTIFUL SIDE OF EVIL

> They have no struggles;
> their bodies are healthy and strong.
> They are free from common human burdens;
> they are not plagued by human ills.
> Therefore pride is their necklace;

---

5   Labberton, *Called*, 74.
6   Quoted in Ross, *Psalms*, 2:555.
7   Okorocha and Foulkes, "Psalms," 678.

they clothe themselves with violence.
From their callous hearts comes iniquity;
their evil imaginations have no limits.
They scoff, and speak with malice;
with arrogance they threaten oppression.
Their mouths lay claim to heaven,
and their tongues take possession of the earth.
Therefore their people turn to them
and drink up waters in abundance.
They say, "How would God know?
Does the Most High know anything?"
This is what the wicked are like—
always free of care, they go on amassing wealth.
                    —Psalm 73:4–12

Asaph is in ethical shock. He is not troubled by the pimp or
prostitute. Ordinary thieves, drug pushers, thugs, common criminals,
and the like are not the ones provoking his envy. He's looking at the
beautiful people. They are athletic, intelligent, photogenic, and envi-
able. He is asking himself, "Why am I writing psalms when I could be
building a palace?" He's eying the elite, the affluent Upper East Side
of a sophisticated culture. What makes these people what they are?
They have pride! They believe in themselves. They radiate their own
special, self-assertive, self-aggrandizing style. They are all dressed up
in ego-power. Their vitality is in their vanity. They clothe themselves
in the violence that sheds no blood but destroys lives. They are armed
with deception and dishonesty. Occasionally goodwill and kind gestures
are part of their deception.

They believe in no-fault morality and insist on making up the rules
as they go. They redefine morality to suit their tastes and whims. Lying
is advertising; manipulation is public relations; infidelity is flexibility;
cheating is evening the odds; immorality is an alternative lifestyle; for-
nication is nothing more than a handshake. "Their mouths lay claim to
heaven," Asaph writes, "and their tongues take possession of the earth"
(v. 9). Talk is everything: flattery, scoffing, threatening, bullying, cursing,
sneering, malicious sarcasm, and cynical disregard for the truth. And
amazingly, people drink up their dogma of success. They have long since
written God off. "They say, 'How would God know? Does the Most
High know anything?'" (v. 11). They have exchanged the living God for

their version of therapeutic deism. Asaph concludes, "This is what the wicked are like—always free of care, they go on amassing wealth" (v. 12).

Ironically, it may have been Solomon and his lavish lifestyle and immorality that provoked Asaph's spiritual struggle. Under Solomon, the character of worship changed, from the relative simplicity of David's time to the elaborate splendor of Solomon's temple. The success of the kingdom was becoming its weakness. Solomon made five hundred shields out of solid gold and a magnificent throne "covered with ivory and overlaid with fine gold" (1 Kings 10:16–18). He imported twelve thousand horses and a zoo of apes and baboons from Africa. He married Pharaoh's daughter and built a new palace for her, because the palace of David had at one time housed the ark of the Lord. He felt uncomfortable bringing a foreign wife into his father's palace (1 Kings 11:2). He reportedly had one thousand wives and concubines. To please them he built shrines to Ashtoreth, Molek, and Chemosh. One can only imagine the difficulty Asaph and his sons must have experienced in leading worship in this pagan, pluralistic atmosphere. Solomon's behavior alone may account for Asaph's crisis of faith.

MORAL PAIN

> Surely in vain I have kept my heart pure
> and have washed my hands in innocence.
> All day long I have been afflicted,
> and every morning brings new punishments.
> —Psalm 73:13–14

For Asaph the arc of devotion began with confession, "Surely God is good to Israel, to those who are pure in heart" (v. 1), and then descended into confusion due to distraction and envy. At this point in the psalm he has hit the murky bottom of despair. Asaph's critique is both valid and dangerous. He is aware of the tension between authentic worship and the world's strategies of success. He is honest with himself, and he is sensitive to moral pain. He discerns how the evil around him, the arrogance, callousness, and injustice is producing evil within him: envy, cynicism, and despair. It is good for Asaph to bring these dark feelings out into the open. His critique of the beautiful side of evil needs to be heard. Honesty is required at every point along the arc of devotion. But

Asaph's spiritual despair is also dangerous. He feels like a fool for refusing to go along with the ways of the world. "I've been stupid to play by the rules; what has it gotten me? A long run of bad luck, that's what—a slap in the face every time I walk out the door" (Ps. 73:13–14 MSG).

We may need to be more honest and allow Asaph's dilemma to surface in our conversations and discussions. I imagine that many have felt either empty or naive for following God's way. At some point we say to ourselves, "Surely in vain I have kept my heart pure" (v. 13). Asaph's feelings are complex and confused. He senses the loss of community. He feels alone and insignificant. He feels the futility and frustration of his longstanding efforts toward faithfulness. He is tempted to buy into the world's quick fixes: fame, wealth, and power. It is at the low point of the arc of devotion that one contemplates alternative paths to significance and self-worth. Impulsive choices are an obvious threat: an affair, extravagant purchases, a distancing between friends, a hardening of one's heart toward worship and others.

THE TURNAROUND

If I had spoken out like that,
I would have betrayed your children.
When I tried to understand all this,
it troubled me deeply
till I entered the sanctuary of God;
then I understood their final destiny.
Surely you place them on slippery ground;
you cast them down to ruin.
How suddenly are they destroyed,
completely swept away by terrors!
They are like a dream when one awakes;
when you arise, Lord,
you will despise them as fantasies.
—Psalm 73:15–20

Asaph's first line of defense against falling away is his loyalty to the people of God. Relationships proved to be a protective buffer. If he said what was on his mind, "Obedience is pointless," or "Faithfulness makes me feel like a fool," he would have betrayed the fellowship of believers. This is sobering because many of us have been raised in a hyper-individualistic culture. Many Christians feel isolated, disconnected, and anonymous. They are out of close fellowship with other Christians. In the Western church this first line of defense is often weak if not nonexistent. The author of Hebrews understood the importance of Christian solidarity. He exhorted believers, "let us draw near to God with a sincere heart. . . . Let us hold unswervingly to the hope we profess. . . . And let us consider how we may spur one another on toward love and good deeds, not giving up meeting together, as some are in the habit of doing, but encouraging one another—and all the more as you see the Day approaching" (Heb. 10:22–25).

Asaph's solidarity with the believing community may keep him faithful, but that doesn't change how he feels. He holds his tongue, but his heart is in turmoil.[8] Ultimately, whether or not we betray "this generation of God's people" depends on our relationship with God. Not letting others down only works for so long. Asaph admits, "When I tried to understand all this, it troubled me deeply till I entered the sanctuary of God; then I understood their final destiny" (vv. 16–17). Asaph's decisive move from "destructive doubt" to "reassuring faith" is made in the sanctuary of God.[9] In worship, Asaph regained perspective. He discovered the importance of faith over feelings. "Worship is an act which develops feelings for God, not a feeling for God which is expressed in an act of worship. When we obey the command to praise God in worship, our deep, essential need to be in relationship with God is nurtured."[10]

Asaph's picture of the beautiful side of evil was shattered in worship. In the sanctuary he discovered the divine perspective. With a renewed focus on the Lord "he was able to put everything in perspective."[11] In the sanctuary he came to understand the human condition in the light

---

8   Okorocha and Foulkes, "Psalms," 679. Cyril Okorocha, Bishop of the Anglican Diocese of Owerri, Nigeria, writes: "It is the mark of Christian maturity to use one's tongue wisely, to encourage rather than discourage others (Prov 12:18). While it is healthy to share our burdens openly with others for prayer and counsel, we must be careful not to discourage others with an attitude of grumbling and complaining, especially if we are in a leadership position or have others to look up to us. Yet there is great blessing in the gift of friends with whom leaders, who are often lonely people, can bare their hearts and experience God's holy refreshing (see Malachi 3:16)."

9   Ross, *Psalms*, 2:561.

10 Peterson, *Long Obedience*, 49–50.

11 Ross, *Psalms*, 2:561.

of God's judgment.[12] Asaph gained a powerful new perspective. He had stated his despair emphatically, "Surely in vain I have kept my heart pure," but now he states his confidence in the judgment of God, "Surely you place them on slippery ground; you cast them down to ruin" (v. 18). Asaph was graphic in his depiction of evil (vv. 3–11), but now he is graphic in his description of judgment. They will be destroyed suddenly, completely swept away. They will vanish like a dream. The wicked are like a nightmare that is over when you wake up. "When you arise, Lord, you will despise them as fantasies" (v. 20).

Solidarity with the people of God was Asaph's first line of defense, but worship in the sanctuary revived his understanding of life's meaning and destiny. He regained God's perspective on true values and moral consequences. Finally, self-examination and repentance restored his personal relationship with God. Instead of being disappointed and disillusioned with God, he became disappointed and disillusioned with himself. The root problem wasn't in God's moral order, nor was it found in the wicked he envied. The problem was in his own heart and soul.

THE STRENGTH OF MY HEART

When my heart was grieved
and my spirit embittered,
I was senseless and ignorant;
I was a brute beast before you.
Yet I am always with you;
you hold me by my right hand.
You guide me with your counsel,
and afterward you will take me into glory.
Whom have I in heaven but you?
And earth has nothing I desire besides you.
My flesh and my heart may fail,
but God is the strength of my heart

---

12 Reardon, *Christ in the Psalms*, 143. Reardon writes: "One of the more characteristic features of the modern world is its growing inability to presume that the moral order, including the social order, is rooted in the metaphysical order. . . . Relatively few people in today's culture seem any longer able to presuppose that they live in a moral universe where the differences between right and wrong, justice and injustice, are fixed in the composition of reality."

and my portion forever.
Those who are far from you will perish;
you destroy all who are unfaithful to you.
But as for me, it is good to be near God.
I have made the Sovereign LORD my refuge;
I will tell of all your deeds.
                                    —Psalm 73:21–28

Although Asaph never acted on his envy, he was greatly disturbed, and it ate away at his soul like a cancer. He never joined the ranks of the wicked or engaged in their self-indulgence. He never participated in their violent and malicious ways—never bullied and oppressed anyone. But he thought about it. He saw how easily his heart was twisted by the prosperity of the wicked. The tension between Asaph's vocational calling and his deep feelings of humiliation could only be resolved through repentance. "When my heart was grieved," Asaph confesses, "and my spirit embittered, I was senseless and ignorant; I was a brute beast before you" (vv. 21–22). His self-description is reminiscent of the patriarch Job, who became convinced that he "must hand the whole matter over completely to God more trustingly, less fretfully."[13] Like Job, Asaph is humbled by God, not humiliated. He does not cower before God; he bows. God's presence is not intimidating; it's inviting. It's not repulsive; it's redemptive. When Job says, "My ears had heard of you but now my eyes have seen you. Therefore I despise myself and repent in dust and ashes" (Job 42:5–6), he is not incriminating himself. He is admitting that he has been woefully ignorant of God's ways. He has misjudged God and drawn wrong conclusions. That is why in the awesome presence of God, Asaph, like Job, is both delighted and ashamed at the same time! He feels like a brute beast—a dumb ox—but whatever foolishness or awkwardness he feels is overwhelmed by the fellowship he experiences. He is chastened, but cherished. Asaph has been learning obedience by the things that he suffered (Heb. 5:8).

The arc of devotion climaxes with Asaph's almost lyrical description of his relationship with Yahweh. The loving bond between them is now more intimate, informed, and enduring. Asaph has gone from distraction and disillusionment to discernment and devotion. "Whom have I

---

13   Andersen, *Job*, 287.

in heaven but you? And earth has nothing I desire besides you" (v. 25). Henry writes, "There is scarcely a verse in all the psalms more expressive than this of the pious and devout affections of a soul to God; here it soars up towards him, follows hard after him, and yet, at the same time, has an entire satisfaction and complacency in him."[14] This is the Old Testament equivalent to the apostle Paul's testimony: "For to me, to live is Christ and to die is gain" (Phil. 1:21), and again, "I have been crucified with Christ and I no longer live, but Christ lives in me. The life I now live in the body, I live by faith in the Son of God, who loved me and gave himself for me" (Gal. 2:20).

Asaph concludes where he began, "But as for me . . ." (Ps. 73:2, 28). Only this time, instead of falling away, he's holding God close. "But as for me, it is good to be near God." He has come full circle. Now he can say with confidence, "Surely God is good to Israel, to those who are pure in heart." As Oliver Wendell Holmes famously said, "I would not give a fig for the simplicity this side of complexity, but I would give my life for the simplicity on the other side of complexity." Asaph has reached the simplicity on the other side of complexity, and he is grateful: "I will tell of all your deeds" (v. 28).

Psalm 73 is at the heart of the Psalms, centered between the profound truth of Psalm 1 and the all-out praise of Psalm 150.[15] Spiritual maturity requires that we experience Asaph's arc of devotion. The journey from Eden's fellowship with God to Christ's rule and reign in the New Jerusalem goes through Calvary.[16] Asaph's turning point came in the sanctuary (Ps. 73:17). Our turning point is at the cross of Christ. This is why the apostle Paul was resolved to know nothing except Jesus Christ and him crucified (1 Cor. 2:2). This is the critical truth that turns everything around. We say with Asaph, "God is the strength of my heart" (v. 26), and we set apart Christ as Lord of our hearts (1 Peter 3:15).

---

14   Henry, *Psalms*, 307.

15   Brueggemann, "Bounded by Obedience and Praise," in *Psalms and the Life of Faith*, 206.

16   Wilcock, *The Message of Psalms*, 2:11. Wilcock writes, "The glories of Psalm 73:24–26, and Psalm 150, and Job 42, and the last two chapters of Revelation, are the glories of Paradise, and Paradise is not Eden. You can get there only by way of Psalm 73:17, which in the New Testament terms is the encounter with God in Christ at Calvary."

The apostles echo the Psalms at every turn, causing us to wonder if the apostle Paul had Asaph's lament in mind when he wrote his powerful defense of the bodily resurrection. Paul concludes 1 Corinthians 15, "'Death has been swallowed up in victory.' . . . The sting of death is sin, and the power of sin is the law. But thanks be to God! He gives us the victory through our Lord Jesus Christ" (vv. 54–57). Paul adds an exhortation that may echo Asaph's lament. Remember what the psalmist said at his lowest point, "Surely in vain I have kept my heart pure and have washed my hands in innocence" (Ps. 73:13). Paul concludes, "Therefore, my dear brothers and sisters, stand firm. Let nothing move you. Always give yourselves fully to the work of the Lord, because you know that your labor in the Lord is not in vain" (1 Cor. 15:58).

WORSHIPING IN A CRISIS

The narrative backstory for Psalm 74 is most likely the Babylonian invasion of Israel in 587/6 BC, when the army of Nebuchadnezzar burned the city of Jerusalem, razed the temple to the ground, and carried anyone or anything of material value back to Babylon. Thousands of Israel's leaders, soldiers, artisans, and skilled craftsmen were taken to Babylon in the first wave of exiles (Jer. 52:28; 2 Kings 24:8–17). The devastation was so extreme that recovery was hardly imaginable (Lam. 2:1–22; Jer. 52:1–30). This powerful communal lament is attributed to the musical tradition of Asaph, whose distinctive poetic style is bold, emotionally raw, and penetrating. It is the spiritual equivalent to being caught in a freezing rainstorm, soaked to the bone and pelted by hail. This kind of worship is not for the fainthearted nominal believer, but is essential for all who follow the Lord Jesus.

The psalmist gives us the words to describe "the extremities of human experience" that we are bound to face.[1] We might like to purge these sorrows from our version of the Christian life, but that is impossible. True faith always suffers. Spurgeon writes, "The history of the suffering church is always edifying; when we see how the faithful trusted and wrestled with their God in times of dire distress, we are thereby taught how to behave ourselves under similar circumstances; we learn moreover, that when fiery trial befalls us, no strange thing happened unto us, we are following the trail of the host of God."[2]

---

1   Brueggemann, *Psalms and the Life of Faith*, 27.
2   Spurgeon, "Psalm 74," *Treasury of David*.

The suffering experienced by Babylon's atrocities is not limited to the sixth century BC. It is consistent with the violence and terror experienced by believers around the world and by believers in the West who run counter to the prevailing worldview. The many forms of violence go beyond the physical to psychological, emotional, and spiritual trauma.

The structure of Psalm 74 is straightforward. The first half describes the utter devastation of everything to do with worship wrought by an enemy zealous to obliterate everything associated with God's name (vv. 1–11). The second half of the psalm appeals to the Lord of the universe whose sovereign power overrules the chaos of nature and who has established his covenant with his people. The psalmist makes a case for the defense of God's defenseless people and for the vindication of God's cause over the fools, foes, adversaries, and enemies that mock and revile his name (vv. 12–23). Against the backdrop of human devastation, the psalmist focuses on what the crisis means for worship. Every aspect of the psalm is intensely God-centered. Everything from destruction to deliverance is under the sovereign will of God. Nothing happens apart from God, and God is the one to address, but God is not to blame for the ruins. Israel's enemies are responsible for waging war against worship, and they will be held accountable.

Lining up Psalm 74 with the persecuted global church is frightfully easy. The burning and desecration of Christian places of worship is a real threat from Syria to Selma. Churches are soft targets for racists, Communists, and Islamic terrorists. Christians living in AD 70, when Rome conquered Jerusalem, had a psalm to pray as Christians do today living in North Korea, Iraq, Syria, China, and northern Nigeria. Even if we are inclined to turn away from the stark reality of evil confronted in this psalm, we are determined to embrace its sober message and turn to God our King. Psalm 74 is a spiritual-formation tool, equipping us with the mental models necessary to focus our attention on the Lord when all hell breaks loose.

RAGE AGAINST WORSHIP

O God, why have you rejected us forever?
Why does your anger smolder against the sheep of your pasture?
Remember the nation you purchased long ago,
the people of your inheritance, whom you redeemed—

Mount Zion, where you dwelt.
Turn your steps toward these everlasting ruins,
all this destruction the enemy has brought on the sanctuary.
Your foes roared in the place where you met with us;
they set up their standards as signs.
They behaved like men wielding axes
to cut through a thicket of trees.
They smashed all the carved paneling
with their axes and hatchets.
They burned your sanctuary to the ground;
they defiled the dwelling place of your Name.
They said in their hearts, "We will crush them completely!"
They burned every place where God was worshiped in the land.
We are given no signs from God;
no prophets are left,
and none of us knows how long this will be.
How long will the enemy mock you, God?
Will the foe revile your name forever?
Why do you hold back your hand, your right hand?
Take it from the folds of your garment and destroy them!
—Psalm 74:1–11

Faith, not unbelief, prompts two heart-wrenching questions to open the psalm and then three at the end to close the first half of the psalm. Faith, not unbelief, addresses God personally, and identifies the worshipers as "the sheep of your pasture." Skeptics and cynics do not address God this way, but believers do. They may be discouraged, even despairing; disoriented, even disgusted—but their devotion to God is real and resilient. When faith is tested and all reason seems to fail, it is faith, not doubt, that asks why. Even in the throes of despair, faith will not let go of the divine reality. The psalmist turns to God in an act of faith. He foreshadows Peter's conviction when Peter spoke on behalf of the disciples, "Lord, to whom shall we go? You have the words of eternal life. We have come to believe and to know that you are the Holy One of God" (John 6:68–69).

Despite the "forever" impact of God's rejection, the communal lament in Psalm 74 is cried in good faith. The psalmist feels like God has walked off and is never coming back. The scene before his eyes must have been post-apocalyptic. The utter devastation goes on forever, as far as the eye can see. The psalmist pleads with the Lord to turn around and come back to "the everlasting ruins" (Ps. 74:3).

Faith, not unbelief, focuses on the destruction of the sanctuary and the dishonor of God. Surely whole villages and towns, along with farms and crops and herds of cattle, were destroyed. The Babylonian conquest meant that men, women, and children were brutally raped, killed, imprisoned, and enslaved. Nevertheless, the psalmist remained focused exclusively on the temple. His passion was centered on the house of God and was consistent with David's plea: "One thing I ask from the LORD, this only do I seek: that I may dwell in the house of the LORD all the days of my life, to gaze upon the beauty of the LORD and to seek him in his temple. For in the day of trouble he will keep me safe in his dwelling" (Ps. 27:4–5). The disaster is wholly understood in the light of its impact on worship and the honor of God, and not on the personal suffering of the people of God.

In the first year of Nebuchadnezzar's reign over Babylon, Jeremiah reminded the people of Judah that for twenty-three years he had spoken the word of the Lord "again and again," but they had not listened (Jer. 25:3). God's warning was as clear as it could be: "Turn now, each of you, from your evil ways and your evil practices, and you can stay in the land the LORD gave to you and your ancestors for ever and ever. Do not follow other gods to serve and worship them; do not arouse my anger with what your hands have made. Then I will not harm you. But," God says, "you did not listen to me" (Jer. 25:5–7).

Reading Psalm 74 against the backdrop of Jeremiah's prophecy (Jer. 25:8–13) causes one to wonder why the psalmist did not allude to the sins of Israel or stress the need for repentance. Surely it is their rejection of God and his ways that precipitated God's rejection of them. But the psalmist says nothing about their culpability and guilt. Instead of discussing sin and repentance, the psalmist equates Nebuchadnezzar's conquest with God's judgment. It is God who is ultimately responsible for the terrible devastation, and the Babylonian army is his instrument of judgment. God has weaponized the enemy.

The time for national confession and repentance is in the past. The sinful nation of Israel has been sentenced and judged. This is why the focus is neither on Israel's sins nor Babylon's conquest. What matters now is how long God's rejection will last. The key word is "forever." "O God, why have you rejected us *forever?*" (Ps. 74:1). The poignancy of the psalm lies in what feels like a never-ending separation—a permanent estrangement. It is into this state of suffering and anguish that the psalmist pleads for God to end his smoldering anger, to acknowledge the sheep of his pasture, to remember his inheritance, to embrace his redeemed and chosen people, and to dwell again on Mount Zion. The psalmist weaves into his communal lament a rich theology of grace that we must not miss in the midst of the suffering. It is right there from the beginning of the psalm.

In the Asaph tradition, the psalmist pictures evil, not in the abstract, but in the vivid detail of an on-the-scene observer who witnesses a mob roaring into the temple, desecrating the sanctuary with pagan graffiti and using axes and hatchets to hack away at the beautiful cedar paneling (1 Kings 6:16–19) as if it were firewood. They smashed the cherubim, stripped the gold, and then lit the Holy of Holies on fire to burn Solomon's temple to the ground. "'We will crush them completely!'" was their cry.

The psalmist's focus here is not on Israel's suffering, but on God's honor. "They defiled the dwelling place of your Name" (Ps. 74:7). His cry is not for the nation but for the name: "How long will the enemy mock you, God? Will the foe revile your name forever?" (v. 10). The psalmist knows that the destiny of the nation lies in the devotion to the name. Only in God is there any hope for salvation, causing the psalmist to cry out, "Why don't you do something? How long are you going to sit there with your hands folded in your lap?" (Ps. 74:11 MSG).

Our praying imagination links Psalm 74 to the apostle John's apocalyptic picture of the suffering saints. When the fifth seal is broken, an extraordinary prayer meeting is revealed (Rev. 6:9–11). The saints who have gone before, who have been "slain because of the word of God and the testimony they had maintained" (Rev. 6:9), are praying for salvation. The saints who can identify with Psalm 74 are those who have suffered for their faith in Christ. Prayer is the link that ties us to the Lord of history. Prayer expresses our shared anticipation of Christ's salvation and judgment and our shared community with those who have gone before.

RISE UP, O GOD, MY KING

Psalm 74, like Psalm 73, makes a decisive shift from lament to confession and from despair to hope. The tale of destruction in the first half of the psalm is matched by a history of God's deliverances. Calvin explains "the simple and natural meaning" of this strategic pivot: "God has wrought on behalf of the chosen people many deliverances, which were as open and manifest as if they had been exhibited in a conspicuous theatre."[3] Who is King Nebuchadnezzar compared to God who reigns in sovereign majesty, and how does the power of the Babylonian army compare to God's power over the universe? As Ross points out, the psalmist reviews "the overwhelming power of God" to tame the chaos of nature and to form the nation of Israel, freeing it from Egyptian bondage. The psalmist appears to have deliberately merged creation and election in language reminiscent of both in order to refute ancient Babylonian and Canaanite myths. He declares in unmistakable ways that the Lord is sovereign over creation and history.[4]

In the midst of political, philosophical, and spiritual wreckage, the psalmist extols the truth of who God is and what God has done. In worship, he reverses the dishonor shown to God and remembers who dried up the Red Sea and split the rock in the wilderness, bringing forth water.[5] The psalmist credits God with the foundational realities that shape life and history: "You own the day, you own the night; you put stars and sun in place. You laid out the four corners of earth, shaped the seasons of summer and winter" (Ps. 74:16–17 MSG).

The psalmist is our worship leader fighting for perspective in the midst of the ruins. He goes back to these fundamental truths and the basic story of God's power to create and redeem. He gives us words to articulate the positive realities hidden in the darkness of evil. He is not reminding God of who he is and what he has done as if God has forgotten. No, his direct address is not for God's benefit but for ours: You split the sea. You broke the heads of the monster. You crushed the heads of Leviathan. You opened up springs and steams. You dried up the ever-flowing rivers. Day is yours. Night is yours. You set the boundaries of the earth. You made summer and winter. He is telling the truth about God, and in the act of worship, we, the people of God, are reminded of the fundament truths that shape our existence and give us hope even when it seems that all is lost.

---

3   Calvin, *Psalms*, 5.2:173.
4   Ross, *Psalms*, 2:586–87.
5   Ross, *Psalms*, 2:588.

By continuing to address God directly, "Remember how the enemy has mocked you, Lord" (v. 18) and "Remember how fools mock you all day long" (v. 22), the psalmist makes his appeal on the basis of God's honor. He pleads with God: "Have regard for your covenant" (v. 20). "Rise up, O God, and defend your cause" (v. 22). The psalmist's primary appeal for God to act rests in his sovereignty rather than in his people's suffering. Nevertheless, he prays on behalf of "the sheep of your pasture" (v. 1), "the nation you purchased long ago" (v. 2), and he pleads with the Lord, "Do not hand over the life of your dove to wild beasts; do not forget the lives of your afflicted people forever" (v. 19). The striking image of the dove endangered by wild beasts underscores the vulnerability, fragility, and weakness of the people of God. We cannot save ourselves. We were never meant to. The church, made up of beatitude-based believers, will never impress the world as anything other than poor and needy. Christians do not belong to the elite. They don't leverage institutional power to shape society. This is not because "they don't believe enough, or try hard enough, or care enough, or think Christianly enough, or have the right worldview."[6] Faithfulness to Christ runs contrary to the dominant culture, and understanding this truth encourages humility, cultivates realism, reduces anxiety, removes false guilt, builds resilience, and encourages prayerful dependence. Futility and cynicism are countered by a realistic appraisal of the power of evil and our dependence upon the Lord.

Nietzsche (1844–1900) despised the biblical description of the believer as a lamb or a dove. He argued that hope in anything other than the will to power is an illusion. If Nietzsche read Psalm 74, he would extol the philosophy of the wild beast and the power of the oppressor. For him there is only the strong man and his will to power. Nietzsche argued that Christianity used the myth of love to foster an illusion. Humanity was falsely educated to believe in something other than the hard fact of exploitation and self-mastery. Nietzsche applied the law of the jungle to the human beast. No one weeps when the lion tears apart its prey, and no one should weep when the noble dominate the weak.

The "forever" possibility played into the deep discouragement of the psalmist. He feared that somehow God's rejection would be forever, that the ruins would be everlasting, and that the Lord would forget the

---

6   Hunter, *To Change the World*, 89.

lives of his afflicted people forever. At the center of the psalm he laments, "We are given no signs from God; no prophets are left, and none of us knows how long this will be" (v. 9). It is understandable that in the wake of the Babylonian invasion and conquest that the psalmist would feel this way. The prophets are silent, and there is no sign of future vindication. Nevertheless Nebuchadnezzar's triumph does not mark the Lord's failure. The Lord's sovereign plan is being worked out "in a manner far more complex, thorough, and slow" than the psalmist can imagine.[7] The trajectory of salvation history leads downward to the manger. God called Abraham out of nowhere to make of him a great nation. Under the patriarchs Isaac, Jacob, and Joseph, the family grew. Then famine led the Israelites into four hundred years of Egyptian bondage. We remember the first exodus when the Israelites escaped from Egypt, crossed the Red Sea, and were led through the wilderness by Moses and Joshua into the Promised Land. The stories of Deborah, Gideon, and Ruth lead us to the epic stories of kings Saul and David. Here Israel is at its height. David's son Solomon begins the descent.

The kingdom is divided between Jeroboam's Israel in the north and Rehoboam's Judah in the south. Against a litany of bad kings, Elijah and Elisha keep Israel's history alive. From there the story line belongs to the prophets. It is hard to keep sixteen prophets straight. Their ministry, from Joel to Malachi, spans four hundred long years. Joel, Jonah, Amos, Hosea, Isaiah, Micah, Nahum, Zephaniah, and Jeremiah tried to turn the hearts of the people to God. Embedded in their message is the story of the coming Messiah. God judges his people and sends them into exile. The Babylonian captivity runs for seventy years. Habakkuk, Daniel, Ezekiel, Obadiah, Haggai, Zechariah, and Malachi cover this period. This is where Nehemiah and Ezra come in as well.

The first exodus was powerful. God's ten plagues, the Passover meal, and the solidarity of the people of Israel leaving Egypt in mass, crossing the Red Sea on dry ground, feeding on manna in the wilderness, and receiving the law on Mount Sinai all add up to a spectacular defining moment. The second exodus from Babylon was nothing by comparison. Israel trekked back to their homeland as refugees. Nehemiah and Ezra describe a beleaguered people, barely hanging on. When the temple was

---

7   Wilcock, *The Message of Psalms*, 2:15.

rebuilt, those who remembered the glory days of Solomon's temple cried, because they knew the difference between the glory of the past and the reality of the present. Malachi's cry for faithfulness is the last word in this downward trajectory, followed by four hundred years of silence. The people of God, through whom God designed to bless all the nations, was taken down to rock bottom. The descent of the Messiah was preceded by the descent of the people of God.

All the work that went into postexilic Israel was God's way of building a cradle for his ultimate revelation. God restored the Jewish people, the Jerusalem temple, the Mosaic law, the Passover, the sacrificial system, the priesthood, and the walls of Jerusalem in order to cradle the Incarnate One. And even though everything was on a smaller scale than the first exodus and Solomon's temple, and even though there was more struggle and less excitement, anticipation grew. There was no room for pride of country and race among a people humbled by God and looking for his mercy and justice. The Promised Land may have been less promising than in the days of Moses, but the Promised One was coming and God was at work. "Today in the town of David a Savior has been born to you; he is the Messiah, the Lord. This will be a sign to you: You will find a baby wrapped in cloths and lying in a manger" (Luke 2:11–12).

THE SET TIME

Psalm 75 is a response to Psalm 74 in several key ways. The negative "forever" reference in Psalm 74 is eclipsed by the psalmist's positive declaration of praise to the God of Jacob—praise that lasts *forever* (v. 9). In Psalm 75 God responds in the first person (vv. 2, 3, 4, 10) to the communal lament of Psalm 74. Instead of using the second person, "you" and "yours," for God, the psalmist quotes God directly, saying, "I choose the appointed time; it is I who judge with equity," and "It is I who hold its pillars firm," and "I will cut off the horns of all the wicked." The psalmist feels God's nearness, not his distance, because he is confident that the Lord will act, knowing that God has set the time for judgment and salvation.

The sequence of Psalms 73–75 may link Asaph's worship tradition with Israel's history of internal apostasy (Psalm 73), followed by the Babylonian conquest (Psalm 74), and climaxing in God's judgment of Israel's oppressors (Psalm 75). Psalm 73 describes the failure of the people of God to maintain even a semblance of faithfulness. The true worshiper struggles against a growing tide of popular religiosity, concluding, "But as for me, it is good to be near God" (Ps. 73:28). Psalm 74 describes the total destruction of the temple, recounts the eternal sovereignty of God, and ends by pleading with God to remember his people and defend his cause. The personal and communal laments of Psalms 73 and 74 give way to praise and the assurance of God's vindication in Psalm 75. The themes of the nearness of God and the certainty of divine judgment are celebrated.

THE NEARNESS OF GOD

> We praise you, God,
>   we praise you, for your Name is near;
> people tell of your wonderful deeds.
>   —Psalm 75:1

The psalm opens with a burst of praise against the backdrop of personal pain and communal lament. With minimal words, the psalmist introduces a sharp reversal of discouragement. The mood of desperation is swept aside, and in its place are praise and thanksgiving for God's nearness and wondrous deeds. All he needs to say is "your Name is near" to eclipse the darkness. The name of God represents who God is and what God has done. It represents everything about God. For today's worshipers, the "nearness of the Name" is best understood in the person of Jesus, the Christ. Jesus is God's autobiography to the world.[1] The only God to be known is the one true and living God revealed in Jesus Christ. God's very own self-representation is manifest through incarnation, mission, passion, ascension, intercession, and the coming consummation. When Jesus says, "I have revealed [your name]," he echoes his previous line, "I have brought you glory" (John 17:4). Jesus has made God visible, his message clear, and his name known. We cannot know God apart from Jesus. The Bible is emphatic on this truth: "No one who denies the Son has the Father; whoever acknowledges the Son has the Father also" (1 John 2:23).

Jesus refers to the *Name* six times in his high priestly prayer in John 17. The *Name* stands for the *personal* revelation of God, his character and his actions. The *Name* sums up everything about the person and work of the triune God. It is more testimony than the whole of doctrinal tradition and more personal narrative than all the wisdom of creedal confession. It is about *who* rather than *what*. Jesus said to Philip, "Anyone who has seen me has seen the Father. . . . Believe me when I say that I am in the Father and the Father is in me" (John 14:9, 11).

The personal nature of the *Name* reminds us that Jesus's legacy is not "a body of teaching preserved in a book—like the Qur'an. He does not leave behind an ideal or a program. He leaves behind a community—the Church."[2] The story—the long story—behind the *Name* goes back to Exodus, when Moses asked for God's name. How could Moses be God's representative to the people and not know the name of God? God said to Moses, "I AM WHO I AM. This is what you are to say to the Israelites: 'I AM has sent me to you'" (Exod. 3:14). By revealing himself in this way, God empowered Moses *personally* to lead the people of Israel out of

---

1   Bruner, *John*, 967.
2   Newbigin, *Light Has Come*, 228.

Egypt. Similarly, the Son's revelation of the *Name*—"If you really know me, you will know my Father as well"—empowers Christ's disciples to be sent out on their mission.[3]

The early church was convinced that Jesus was the revelation of God, the culmination of a long history of revelation, the very self-disclosure of God. The exclusive truth claim of the gospel fits with the purpose of God's promise from the beginning. God chose one, small, weak, insignificant nation through which to make himself known and bless the world. The exclusiveness of the gospel is consistent with the character of revelation and the nature of God's own self-disclosure.

There are not many gods to know, as the Canaanites or the Greeks or Hindus believed, but only one God. All the rest are idols. Neither is God a vague abstraction, a nameless, undefined, indistinguishable being or force or feeling or projection. God's self-disclosure is more definite, definable, specific, and singular than we can fully grasp—more than we can completely comprehend, not less! If we consider our own person-hood as distinctive and unique, how could God, the very Author of Life and Maker of the Universe, be any less? If our sense of self recoils at the notion of being just one of the masses, we can be assured that the Lord God is no less a person than we are. There is in fact only one you! And there is in truth only one God! The Word of God declares, "I am the LORD your God. . . . You shall have no other gods before me. You shall not make for yourself an [idol]" (Exod. 20:3–4). "Hear, O Israel: The LORD our God, the LORD is one. Love the LORD your God with all your heart and with all your soul and with all your strength" (Deut. 6:4–5).

The apostles believed that the promise of God given to Abraham, that "all peoples on earth will be blessed through you" (Gen. 12:3), is fulfilled in Jesus. And each subsequent stage of salvation history, from Moses to the prophets, from Jeremiah to David, anticipated the Savior—not an ethnic Savior, not a cultural religion, nor a tribal deity, but the Savior of the world (John 3:16). The one and only way makes sense because of the one and only Son![4] We cannot celebrate the wondrous deeds of God without telling about the one who has made God known in the most personal way possible. God has drawn near in person.

---

3   Webster, *God Who Prays*, 66–69.
4   Webster, *God Who Prays*, 59.

THE SOVEREIGNTY OF GOD

> You say, "I choose the appointed time;
> it is I who judge with equity.
> When the earth and all its people quake,
> it is I who hold its pillars firm.
> To the arrogant I say, 'Boast no more,'
> and to the wicked, 'Do not lift up your horns.
> Do not lift up your horns against heaven;
> do not speak so defiantly.'"
>   —Psalm 75:2–5

The psalmist's reference to Elohim emphasizes the universal truth and testimony of God's sovereignty. God's set time for judgment and salvation is not peculiar to the people of God, but universally applicable for all people everywhere. The psalmist quotes God's direct address to everyone, not just to the people of God. Four first-person "I" statements emphatically declare that God is sovereign over the timing of judgment, the administration of justice, the moral order of the universe, and the bravado of the wicked.

The "set time" of judgment has never been in doubt, but the day and hour remains a mystery. Jesus said, "But about that day or hour no one knows, not even the angels in heaven, nor the Son, but only the Father. Be on guard! Be alert! You do not know when that time will come" (Mark 13:32–33). Even "when the earth and all its people quake" (Ps. 75:3), God is in control of the physical universe and the social and political structures of the human race.[5] The earth is in its God-ordained orbit; "he is before all things, and in him all things hold together" (Col. 1:17). The apostles attribute this sovereignty to the Son, through whom God made the universe; he "[sustains] all things by his powerful word" (Heb. 1:2–3).

The psalmist quotes God's staccato commands to the arrogant and the wicked *verbatim*. The image of the ram's "horn" stands for strength and power (Deut. 33:17; 1 Sam. 2:1, 10), and stiff-necked arrogance symbolizes smart-aleck resistance. But with God nothing is left to chance. His commands are emphatic. There is no ambiguity in "Boast no more!" There is no doubt in God's "do nots:" "Do not lift your horns against heaven; do not speak so defiantly" (Ps. 75:5). The voice of God renders

---

5   Wilcock, *The Message of Psalms*, 2:15.

the wicked power brokers powerless. Psalm 75 echoes Hannah's prayer (1 Sam. 2:1–10) against the arrogant talk of the wicked and foreshadows Mary's song of deliverance (Luke 1:46–55). God brings down the wicked and exalts the poor.

THE JUST JUDGMENT OF GOD

> No one from the east or the west
> or from the desert can exalt themselves.
> It is God who judges:
> He brings one down, the exalts another.
> In the hand of the LORD is a cup
> full of foaming wine mixed with spices;
> he pours it out, and all the wicked of the earth
> drink it down to its very dregs.
> [But] As for me, I will declare this forever;
> I will sing praise to the God of Jacob,
> who says, "I will cut off the horns of all the wicked,
> but the horns of the righteous will be lifted up."
> —Psalm 75:6–10

Israel's kings tried to establish alliances with surrounding nations for protection and security. Since Babylon is identified as the enemy from the north, Israel may very well be tempted to look east, west, and south for help.[6] The psalmist, like the prophets, counseled against these alliances. Israel's hope must be in the Lord alone. Humble dependence upon God is essential for their deliverance. Jesus's Beatitudes echo this theme. We cannot save ourselves. Blessed are those who know they are poor and needy and who see themselves as completely dependent upon the Lord for their salvation. Any effort toward self-salvation exposes the myth of self-sufficiency. The implication is that we are quick to measure our lives by what we achieve rather than what we receive from the Lord. We prefer our own means and methods to the mercy of God and the state of grace.

The psalmist reminds us that God alone saves and judges: "He brings one down, he exalts another" (Ps. 75:7). The cup of wrath symbolizes God's judgment against the arrogant and wicked who refuse to turn to God for mercy. The metaphor of the cup of judgment is used throughout

---

6   See Ross, *Psalms*, 2:603; Delitzsch, *Psalms*, 2:340.

Scripture (Isa. 51:17; Jer. 25:15–38; 49:12; 51:7; Rev. 16:19; 18:6). In the end, Babylon the Great, the biblical symbol for all cultures and peoples that are antithetical to the kingdom of God, is given "the cup filled with the wine of the fury of [God's] wrath" (Rev. 16:19).

The end of evil will not come about through legal reform or advances in education or a thriving global economy or international efforts for world peace. Evil will only come to an end in God's final judgment. The will to power and the weapons of this world will not achieve the end of evil. With that said, the Christian is called to be salt and light in a decaying and dark world, not because of the promise of reform, but because of the promise of salvation. Jesus intends his followers to penetrate their culture the way rubbed-in salt penetrates meat to prevent it from going bad. Jesus does not say, "You are the sugar of the earth" or "You are the honey of the world." German theologian Helmut Thielicke speaks of the biting quality of true Christian witness: there is a natural temptation for Christians to "sweeten and sugar the bitterness of life with an all too easy conception of a loving God."[7] Jesus expected his followers to be an essential preservative in a culture bent on evil. We enter into this mission for the good of the world, knowing that the evil of the world will not end until God's wrath is poured out.[8]

The Asaph tradition characteristically casts a large vision that is applied personally (Pss. 73:28; 74:12; 75:9). Psalm 75 concludes decisively: "[But] as for me, I will declare this forever; I will sing praise to the God of Jacob" (v. 9). The hopeless fear of rejection forever (Ps. 74:1, 19) is overcome in the psalmist's personal declaration to praise the God of Jacob forever. The emphatic "I" statements of God (Ps. 75:2, 4) inspire the psalmist's own "I" statements. He is empowered to say, "I will declare. . . . I will sing praise," because God is sovereign over judgment and salvation: "I will cut off the horns of all the wicked, but the horns of the righteous will be lifted up" (v. 10). The psalmist's emphatic "I" statements point forward to the apostle Paul's "I" statement: "But by the grace of God I am what I am, and his grace to me was not without effect" (1 Cor. 15:10).

---

7   Thielicke, *Life Can Begin Again*, 28.
8   Webster, *Follow the Lamb*, 224.

GOD BREAKS THE POWER OF EVIL

Psalm 76 links God's renown in Judah with the universal judgment of God at the end of time. God's defense of Jerusalem against vicious and valiant warriors by means of a mere rebuke is a precursor to the finality of his wrath against humankind. Such power inspires God's people to praise and motivates the kings of neighboring lands to submit reverently and to humbly "bring gifts to the One to be feared" (Ps. 76:11).

The Asaph tradition keeps the big picture of God's story before us. The total destruction of Jerusalem by Nebuchadnezzar and the Babylonian army (Psalm 74) is a marked exception to God's protection of Israel made necessary by her flagrant apostasy (Psalm 73). The psalmist sees the just judgment of Israel as a precedent for God's universal judgment and calls on God to remember his people and vindicate his name (Psalm 75). Psalm 76 celebrates the victory of that historical judgment as proof of God's ultimate power and justice and looks forward to the time when God will break "the spirit of rulers" and the kings of the earth will submit (v. 12).

When Jesus said to Pilate, "My kingdom is not of this world" (John 18:36), he signaled the underlining truth that shaped salvation history from the beginning (Gen. 12:3). He exchanged ethnic privilege and local geography for the global church. The Great Commission and Pentecost ushered in the Gentile mission and a new perspective on the universal impact of the gospel. "What neither the Old Testament nor Jesus revealed [explicitly] was the radical nature of God's plan, which was that the theocracy (the Jewish nation under God's rule) would be terminated, and replaced by a new international community, the church."[1] This is why Paul says, "God placed all things under his feet and appointed him to be head over everything for the church, which is his body" (Eph. 1:22–23). The scope of salvation is as global as it is personal. The church encompasses "the fullness of him who fills everything in every way" (Eph. 1:23). God's plan is "to bring unity to all things in heaven and on earth under Christ" (Eph. 1:10).

The true Jew is no longer a matter of race and ritual. As the apostle Paul explains, "No, a person is a Jew who is one inwardly; and circumcision is circumcision of the heart, by the Spirit, not by the written code" (Rom. 2:29). The true children of Abraham received Christ, who was not only the Messiah to the Jews, but the Savior of the world. They proclaimed the gospel to Jew and Gentile alike. "So in Christ Jesus you are all children of God through faith, for all of you who were baptized into Christ have clothed yourselves with Christ. There is neither Jew nor Gentile, neither slave nor free, nor is there male and female, for you are all one in Christ Jesus. If you belong to Christ, then you are Abraham's seed, and heirs according to the promise" (Gal. 3:26–29). Jesus prayed Psalm 76 in a radically new way, and Christians today follow his lead. The Lion of Judah has become the Savior of the world.[2]

GOD'S REBUKE

> God is renowned in Judah;
> in Israel his name is great.
> His tent is in Salem,
> his dwelling place in Zion.
> There he broke the flashing arrows,
> the shields and the swords, the weapons of war.
> You are radiant with light,

---

1   Stott, *God's New Society*, 118.
2   Augustine, *Expositions on the Book of Psalms*, 8:356. Commenting on the true Jew, Augustine writes: "They then are more truly Jews, who have been made Christians out of Jews: the rest of the Jews, who in Christ have not believed, have deserved to lose even the very name. The true Judea, then, is the Church of Christ, believing in that King, who hath come out of the tribe of Judah through the Virgin Mary; believing in Him of whom the Apostle [spoke], 'Be thou mindful that Jesus Christ hath risen from the dead, of the seed of David, after my Gospel' (2 Tim 2:8). For of Judah is David, and out of David is the Lord Jesus Christ."

more majestic than mountains rich with game.
The valiant lie plundered,
they sleep their last sleep;
not one of the warriors
can lift his hands.
At your rebuke, God of Jacob,
both horse and chariot lie still.

—Psalm 76:1–6

Secular history examines "the great civilizations of Assyria and Egypt, of Babylon, Persia, Greece and Rome, but Israel (if it figures at all) will hardly be more than a blip on their mental horizon," Bray writes. He continues, "To write the history of antiquity putting Israel at the center is rather like writing the history of Europe from the standpoint of Luxembourg, a country that is geographically central but otherwise insignificant."[3] Salvation history departs from the world's criteria of greatness and focuses on God's strategy of redemption. God chose a small, insignificant people through whom to bless all people. He pitched his metaphoric tent in the arid land of Palestine, in a town named Salem, meaning "peace" (Gen. 14:18). This shocking particularity narrows salvation's course of action to a specificity that seems incredible, yet perfectly consistent with everything else about creation and redemption. Lewis writes,

> Out of enormous space a very small portion is occupied by matter at all. Of all the stars, perhaps very few, perhaps only one, have planets. Of the planets in our own system probably only one supports organic life. In the transmission of organic life, countless seeds and spermatozoa are emitted: some few are selected for the distinction of fertility. Among the species only one is rational. Within that species only a few attain excellence of beauty, strength, or intelligence.[4]

Divine selection is based on mercy, not merit. Covenant love is extended to the smallest and the weakest, not the best and brightest (Deut. 7:7–9). "The 'chosen' people are chosen not for their own sake (certainly not for their own honor or pleasure) but for the sake of the unchosen. Abraham is told that 'in his seed' (the chosen nation) 'all nations will be

---

3   Bray, *God Is Love*, 38.
4   Lewis, *Miracles*, 121.

blest.' That nation has been chosen to bear a heavy burden. Their sufferings are great: but, as Isaiah recognized, their sufferings heal others."[5]

The descent of God into human history reaches its climax in the
incarnation. "The Word became flesh and made his dwelling among us.
We have seen his glory, the glory of the one and only Son, who came from
the Father, full of grace and truth" (John 1:14). We can hardly imagine
the shocking truth of the incarnation—the "vastness of God confined in
the womb of a maid."[6] In God's redemptive strategy, Jesus was "born of a
woman, born under the law, to redeem those under the law" (Gal. 4:4–5).
His lowly birth in Bethlehem symbolizes the shock of God's descent into
human history. The humility of God "dwelling in the land of Zion" is
transcended by an even greater humility. The Incarnate One, Jesus Christ,
"who, being in very nature God . . . made himself nothing by taking the
very nature of a servant, being made in human likeness" (Phil. 2:6–7).

The word the psalmist uses to describe God's "abode" or "dwelling place"
in Zion may refer to a dense thicket or lion's lair (Amos 3:4; Jer. 25:38), implying that Zion is home to the Lion of the tribe of Judah.[7] God is powerful
to protect his people against the weapons of war. The Israelite foot soldier
feared a squadron of horse-driven chariots. Today we fear a suitcase-sized
nuclear smart bomb. But no matter how ingenious the weapons of war
may be, they are no match for God's thunderbolts and pathogens. The
God of Jacob is able to stop an army in its tracks and render the powerful
powerless with a simple rebuke (Isa. 37:36; 2 Kings 19:35). The image of
God fighting for his people finds its ultimate redemptive trajectory in God's
defeat of sin and death. "In this world you will have trouble," Jesus said,
"But take heart! I have overcome the world" (John 16:33). And in the face
of danger the apostle Paul said, "But thanks be to God, who always leads
us as captives in Christ's triumphal procession and uses us to spread the
aroma of the knowledge of him everywhere" (2 Cor. 2:14).

GOD'S WRATH

It is you alone who are to be feared.
Who can stand before you when you are angry?

---

5   Lewis, *Miracles*, 122.
6   Clarkson, *A Singing Heart*, 104.
7   Ross, *Psalms*, 2:615; Delitzsch, *Psalms*, 2:344.

From heaven you pronounced judgment,
and the land feared and was quiet—
when you, God, rose up to judge,
to save all the afflicted of the land.
Surely your wrath against mankind brings you praise,
and the survivors of your wrath are restrained.
Make vows to the LORD your God and fulfill them;
let all the neighboring lands
bring gifts to the One to be feared.
He breaks the spirit of rulers;
he is feared by the kings of the earth.

—Psalm 76:7–12

The psalmist moves from God's protection of Israel to God's ultimate eschatological fulfillment. "The action is no longer localized, or past, or defensive. God is foreseen striking the final blow against evil everywhere, as Judge."[8] Far from being an embarrassment, the wrath of God is cause for praise. God's wrath does not mean "the intemperate outburst of an uncontrolled character. It is rather the temperature of God's love, the manifestation of his will and power to resist, to overcome, to burn away all that contradicts his counsels of love."[9] The wicked are condemned; the righteous vindicated. The psalmist's rhetorical question to God, "Who can stand before you when you are angry?" is echoed by the prophet Malachi in his prophecy of the Lord's second coming (Mal. 3:2). It is also vividly described in the opening of the sixth seal in the apostle John's apocalypse (Rev. 6:12–17). John elaborates on the meaning of Psalm 76 as he captures the finality of the end. The sixth seal moves from the chaos of evil to the coming cataclysmic undoing of everything that opposes God. The reality of judgment reassures believers that justice will prevail. Evil will come to an end in God's final judgment.

The purpose of God's wrath is salvation, "to save all the afflicted [meek, humble] of the land" (Ps. 76:9). The scope of God's justice is not limited to the land of Israel, but extends to the whole world. Kidner writes, "His little kingdom of verses 1–3 was His bridgehead, never His boundary. This was as wide as the earth, and His objective the salvation

---

8   Kidner, *Psalms 73–150*, 275.
9   Barth, *Ephesians 1–3*, 231–32.

of 'all poor men and humble' (Ps. 76:9b)."[10] Human anger and wrath is like fuel for the fire of God's purifying wrath. God consumes everything that is used against him. The psalmist pictures God taking the wrath of humankind and belting it around his waist, arming himself for battle with the evil of humanity. The image implies that humanity brings down upon itself the judgment of its own evil ways.

Spurgeon captures the truth of the psalm when he writes,

> Let men and devils rage as they may, they cannot do otherwise than subserve the divine purposes. The remainder of wrath shalt thou restrain. Malice is tethered and cannot break its bounds. The fire which cannot be utilised shall be damped. Some read it "thou shalt gird," as if the Lord girded on the wrath of man as a sword to be used for his own designs, and certainly men of the world are often a sword in the hand of God, to scourge others. The verse clearly teaches that even the most rampant evil is under the control of the Lord, and will in the end be overruled for his praise.[11]

In the meantime, while we wait for God's final judgment and the end of evil, the psalmist counsels obedience—deep obedience and sacrificial gifts to "the One to be feared" (Ps. 76:11). We are encouraged to submit to the One who has the power to break "the spirit of rulers" (v. 12). The psalmist's universal warning to "the neighboring lands" (v. 11) and "the kings of the earth" (v. 12) corresponds to the warning given in Psalm 2: "Therefore, you kings, be wise; be warned, you rulers of the earth. Serve the LORD with fear and celebrate his rule with trembling" (Ps. 2:10–11; see Rev. 19:11–16).

---

10   Kidner, *Psalms 73–150*, 275.
11   Spurgeon, "Psalm 76," *Treasury of David*.

PSALM 77

THE ARC OF GRIEF

Psalm 77 is in the Asaph tradition, and not surprisingly the poet expresses raw emotion and deep anguish over intense suffering. The psalmist feels this suffering is unjust and out of character with God's promises. He feels utterly rejected and abandoned by God. It is as if everything he ever believed about God, his promises, his unfailing love, and his compassion, has vanished into thin air *forever* (Ps. 74:1, 10, 19). But then the poet makes a sudden transition that raises in sharp relief the miraculous history of God's redemptive intervention and salvation. These quick transitions are part of the Asaph style (Pss. 73:15; 74:12; 75:9). The psalmist remembers the exodus miracle and the power of God over the forces of nature. Great grief is transformed into the genuine hope of salvation history.

If the underlying historical crisis is the Babylonian captivity, as described in Psalm 74, we can see how sincere and faithful believers who have not "lost their foothold" nor "envied the arrogant" nor "clothed themselves in violence" (Ps. 73:2, 3, 6) could feel deep anguish and righteous sorrow as they experience the total destruction of Jerusalem. Psalm 77 stands in the faithful tradition of Jeremiah, as well as Asaph. It wrestles with the harsh realities of becoming collateral damage in God's judgment. Faithful, innocent people suffered along with evildoers and idolaters. The vicarious experience of abandonment foreshadows the vicarious suffering of Christ, when "God made him who had no sin to be sin for us, so that in him we might become the righteousness of God" (2 Cor. 5:21).

A GRIEF OBSERVED

I cried out to God for help;
I cried out to God to hear me.
When I was in distress, I sought the Lord;

at night I stretched out untiring hands,
and I would not be comforted.
I remembered you, God, and I groaned;
I meditated, and my spirit grew faint.
You kept my eyes from closing;
I was too troubled to speak.
I thought about the former days,
the years long ago;
I remembered my songs in the night.
My heart meditated and my spirit asked:
"Will the Lord reject forever?
Will he never show his favor again?
Has his unfailing love vanished forever?
Has his promise failed for all time?
Has God forgotten to be merciful?
Has he in anger withheld his compassion?"
                                        —Psalm 77:1–9

There is no hint of repentance, suggesting that the psalmist did not
bring on this distress. He is caught up in consequences not of his making,
actions provoked by others for which he is not responsible. Nevertheless
he suffers. He is distraught, exhausted, and conflicted. He questions God's
favor. He doubts God's unfailing love, which it seems has vanished forever.
He longs for God's mercy, but what he feels is God's anger. "No one ever
told me," wrote Lewis, "that grief felt so like fear. I am not afraid, but
the sensation is like being afraid. The same fluttering in the stomach, the
same restlessness, the yawning. I keep on swallowing."[1]

First-person singular pronouns heighten the poignancy of the psalmist's
plea, but his lament is thoroughly God centered. With every ounce of energy and in every waking moment, he cries out to God for help. Instead of
escape, he seeks the Lord in his distress. "I cried . . . I sought . . . I stretched
out untiring hands . . . I remembered . . . I groaned . . . [I] meditated,"
but all of his effort is to no avail. Doubt surges, comfort eludes him, and
his soul grows faint. He cannot sleep; he cannot speak. Every memory of
God's blessing only causes him pain. He remembers his songs in the night,
but now they seem like a cruel joke, because he feels rejected, forgotten,
abandoned. Nevertheless, the lament is radically God-centered.

---

1   Lewis, *Grief Observed*, 1.

The psalmist gives free reign to his doubt and pain. He asks six heart-wrenching rhetorical questions, beginning with, "Will the Lord reject forever?" and ending with, "Has he in anger withheld his compassion?" Implicit in these questions is the fact that the Lord, and no one else, is the psalmist's principal source for communion, favor, love, promise, mercy, and compassion. The absence of these vital provisions means the absence of life itself. For the psalmist and the people of God, this is the most graphic way to describe their dire situation. He therefore prays, expecting God to answer him and to prove that God has not forgotten his people. The questions may be "a not-so-subtle prod for God to demonstrate his favor, love, grace, and compassion here and now."[2]

The psalmist did not choose this suffering, but a crisis not of his making presented him with a choice: reject God, indulge in self-pity, or turn to God in faith. Theologian Jerry Sittser suffered the loss of his wife, daughter, and mother in a terrible car crash caused by a drunk driver. Sittser came to see that choice is key. "We can run from the darkness, or we can enter into the darkness and face the pain of loss. . . . We can return evil for evil, or we can overcome evil with good. It is this power to choose that adds dignity to our humanity and gives us the ability to transcend our circumstances, thus releasing us from living as mere victims. These choices are never easy."[3] The psalmist exercises his choice by bringing his lament to God with everything he has. All of his doubts and fears, all of his despair and anger, are brought raw into the presence of God through prayer. Devotion to God becomes the means by which loss is vented, examined, and offered up to God.

The first half of the psalm ends on a question. The psalmist's life is up in the air, held in suspension between doubt and devotion. "And grief still feels like fear," wrote Lewis. "Perhaps, more strictly, like suspense. Or like waiting; just hanging about waiting for something to happen. It gives life a permanently provisional feeling."[4] We have no way of knowing how long these questions filled the psalmist's mind or how long his memories of God's blessing caused more torment than comfort. It is fair to say that the psalm edits the narrative of hours of waiting and longing—the blank

---

2   Ross, *Psalms*, 2:636.
3   Sittser, *Grace Disguised*, 46.
4   Lewis, *Grief Observed*, 38.

space that cannot be put into words. "Loss creates a barren present, as if one were sailing on a vast sea of nothingness." Sittser continues, "Those who suffer loss live suspended between a past for which they long and a future for which they hope."[5]

A GRIEF TRANSCENDED

> Then I thought, "To this I will appeal:
> the years when the Most High stretched out his right hand.
> I will remember the deeds of the LORD;
> yes, I will remember your miracles of long ago.
> I will consider all your works
> and meditate on all your mighty deeds."
> Your ways, God, are holy.
> What god is as great as our God?
> You are the God who performs miracles;
> you display your power among the peoples.
> With your mighty arm you redeemed your people,
> the descendants of Jacob and Joseph.
> The waters saw you, God,
> the waters saw you and writhed;
> the very depths were convulsed.
> The clouds poured down water,
> the heavens resounded with thunder;
> your arrows flashed back and forth.
> Your thunder was heard in the whirlwind,
> your lightning lit up the world;
> the earth trembled and quaked.
> Your path led through the sea,
> your way through the mighty waters,
> though your footprints were not seen.
> You led your people like a flock
> by the hand of Moses and Aaron.
> —Psalm 77:10–20

The turning point in the psalm comes suddenly and unexpectedly without reference to outside wisdom or a change in the situation. The language is terse, and linguists have wrestled with the psalmist's

---

5   Sittser, *Grace Disguised*, 66.

intended meaning.[6] The NIV anticipates the verbs that follow, "I will remember," "I will consider . . . and meditate," by adding the phrase, "Then I thought . . .". This signals a remarkable shift from doubt and despair to the first inklings of confidence and hope. Spurgeon clarifies the terse poetry of Psalm 77:10 and draws out the meaning of this critical pivot:

> Here a good deal is supplied by our translators, and they make the sense to be that the psalmist would console himself by remembering the goodness of God to himself and others of his people in times gone by: but the original seems to consist only of the words, "the years of the right hand of the most High," and to express the idea that his long continued affliction, reaching through several years, was allotted to him by the Sovereign Lord of all. It is well when a consideration of the divine goodness and greatness silences all complaining, and creates a childlike acquiescence.[7]

"Feelings, and feelings, and feelings," remarked Lewis. "Let me try thinking instead."[8] The psalmist endeavored to remember the Lord's great acts of deliverance so as to build his confidence.[9] Instead of comparing his immediate troubles with previous personal blessings, he aimed for the big picture of God's miraculous acts of salvation. He exchanged the long-range view for the short-range view. Augustine characterized the psalmist's change as "leaping over himself" to contemplate the works of God's mercy.[10] Instead of succumbing to his dark and depressed feelings, he is ready now to "remember the deeds of the LORD" (Ps. 77:11). Augustine describes the psalmist: "Now behold him roaming among the works of the Lord."[11]

The pivot from lament's raw feelings to God's real mercy challenges our capacity to remember what the Lord has done. Lewis writes, "I have gradually been coming to feel that the door is no longer shut and bolted.

---

6   There is considerable translation debate over verse 10. The ESV reads, "Then I said, 'I will appeal to this, to the years of the right hand of the Most High.'" The 1662 Book of Common Prayer version reads, "And I said, 'It is mine own infirmity: but I will remember the years of the right hand of the most Highest.'"
7   Spurgeon, "Psalm 77," *Treasury of David*.
8   Lewis, *Grief Observed*, 41.
9   Ross, *Psalms*, 2:637.
10 Augustine, *Expositions on the Book of Psalms*, 8:363.
11 Augustine, *Expositions on the Book of Psalms*, 8:363.

Was it my own frantic need that slammed it in my face? The time when there is nothing at all in your soul except a cry for help may be just the time when God can't give it: you are like the drowning man who can't be helped because he clutches and grabs. Perhaps your own reiterated cries deafen you to the voice you hope to hear."[12]

It is only when we begin to realize that our anger and self-pity do not define reality that we begin to be open to "remembering" and "meditating" on the big picture of God's mercy. Sittser writes, "The feeling self is not the center of reality. God is the center of reality. To surrender to God, however contrary to our emotions, will lead to liberation from self and will open us to a world that is much bigger and grander than we are."[13]

The whole demeanor of the psalmist changes.[14] Kidner observes, "By the end of the psalm the pervasive 'I' has disappeared and the objective facts of the faith have captured all [the psalmist's] attention and all of ours."[15] Before he cried and groaned all through the night and refused comfort and sleep, but now he calmly ponders the mighty deeds of the Lord. The depth of his despair is matched and transcended by his unrestrained reveling in God's miraculous acts of redemption. He declares to God for all to hear, "Your ways, God, are holy" (Ps. 77:13). The shift from personal pain and sorrow to the shared hope of salvation is remarkable: "With your mighty arm you redeemed your people, the descendants of Jacob and Joseph" (v. 15).

The psalmist returns to the song of Moses and Miriam for inspiration (Exod. 15:1–18). He paraphrases and embellishes the Exodus text. "Poetic freedom . . . heightens and personalizes the drama. . . . But it is a true picture of God's sway over nature."[16] To pray this psalm today is to remember the miraculous power of the Incarnate One who rebuked the wind and said to the waves, "Quiet! Be still!" (Mark 4:39). The psalmist is mindful that Yahweh is the Lord of history and that the

---

12 Lewis, *Grief Observed*, 54.
13 Sittser, *Grace Disguised*, 101.
14 Boice, *Psalms*, 2:638. Boice notes, "As we go through the psalm, one thing to pay special attention to is the pronouns. In the NIV, in the first six verses of the psalm there are eighteen occurrences of the first person singular pronoun (I or me), and six references to God by name, title, and pronoun. In the last eight verses (vv. 13–20) there are twenty-one mentions of God and no personal references at all."
15 Kidner, *Psalms 73–150*, 277.
16 Kidner, *Psalms 73–150*, 280.

essential fact of human existence is not oppression and revolution, but atonement and salvation. The book of Exodus bears witness to God's strategy for redemption. We see God's saving action running like a thin red line through human history. As civilizations and empires come and go, Israel's exodus may not even show up as a blip on history's timeline, but what God did for Israel is what he seeks to do for all people. The Passover and the blood of the lamb are not referenced explicitly, but they stand behind everything that is said and point forward to the propitiatory sacrifice of Christ.

The redemptive power of God is expressed in images of thunder, lightning, whirlwind, and earthquake. By noting the absence of God's footprints, the psalmist, without meaning to, causes Christians to think of the Incarnate One. Jesus literally walked this earth. He left actual footprints, and John the Baptist claimed he wasn't worthy to even untie his sandals (John 1:27). Ross concludes, "Whereas the psalmist recalled the greatest act of salvation in Israel's history, the exodus, Christians recall a greater salvation provided for them in the death and resurrection of Christ Jesus. Deliverance for all suffering and death is thereby assured; but until that happens, we are to follow Jesus's example and seek to use our suffering to help others (1 Peter 2:19)."[17]

The psalm's abrupt ending is consistent with Asaph's literary style. The brief mention of Moses and Aaron's shepherding of the flock of Israel serves as a fitting segue to Psalm 78 and its historical review of God's mercy and Israel's stubborn failure to trust in Yahweh. The prophet Habakkuk may have drawn on Psalm 77 in his description of the exodus redemption and God's deliverance. Delitzsch concludes, "Where our Psalm leaves off, Hab. 3 goes on, taking it up from that point like a continuation."[18] Boice suggests that the prophet's statement "The righteous will live by his faith" (Hab. 2:4) would be a fitting end for Psalm 77.[19]

---

17 Ross, *Psalms*, 2:640.
18 Delitzsch, *Psalms*, 2:349. Delitzsch argues that Psalm 77 is dependent on Habakkuk rather than the other way around. He claims to have proven in his commentary on Habakkuk (1843) "that the mutual relationship is one that is deeply grounded in the prophetic type of Habakkuk, and that the Psalm is heard to re-echo in Habakkuk, not Habakkuk in the language of the psalmist."
19 Boice, *Psalms*, 2:643.

FORGETTING THE UNFORGETTABLE

Asaph uses the five-hundred-year history of Israel from the exodus to King David to prove two things, the covenant faithfulness of Yahweh and the hardhearted, stubborn rebelliousness of Israel.[1] Asaph's psalm sounds more like a sermon preached at the city gate by a prophet than a song sung by the chief musician. He warns the people not to follow in the footsteps of their ancestors. Israel's worship leader levels a scathing rebuke against those who refuse to remember the Lord's unforgettable and miraculous acts of redemption. "Again and again they put God to the test; they vexed the Holy One of Israel. They did not remember his power—the day he redeemed them from the oppressor" (Ps. 78:41–42).

The sequence of psalms begins with Asaph's personal struggle with apostasy (Psalm 73), followed by a communal lament over the total devastation of the Jerusalem temple (Psalm 74). Psalm 75 stresses the nearness of God's faithfulness and the certainty of his judgment and vindication. Psalm 76 continues the theme of judgment by celebrating the victory of God's justice and power in a final judgment. God will break "the spirit of rulers," forcing the kings of the earth to submit to him forever (Ps. 76:12). Psalm 77 captures the personal struggle of the faithful who suffer because of Israel's faithlessness. They make their appeal to the Most High and remember the deeds of the Lord. Psalm 78 picks up on the theme of remembering and chronicles Israel's history of

---

1   Waltke, *An Old Testament Theology*, 881. "Narrative or storytelling psalms aim to instruct Israel from its sacred history." Waltke identifies the following psalms in this category: Psalms 78, 105, 106, 135, 136.

woeful and willful stubbornness. Asaph accuses them of forgetting the unforgettable mercy of God.

The Israelites played out a sad history of faithlessness, first in the wilderness and then in the Promised Land (Ps. 78:8, 17, 22, 36, 56, 58). The apostles drew on Psalms 78 and 95 to warn the early church of drifting away from so great a salvation. Paul was concerned that history would repeat itself. He wrote, "These things happened to them as examples and were written down as warnings for us, on whom the culmination of the ages has come. So, if you think you are standing firm, be careful that you don't fall!" (1 Cor. 10:11–12; see Heb. 3:1–4:11).

Psalm 78 tells an epic story in two overlapping parts. Part one is the story of the exodus and Israel's wilderness rebellion (Ps. 78:9–40). Part two repeats the story of the exodus, with an emphasis on the plagues, followed by Israel's apostasy in the Promised Land (vv. 41–72). Both parts end with a description of Israel's rebellious ancestors as a warning to all believers. Yet through it all God remains faithful to his people. Asaph's pedagogical strategy is pastoral and prophetic. He seeks to warn believers against falling away, even as he seeks to encourage believers to remain faithful (vv. 1–8).

WISDOM'S LEGACY

My people, hear my teaching;
listen to the words of my mouth,
I will open my mouth with a parable;
I will utter hidden things, things from of old—
things we have heard and known,
things our ancestors have told us.
We will not hide them from their descendants;
we will tell the next generation
the praiseworthy deeds of the LORD,
his power, and the wonders he has done.
He decreed statutes for Jacob
and established the law in Israel,
which he commanded our ancestors
to teach their children,
so the next generation would know them,
even the children yet to be born,
and they in turn would tell their children.

Then they would put their trust in God
and would not forget his deeds
but would keep his commands.
They would not be like their ancestors—
a stubborn and rebellious generation,
whose hearts are not loyal to God,
whose spirits were not faithful to him.
                              —Psalm 78:1–8

Right from verse 1 the impassioned tone of a caring prophet is set. "My people" implies solidarity and endearment. "My teaching" implies ownership and investment. "My mouth" implies integrity and relationship. The double emphasis on reception is stressed with two key verbs: hear and listen. The introduction calls for attention without any claim of authority other than the shared solidarity of "my people" and the sincerity of personal integrity. This is the basis for Christian communication shared by pastors, prophets, parents, and friends. All we can do is invite a hearing based on the Word of God. We open our mouths, and the Spirit of God fills us with his message.

Asaph introduces his epic as a parable wrapped in history. We are not in the habit of linking history, seasoned with times and places, with the literary genre of parable, which we tend to associate with creative stories designed to tell the truth slant. The word "parable" is made up of "para," which means "alongside of," and "ballein," which means "to throw." What Asaph seeks to do in his epic is to set up a comparison between history and meaning. History as simply a collection of dates and events yields little insight, but when those facts interface with God's revelation—the hidden things—world-changing, salvation-shaping meaning is communicated. This is why "parable," or Hebrew "mashal," has come to mean "wisdom." The plural form of "mashal" entitles the book of Proverbs. The comparison of life and revelation yields life-transforming meaning.[2]

---

2   Calvin, *Psalms*, 5.3:227–28. Calvin concludes that the reference to using parables "denotes grave and striking sentences, such as adages, or proverbs, and apophthegms." Calvin implies a degree of sophistication and eloquence lies behind this effort: "The inspired penman affirms that it is his purpose to utter only striking sentences and notable sayings." This misinterpretation of the term distorts his understanding of Christ's reason for speaking in parables. Calvin writes, "Christ's object in doing so, was to prove that he was a distinguished prophet of God, and that thus he might be received with greater reverence. Since he then resembled a prophet because he preached sublime mysteries in a style of language above the common kind, that which the sacred writer

When Asaph tells the "the praiseworthy deeds of the LORD" and presents the "decreed statutes for Jacob" (vv. 4–5), he is not revealing anything new that the people didn't already know. The problem was that God's unforgettable actions and commands had been rejected and forgotten by a "stubborn and rebellious generation" (v. 8). Asaph's purpose for writing was to remind the people of God to be faithful and obedient to the steadfast love of the Lord.

WILDERNESS WARNING

The men of Ephraim, though armed with bows,
turned back on the day of battle;
they did not keep God's covenant
and refused to live by his law.
They forgot what he had done,
the wonders he had shown them.
He did miracles in the sight of their ancestors
in the land of Egypt, in the region of Zoan.
He divided the sea and led them through;
he made the water stand up like a wall.
He guided them with the cloud by day
and with light from the fire all night.
He split the rocks in the wilderness
and gave them water as abundant as the seas;
he brought streams out of a rocky crag
and made water flow down like rivers.
But they continued to sin against him,
rebelling in the wilderness against the Most High.
They willfully put God to the test
by demanding the food they craved.
They spoke against God;
they said, "Can God really
spread a table in the wilderness?
True, he struck the rock,
and water gushed out,
streams flowed abundantly,

---

here affirms concerning himself, is with propriety transferred to him." On the contrary, Jesus used parables to hold in check hard-hearted religious resistance and popular messianic fervor, even as he communicated the gospel subversively to the disciples.

but can he also give us bread?
Can he supply meat for his people?"
When the LORD heard them, he was furious;
his fire broke out against Jacob,
and his wrath rose against Israel,
for they did not believe in God
or trust in his deliverance.
Yet he gave a command to the skies above
and opened the doors of the heavens;
he rained down manna for the people to eat,
he gave them the grain of heaven.
Human beings ate the bread of angels;
he sent them all the food they could eat.
He let loose the east wind from the heavens
and by his power made the south wind blow.
He rained meat down on them like dust,
birds like sand on the seashore.
He made them come down inside their camp,
all around their tents.
They ate till they were gorged—
he had given them what they craved.
But before they turned from what they craved,
even while the food was still in their mouths,
God's anger rose against them;
he put to death the sturdiest among them,
cutting down the young men of Israel.
In spite of all this, they kept on sinning;
in spite of his wonders, they did not believe.
So he ended their days in futility
and their years in terror.
Whenever God slew them, they would seek him;
they eagerly turned to him again.
They remembered that God was their Rock,
that God Most High was their Redeemer.
But then they would flatter him with their mouths,
lying to him with their tongues;
their hearts were not loyal to him,
they were not faithful to his covenant.
Yet he was merciful;
he forgave their iniquities

and did not destroy them.
Time after time he restrained his anger
and did not stir up his full wrath.
He remembered that they were but flesh,
a passing breeze that does not return.
How often they rebelled against him in the wilderness
and grieved him in the wasteland!
—Psalm 78:9–40

Ephraim factors into the beginning and end of Asaph's epic review of
Israel's history from the exodus to David (vv. 9, 67). Ephraim was one of
the twelve Jewish tribes named after the younger of the two sons born to
Joseph (Gen. 41:50–52). Against his father's objections, Ephraim received
from the hand of his grandfather, Jacob, a greater blessing than his older
brother Manasseh. Ephraim's prominence grew because Joshua, Moses's
successor, was an Ephraimite, and the tabernacle was erected in Shiloh
in the territory of Ephraim. The ark of the covenant remained there until
the incident alluded to by Asaph when the Ephraimites were defeated
in battle by the Philistines and the ark of God was captured (1 Sam.
4:1–11). Asaph discloses the "hidden" reason for Ephraim's defeat. "They
did not keep God's covenant and refused to live by his law" (Ps. 78:10).
    Asaph's theme throughout his account is God's great faithfulness,
even when Israel proves faithless. But Asaph is also honest about the sad
and unnecessary consequences for willful disobedience and sinful craving.
Ephraim was "exhibit A," a tragic casualty of spiritual negligence and
rebellion. "They forgot what he had done, the wonders he had shown
them" (v. 11). Asaph implies that God "abandoned the tabernacle of
Shiloh" (v. 60), "rejected the tents of Joseph," and "did not choose the
tribe of Ephraim" (v. 67) because the Ephraimites were found faithless.
This is how Asaph begins and ends the psalm in order to emphasize the
high cost of disobedience and idolatry.
    Asaph describes the exodus twice (vv. 12–13; 43–53). The pur-
pose of this parallel description was to emphasize the power of God to
overcome the preeminent superpower of the day. The people of God
witnessed firsthand the power of God to overrule Egypt in the land of
Zoan (Exod. 1:11).[3] They saw the miracles: the great escape, the divided

---

3   Zoan is identified with Rameses, the capital city that the Israelites helped build.

sea, the cloud by day, and the pillar of fire by night. Up until the cross of the crucified Messiah and the empty tomb of the risen Christ, the exodus was the epicenter of God's redemptive mercy. However, the power of God to redeem, lead, and provide was not enough for the Israelites. "They willfully put God to the test by demanding the food they craved" (Ps. 78:18; see Exod. 16:1–17:7; Num. 11:4–32; 14:22). The problem was not that they needed food and water. God knew their need. The problem was their ingratitude and unbelief.[4] When Jesus fed more than five thousand, the people invoked this very same wilderness experience to make Jesus prove himself. They said, "Our ancestors ate the manna in the wilderness; as it is written: 'He gave them bread from heaven to eat'" (John 6:31; see Exod. 16:4; Ps. 78:24–25). They had already eaten their full, but that wasn't enough. They wanted more. Jesus said to them, "Very truly I tell you, it is not Moses who has given you the bread from heaven, but it is my Father who gives you the true bread from heaven. For the bread of God is the bread that comes down from heaven and gives life to the world" (John 6:32–33). The physical need for nourishment was never in question, but Jesus pointed to a deeper need, the need for the bread of life. But like the Israelites, the people grumbled and complained and ridiculed the notion that Jesus was the bread of life that comes down from heaven.

The people's ingratitude and their insatiable hunger for more and more infuriated the Lord, and "his fire broke out against Jacob" (v. 21). We might reasonably conclude that this "fire" was a vivid metaphor, but Numbers describes how an actual "fire from the LORD burned among them and consumed some of the outskirts of the camp" (Num. 11:1). But even this fire did not quell the Israelites' craving for quail. They wanted meat so badly that God gave them meat—literally, tons of meat. He used a strong east wind to drive inland tens of thousands of low-flying quail from the sea. The greed of the people knew no bounds, and they consumed the meat like there was no tomorrow. Moses tells us that "while the meat was still between their teeth and before it could be consumed, the anger of the LORD burned against the people, and he struck them with a severe plague" (Num. 11:33). Kidner writes, "The swift judgment of [God; Ps. 78:30–31] shows not

---

4   Boice, *Psalms*, 2:647.

that God acted prematurely but that this behavior was symptomatic, this attitude contagious and this moment crucial."[5]

As much as we might like to think that Asaph's description of persistent sin, shallow repentance, hollow confession, and pseudo-faithfulness applies only to the Israelites in the wilderness, we have to admit that what he says is sadly true of many Christians today. Asaph draws out the dramatic irony of the situation. The people "kept on sinning" (Ps. 78:32), whether God judged them for their sin or miraculously did wonders for their benefit. The results were frustratingly similar. Even when they truly remembered "that God was their Rock, that God Most High was their Redeemer," they persisted in ostentatious sacrilege and ethical duplicity (vv. 35–37). Yet, in spite of everything, God remained merciful; "he forgave their iniquities and did not destroy them" (v. 38). We should not minimize the tragic cost of disobedience and faithlessness that many suffered because of God's just judgment, but as Asaph emphasized, God's mercy far exceeded his righteous judgment. The apostle Paul makes a similar point when he quotes a trustworthy saying in the early church: "If we died with him, we will also live with him; if we endure, we will also reign with him. If we disown him, he will also disown us; if we are faithless, he remains faithful, for he cannot disown himself" (2 Tim. 2:11–13).

IDOLATRY IN THE PROMISED LAND

> Again and again they put God to the test;
> they vexed the Holy One of Israel.
> They did not remember his power—
> the day he redeemed them from the oppressor,
> the day he displayed his signs in Egypt,
> his wonders in the region of Zoan.
> He turned their river into blood;
> they could not drink from their streams.
> He sent swarms of flies that devoured them,
> and frogs that devastated them.
> He gave their crops to the grasshopper,
> their produce to the locust.
> He destroyed their vines with hail

---

5   Kidner, *Psalms 73–150*, 283.

and their sycamore-figs with sleet.
He gave over their cattle to the hail,
their livestock to bolts of lightning.
He unleashed against them his hot anger,
his wrath, indignation and hostility—
a band of destroying angels.
He prepared a path for his anger;
he did not spare them from death
but gave them over to the plague.
He struck down all the firstborn of Egypt,
the firstfruits of manhood in the tents of Ham.
But he brought his people out like a flock;
he led them like sheep through the wilderness.
He guided them safely, so they were unafraid,
but the sea engulfed their enemies.
And so he brought them to the border of his holy land,
to the hill country his right hand had taken.
He drove out nations before them
and allotted their lands to them as an inheritance;
he settled the tribes of Israel in their homes.
But they put God to the test
and rebelled against the Most High;
they did not keep his statutes.
Like their ancestors they were disloyal and faithless,
as unreliable as a faulty bow.
They angered him with their high places;
they aroused his jealousy with their idols.
When God heard them, he was furious;
he rejected Israel completely.
He abandoned the tabernacle of Shiloh,
the tent he had set up among humans.
He sent the ark of his might into captivity,
his splendor into the hands of the enemy.
He gave his people over to the sword;
he was furious with his inheritance.
Fire consumed their young men,
and their young women had no wedding songs;
their priests were put to the sword,
and their widows could not weep.
Then the Lord awoke as from sleep,

as a warrior wakes from the stupor of wine.
He beat back his enemies;
he put them to everlasting shame.
Then he rejected the tents of Joseph,
he did not choose the tribe of Ephraim;
but he chose the tribe of Judah,
Mount Zion, which he loved.
He built his sanctuary like the heights,
like the earth that he established forever.
He chose David his servant
and took him from the sheep pens;
from tending the sheep he brought him
to be the shepherd of his people Jacob,
of Israel his inheritance.
And David shepherded them with integrity of heart;
with skillful hands he led them.
—Psalm 78:41–72

Asaph recalls the many times the Israelites "put God to the test" and "vexed the Holy One of Israel" (v. 41; see Num. 14:22). He found their willful incapacity to remember God's redemptive power inexplicable. How could they forget the unforgettable? Once again Asaph remembers the epicenter of God's redemptive power: the exodus. He recalls the wonders that freed Israel from her oppressor by God's sending plagues of blood, flies, frogs, locusts, hail, and lightning. God unleashed "a band of destroying angels" and "struck down all the firstborn of Egypt" (Ps. 78:49, 51). The ten plagues exposed the emptiness of evil and the weakness of the Egyptian superpower. God worked wonders "to purge the Hebrew minds of all envious admiration of evil, to systematically demolish every god-illusion or god-pretension that evil uses to exercise power over men and women."[6] God exercised his sovereignty. He overcame Egypt, guided Israel safely through the wilderness, and drove out the nations of Canaan. But in spite of what God did, Israel rebelled. They put God to the test and became disobedient, disloyal, and idolatrous. Israel was no better in the Promised Land than they had been in the wilderness.

Once again, Asaph focuses on Ephraim as a symbol of Israel's apostasy. Their idolatry infuriated God and led to their defeat at the hands of the

---

6   Peterson, *Christ Plays*, 162.

Philistines (1 Samuel 4–5). Disaster followed disaster. God abandoned the tabernacle of Shiloh, and so many young men died in battle that young women had no one to marry. Even the priests were massacred, and their widows were too weary to weep. But then, inexplicably, God steps up to defend his people. The abrupt reversal is characteristic of Asaph's style. As Kidner remarks, "By this point in the psalm such a development is utterly unexpected, and shows the steadfast love of God in the most robust and unsentimental colors."[7] The Lord is likened to a warrior who is aroused suddenly from his wine-induced sleep. He is ready to do battle, and he "[beats] back his enemies" and puts them to "everlasting shame" (v. 66). The sovereign Lord rejects the descendants of Joseph and the tribe of Ephraim and chooses instead the tribe of Judah. Mount Zion becomes his sanctuary and David his chosen servant (1 Samuel 16). He gives the people a new beginning and new leadership. Like Abraham and Moses before him, David does not merit this selection. God takes him from the fields and puts him on the throne. "One day he was caring for the ewes and their lambs, the next day God had him shepherding Jacob, his people Israel, his prize possession" (Ps. 78:71 MSG). The psalm ends on a positive note of good news and hope. By God's grace, a man after God's own heart has been appointed to rule his people (1 Sam. 13:14; Acts 13:22). Psalm 78 tracks salvation history from the exodus to David's reign, bearing witness to God's great faithfulness even when his people are faithless. Asaph calls us to remember the unforgettable grace and mercy of God.

---

7   Kidner, *Psalms 73–150*, 285.

VOICE OF THE PERSECUTED

The psalmist is outraged. Dead bodies lie in the street, and there is no one left to bury the dead. Blood runs in the street like water. Jerusalem is reduced to rubble, and neighboring nations heap scorn on God's inheritance. It is hard to imagine a more devastating picture of human loss and destruction. The raw emotion of Psalm 79 fits the Asaph tradition and the reality of extreme suffering. It fulfills its canonical purpose by causing worshipers to put words to unspeakable anguish. The human soul and the collective spirit of God's people are pushed past fear and hate to prayer.

Our Christian brothers and sisters in Syria and North Korea can identify with this psalm. Their persecution and suffering has not been brought on by disobedience and idolatry, but they, like the psalmist, suffer brutal political violence and indescribable atrocities. As discouraging as this psalm may be and as much as we might wish it away, it is an essential resource for the suffering people of God. Only such a prayer, in the Spirit of God, can answer the intense anger and hatred generated by such evil. "We might think this is 'un-Christian,' for it tells of anger and a desire for revenge, but we too have had those feelings."[1]

The focus in Psalm 79 on extreme suffering and loss of life is a fitting companion to the description in Psalm 74 of the utter destruction and desecration of the Jerusalem temple. Since both psalms appear to be responding to the Babylonian conquest of Israel, why were these two psalms not placed together? What is the purpose of the intervening psalms? Is the sequence of Psalms 75–79 important? Following the destruction of the

---

1   DeClaissé-Walford, Jacobson, and Tanner, *Book of Psalms*, 629.

sanctuary (Psalm 74), Psalm 75 reassures the worshiper of the nearness of God and his set time for righteous judgment. Psalm 76 moves from the just vindication of Israel to God's ultimate eschatological fulfillment. Like Psalm 73, Psalm 77 wrestles with the tragedy of Jerusalem's fall from the perspective of the person who remains faithful. He struggles for the long-range view of God's mighty salvation and takes comfort in the fact that the Lord led his flock "by the hand of Moses and Aaron" (Ps. 77:20). Even though Psalm 78 ends on a positive note, stressing the integrity of David's heart, the thrust of the psalm records the long and tragic history of hard-hearted rebellion, idolatry, and apostasy. This brings us back to the reality of the Babylonian captivity and the fall of Jerusalem, only this time it is not the temple that is in view (Psalm 74) as much as the people (Psalm 79).

HOW LONG?

O God, the nations have invaded your inheritance;
they have defiled your holy temple,
they have reduced Jerusalem to rubble.
They have left the dead bodies of your servants
as food for the birds of the sky,
the flesh of your own people for the animals of the wild.
They have poured out blood like water
all around Jerusalem,
and there is no one to bury the dead.
We are objects of contempt to our neighbors,
of scorn and derision to those around us.
How long, LORD? Will you be angry forever?
How long will your jealousy burn like fire?
—Psalm 79:1–5

Believers pray this psalm today holding the persecuted church in their hearts. We are mindful of the heavy cost many pay for following Jesus Christ. The Babylonian captivity prompted psalms and prophecies that serve the church today. Israel suffered because of their hard-hearted rebellion and apostasy (Psalms 73, 78), but the persecuted church suffers for their witness and obedience. These Asaph-style prayers resonate with the perspective of the prophets. They represent the faithful remnant who suffer the consequences of national apostasy and the judgment of God, even though they have made the Sovereign Lord their refuge (Ps. 73:28). They are like innocent civilians who become collateral damage in a war they didn't ask for or deserve. Calvin writes, "The most eminent of the servants of God may be put to a cruel and ignominious death—a punishment which we know is often executed upon murderers, and other despisers of God; but still the death of the saints does not cease to be precious in his sight: and when he has suffered them to be unrighteously persecuted in the flesh, he shows, by taking vengeance on their enemies, how dear they are to him."[2]

Even when the early church was not suffering severe, state-sponsored persecution, they saw themselves in the psalmist's description of cultural alienation. What was true for the people of God, "We are objects of contempt to our neighbors, of scorn and derision to those around us" (Ps. 79:4), could have easily been written by the apostles. Peter encouraged faithfulness in spite of false accusations and unjust suffering (1 Peter 2:12, 19). He wrote, "Even if you should suffer for what is right, you are blessed. 'Do not fear their threats; do not be frightened'" (1 Peter 3:14; quoting Isa. 8:12). He called Christ's followers to keep a clear conscience, "so that those who speak maliciously against your good behavior in Christ may be ashamed of their slander" (1 Peter 3:16).

The psalmist's question "How long, Lord?" must have resonated with the apostle John, because it is the pivotal question of the heavenly martyrs' prayer meeting in the book of Revelation. When the fifth seal is broken, we hear the cry of martyrs, whose "untimely deaths on earth are from God's perspective a sacrifice on the altar of heaven."[3] The fifth seal reveals an extraordinary prayer meeting. The saints who have gone before have been "slain because of the word of God and the testimony they had maintained" (Rev. 6:9). In line with Psalm 79, they humbly confess their need for God's grace and zealously pray for the salvation and judgment of God.[4]

The faithful saints cry out to the "Sovereign Lord, holy and true," asking how long the wild horses of judgment and persecution will be allowed to run wild? The answer comes back: "until the number of their

---

2   Calvin, *Psalms*, 5.3:284.
3   Mounce, *Revelation*, 157.
4   Webster, *Follow the Lamb*, 137–39.

fellow servants and their brothers and sisters who were to be killed even as they had been, was completed" (Rev. 6:11 NASB). We are sobered by the fact that time is measured, not in conversions, but in martyrdoms. "God's patience is costly, not simply for God, but for the innocent."[5] These are the saints who suffered Taliban atrocities in Afghanistan and the crackdown against Christians in Iraq. Some of these martyrs are from Nigeria, slain by the ruthless Boko Haram. Many are victims from North Korea's brutal persecution. Under the altar there are new converts from Sri Lanka, who were targeted and killed by radical Buddhists. Some of the praying saints are from Saudi Arabia and Iran. There are Egyptian and Syrian believers who are praying, "How long?"

Prayer is the link that ties us to the Lord of history.[6] Prayer expresses our shared anticipation of Christ's second coming and our shared community with those who have gone before. Their longing becomes our longing. Their hope, our hope. They are not dead and buried, but alive and waiting! We may place a premium on personal security, but the fifth seal offers the perspective of the martyrs: "They called out in a loud voice, 'How long, Sovereign Lord, holy and true, until you judge the inhabitants of the earth and avenge our blood?'" (Rev. 6:10). In the company of the saints who have gone before, we confront real life and feel the weight of glory. John's Spirit-inspired vision calls for courage, endurance, and perseverance. When the peace and power of Christ are available, why settle for the survival tactics of the world? Christians believe that there is real hope in a world that is constantly trying to adapt to hopelessness.

PLEA FOR GOD'S RESPONSE

> Pour out your wrath on the nations
> that do not acknowledge you,
> on the kingdoms
> that do not call on your name;
> for they have devoured Jacob
> and devastated his homeland.
> Do not hold against us the sins of past generations;
> may your mercy come quickly to meet us,

---

5   Volf, *Exclusion and Embrace*, 299–300.
6   Webster, *Follow the Lamb*, 138–39.

for we are in desperate need.
Help us, God our Savior,
for the glory of your name;
deliver us and forgive our sins
for your name's sake.
Why should the nations say,
"Where is their God?"
Before our eyes, make known among the nations
that you avenge the outpoured blood of your servants.
May the groans of the prisoners come before you;
with your strong arm preserve those condemned to die.
Pay back into the laps of our neighbors seven times
the contempt they have hurled at you, Lord.
Then we your people, the sheep of your pasture,
will praise you forever;
from generation to generation
we will proclaim your praise.
                    —Psalm 79:6–13

The questions "How long, Lord? Will you be angry forever?" bridge the two halves of the psalm. The psalmist shifts the focus of the psalm from catastrophe—the tragic fall of Jerusalem due to Israel's apostasy—to God's just judgment of the nations responsible for oppressing Israel. Like a father, God has disciplined Israel, but now the psalmist calls on God as Israel's Savior and Defender: "Pour out your wrath on the nations" (v. 6). The psalmist identifies these nations to the Lord as kingdoms "that do not call on your name" (v. 6). They have "devoured Jacob," "devastated" the land of Israel, shed the blood of "your servants," and have "hurled" contempt at the Lord (vv. 7, 10, 12).

In the midst of all of this tragedy and vented pain, the psalmist pleads for forgiveness, but he does so in such a way as to corroborate the perspective that these Asaph psalms are composed by a faithful remnant. He prays the way Asaph did in Psalm 73 and the way the prophet Jeremiah prayed (Jer. 10:23–25). No sincere believer would ever claim not to need forgiveness. All of us, and especially the most faithful and mature believers among us, embrace the need to pray: "Help us, God our Savior, for the glory of your name; deliver us and forgive our sins for your name's sake" (Ps. 79:9). This is the reason every Christian worship service includes a prayer of confession, not because someone may have sinned, but because we all need to confess our sins and pray for forgiveness. With that said, we can safely assume that the psalmist distances himself, along with all those who share his conviction and practice, from the disobedience, idolatry, and apostasy that brought down God's judgment on Jerusalem through the agency of Nebuchadnezzar and his army (2 Kings 25). He boldly prays, "Do not hold against us the sins of past generations; may your mercy come quickly to meet us, for we are in desperate need" (Ps. 79:8). The prayer itself indicates that the reason no longer exists for God to distance himself from his people. It is this truth that prompts the psalmist to ask rhetorically, "Why should the nations say, 'Where is their God?'" (v. 10).

Asaph and the worship pastors who followed in his tradition may not have comprehended Christ's radical love for our enemies. The ultimate Son of David called his followers to love their enemies and pray for their persecutors (Matt. 5:44), and the apostles called all disciples to follow in Christ's footsteps to the cross (1 Peter 2:21). Even so, we continue to embrace the message of God's just judgment, and we affirm with the psalmist the reality of God's final judgment. We join the psalmist in praying, "Pay back into the laps of our neighbors seven times the contempt they have hurled at you, Lord" (Ps. 79:12), even as we acknowledge with the apostle that the Lord is patient, "not wanting anyone to perish, but everyone to come to repentance" (2 Peter 3:9).

The apostle John's fifth apocalyptic seal is a call to honor the eighth beatitude: "Blessed are those who are persecuted because of righteousness, for theirs is the kingdom of heaven" (Matt. 5:10). The saints who have gone before are praying the Psalms just like we are. Their prayers are reminiscent of Asaph's prayer: "Why should the nations say, 'Where is their God?' Before our eyes, make known among the nations that you avenge the outpoured blood of your servants" (Ps. 79:10). They cry out, "When the foundations are being destroyed, what can the righteous do?" The saints respond, "The LORD is in his holy temple; the LORD is in his heavenly throne. He observes everyone on earth; his eyes examine them. The LORD examines the righteous, but the wicked, those who love violence, he hates with a passion. On the wicked he will rain fiery coals and burning sulfur; a scorching wind will be their lot. For the LORD is righteous, he loves justice; the upright people will see his face" (Ps. 11:3–7).

The psalm ends on a note of praise, an easily overlooked characteristic of the Asaph tradition, given the psalmist's raw emotion and blunt descriptions of disaster, but perfectly consistent with the big picture of God's salvation and judgment. Each of the psalms in this sequence praises God for his guidance and looks forward to God's eschatological fulfillment. For Asaph, the arc of devotion ends with praise to God for the guidance that reaches into eternity: "You guide me with your counsel, and afterward you will take me into glory" (Ps. 73:24).

Psalms 74 and 75 are brought to a similar conclusion with Asaph stating his conviction: "[But] as for me, I will declare this forever; I will sing praise to the God of Jacob" (Ps. 75:9). Psalm 76 emphasizes God's righteous judgment: "He breaks the spirit of rulers; he is feared by the kings of the earth" (Ps. 76:12), and Psalm 77 concludes, "You led your people like a flock by the hand of Moses and Aaron" (Ps. 77:20).

Psalm 78 continues the theme of shepherding. God calls David "to be the shepherd of his people Jacob," and the psalmist concludes, "David shepherded them with integrity of heart; with skillful hands he led them" (Ps. 78:71–72). So it is significant that Psalm 79 ends on this theme of God's everlasting shepherding: "Then we your people, the sheep of your pasture, will praise you forever; from generation to generation we will proclaim your praise" (Ps. 79:13). This brings us to a climax and a fulfillment that points forward to Jesus Christ, the Good Shepherd, who lays down his life for the sheep and who has sheep that are not of this pen (John 10:11, 16).

SHEPHERD OF ISRAEL

I n the light of the work of Christ, Psalm 80 is a gospel parable that sees Israel's tragic history as a type that points forward to God's redemptive fulfillment of his covenant promises. When interpreted within the sequence of Asaph psalms, it inspires the believer to see the full spectrum of salvation history. Psalm 78 introduces the use of parable and offers an interpretative rationale for how the Psalms should be used: "I will open my mouth with a parable; I will utter hidden things, things from of old—things we have heard and known, things our ancestors have told us" (Ps. 78:2–3). What was said in the past, in the Spirit, has importance for us today because it points to Christ.

Psalm 80 is a national lament over the collapse of the northern kingdom of Israel in 722 BC. It may have been written when Shalmaneser, king of Assyria, was either about to or had already conquered the northern kingdom in Samaria and deported the Israelites. The book of Kings spells out in blunt detail Israel's history of apostasy and idolatry and gives ultimate responsibility to the Lord for Israel's defeat and exile. "Therefore the LORD rejected all the people of Israel; he afflicted them and gave them into the hands of plunderers, until he thrust them from his presence" (2 Kings 17:20).

The psalmist pleads with God to reverse the disaster that has come upon the northern kingdom. As we have seen, Ephraim stands as a type representing willful unbelief and hardened resistance against God (Ps. 78:9, 67). But God never did reverse the judgment of Ephraim, at least not in the way the psalmist hoped. There was no restoration of the northern kingdom, and there never will be. The psalm points forward to the global gospel and a new definition of the true Jew. Only in Christ is the plea of the psalmist answered and the promise of the one new human fulfilled.

To pray this psalm with Jesus is to open up the meaning of the psalm for the church today. The psalm is filled with gospel allusions, including Jesus's encounter with the Samaritan woman (John 4:1–26), his description of the Good Shepherd (John 10:1–18), his parable of the vineyard owner who sent his son (Matt. 21:33–46), and his Upper Room Discourse on the vine and the branches (John 15:1–17). These gospel allusions are embedded in Psalm 80.

SAVE US!

> Hear us, Shepherd of Israel,
> you who lead Joseph like a flock.
> You who sit enthroned between the cherubim,
> shine forth before Ephraim, Benjamin and Manasseh.
> Awaken your might;
> come and save us.
> Restore us, O God;
> make your face shine on us,
> that we may be saved.
> —Psalm 80:1–3

Psalm 80 opens with the same shepherding theme that concludes Psalms 77, 78, and 79. This theme not only links the psalms together but builds expectancy. Israel is God's flock, "the sheep of his pasture," and the Lord is their shepherd (Ps. 23:1). But this shepherd is unlike any other. He sits "enthroned between the cherubim" (Ps. 80:1). He is superior in rank and more powerful than the most powerful angels. The light of his glory emanates from a transcendent, cosmic throne that rules over all (Ezek. 1:19–24). Human and divine images merge into one as the psalmist calls for the Lord to pay attention and bring his power to bear on a desperate situation. Ross translates the psalmist's plea, "Stir up your power," and "come to our salvation."[1]

If the apostles were asked how this appeal was answered, they would not hesitate to say that the crucified and risen Lord Jesus Christ fulfills the restoration of Israel. The work of redemption took much longer than expected, and the promise was not fulfilled as some imagined, nationalistically and geographically. But it was fulfilled cosmically, in a way that befit the one "enthroned between the cherubim." The author of Hebrews makes a strong case for the superiority of the Son over the angels when he writes, "So he became as much superior to the angels as

---

1   Ross, *Psalms*, 2:691.

the name he has inherited is superior to theirs" (Heb. 1:4), and "It is not to angels that he has subjected the world to come" (Heb. 2:5). Hebrews describes Jesus as "that great Shepherd of the sheep" (Heb. 13:20), and 1 Peter describes him as "the Chief Shepherd" (1 Peter 5:4).

A refrain with variations on the Lord's title concludes each stanza (Ps. 80:3, 7, 19). The psalmist draws on Aaron's blessing (Num. 6:24–26) and repeats three times for emphasis an earnest longing for the friendship and kindness of God. We hear this blessing today and acknowledge that "in Christ the blessing of God is made personal in the shining face: 'And his face was like the sun shining in full strength.' God in Christ is warmth and sunlight."[2]

HOW LONG?

> How long, LORD God Almighty,
> will your anger smolder
> against the prayers of your people?
> You have fed them with the bread of tears;
> you have made them drink tears by the bowlful.
> You have made us an object of derision to our neighbors,
> and our enemies mock us.
> Restore us, God Almighty;
> make your face shine on us,
> that we may be saved.
> —Psalm 80:4–7

Instead of responding to the warmth of God's smile, the tear-streaked, ash-smudged faces of God's people reflect deep sorrow and hopelessness. The prayers of the people provoke God's burning wrath rather than his glorious blessing. The solidarity of sin marks all the people of Israel for judgment. They suffer the consequences of past sins so that even the faithful who pray earnestly cannot escape the divine necessity of corporate judgment. It is in the midst of this kind of tragedy, the result of years of cultural rebellion, disobedience, idolatry, and apostasy, that the psalmist cries out, "How long, LORD God Almighty, will your anger smolder . . . ?" (Ps. 80:4). We don't like this kind of solidarity, but on this side of eternity, the faithful remnant often suffer right along with idolaters and abusers.

---

2   Peterson, *Reversed Thunder*, 38.

Evil is bound to impact our lives. We are fools to think that our Christianity is not shaped by the autonomous Western self, who is typically self-centered, self-indulgent, and materialistic. We know how difficult it is to shun the obsessions of our high places: food, sex, sports, entertainment, appearance, adventure, technology, control, money, and success. The list of idols in our late modern pantheon is long. And the moment a brave Christian dares to break away from the spirit of the age, she invites derision from her neighbors and colleagues. This stanza is not just about other people living at another time. It is not a historical artifact subject to a scholar's analysis and cataloging. It addresses the people of God today.

Some of us are on a diet of tears because we prioritize work over worship and meaningless entertainment over wisdom. We are drinking from a "bucket of salty tears" because we are eating, working, and indulging ourselves to death. We are constantly giving ourselves grace—permission to do what is antithetical to the gospel—without ever even thinking about the costly grace of Christ. What did Bonhoeffer say? "When Christ calls a man, he bids him come and die."[3] That sounds like something Asaph might have said if he lived today.

THE VINE AND THE SON

> You transplanted a vine from Egypt;
> you drove out the nations and planted it.
> You cleared the ground for it,
> and it took root and filled the land.
> The mountains were covered with its shade,
> the mighty cedars with its branches.
> Its branches reached as far as the Sea,
> its shoots as far as the River.
> Why have you broken down its walls
> so that all who pass by pick its grapes?
> Boars from the forest ravage it,
> and insects from the fields feed on it.
> Return to us, God Almighty!
> Look down from heaven and see!

---

3   Bonhoeffer, *Cost of Discipleship*, 99.

> Watch over this vine,
> the root your right hand has planted,
> the son you have raised up for yourself.
> —Psalm 80:8–15

The psalmist uses the exodus, the epicenter of salvation history, to introduce an extended allegory comparing Israel to a vine. God "transplanted a vine from Egypt" and "drove out the nations" of Canaan. Miraculously, the vine took root and grew so abundantly that it covered the mountains and the mighty cedars. The vine spread out over the land. It reached from the Mediterranean Sea in the west to the river of Euphrates in the east. The allegory traces the tremendous expansion of the kingdom under David's and Solomon's rules. But then the blessing of God comes to an abrupt end. The psalmist confronts God, the gardener, with an accusatory lament: "Why have you broken down the walls?" The unprotected vine represents a defenseless Israel that is ravaged by humans, wild boars, and insects.

The vine was the iconic symbol of Israel, used by the prophets to indict Israel. Hosea charged that even though God made Israel fruitful, the nation persisted in worshiping other gods (Hos. 10:1–2). Isaiah declared, "The vineyard of the LORD Almighty is the nation of Israel." On a fertile hillside, Yahweh planted only the choice vines and did everything possible to care for his crop, but his vine only produced bad fruit (Isa. 5:1–7). Jeremiah accused this "choice vine" of becoming "a corrupt, wild vine" (Jer. 2:21). Ezekiel likened Israel to a useless vine and lamented that wood from a vine was good for nothing but to be burned (Ezek. 15:1–5).

The prophet Isaiah develops the vineyard allegory as a love song: "My loved one had a vineyard on a fertile hillside," but the song quickly turns tragic and the people of Judah are asked to bear witness (Isa. 5:1–7). God did everything he could to assure a fruitful vineyard, but instead of good grapes there were only bad grapes. Isaiah uses the psalmist's allegory as a preface to his message of "woe" (Isa. 5:8–30). The decision to take away the protective wall of hedges is God's, and in no time the beautiful vineyard becomes a wasteland of briars and thorns.

In spite of Israel's willful rebellion, the psalmist cries out, "Return to us, God Almighty!" (Ps. 80:14). But on what grounds should God return to a people who have consistently rejected him and gone their own way? Clearly, there is nothing they have done to merit the blessing of God's merciful return. Knowing this, the psalmist introduces what he hopes is a persuasive reason that lies outside the actions of the people. "Watch over this vine," he pleads (v. 14). Why? Because you planted it. The vineyard belongs to you. But then he breaks out of the allegory as only a poet can do and likens Israel to "the son you have raised up for yourself" (v. 15). His appeal rests not on the merit of the people but on the mercy of God. The redemptive meaning of these images belongs to God's inspired revelation, and they point forward to the Incarnate One, the Son of God. Jesus himself makes the messianic connection and encourages us to follow his lead.

THE SON OF MAN

> Your vine is cut down, it is burned with fire;
> at your rebuke your people perish.
> Let your hand rest on the man at your right hand,
> the son of man you have raised up for yourself.
> Then we will not turn away from you;
> revive us, and we will call on your name.
> Restore us, LORD God Almighty;
> make your face shine on us,
> that we may be saved.
> —Psalm 80:16–19

When Jesus left the upper room with his disciples, they may have passed by the temple on their way to the Kidron Valley and up the Mount of Olives to Gethsemane. Above the temple gate in stone relief were golden vines with grape clusters as big as a person. The evening shadows may have obscured the image, but Jesus's metaphor of a vine and the branches (John 15:1–17) invoked deep biblical roots. The indictment of the prophets and the hope of the psalmist is answered in the one who says, "I am the true vine" (John 15:1). This is the seventh and final "I am" saying of Jesus in the gospel of John.[4] Jesus used descriptive images like the vine to develop a messianic self-portrait free from nationalistic

---

4   "I am the bread of life" (John 6:35); "I am the light of the world" (8:12); "I am the gate for the sheep" (10:7); "I am the good shepherd" (10:11); "I am the resurrection and the life" (11:25); "I am the way and the truth and the life" (14:6).

and political triumph. The comparison is straightforward: Israel is the false vine, destined for judgment. Jesus is the true vine, Israel's only hope. The prophets used the image of the vine to indict Israel, but the psalmist takes the image further as a sign of hope. Jesus develops that theme of hope in himself. Jesus invites us—his followers—to be rooted and grounded in him, to be at home with him. Only in him, the Lord's right-hand man, the Son of Man whom the Lord raised up for himself, will we find redemption. Only in him will the Abrahamic covenant and the Aaronic blessing be fulfilled. The psalmist cries out, "Restore us, God Almighty; make your face shine on us, that we may be saved" (Ps. 80:7). And the apostle declares, "Salvation is found in no one else, for there is no other name under heaven given to mankind by which we must be saved" (Acts 4:12).

WORSHIP AND OBEDIENCE

The psalmist's theme is once again "the Exodus from Egyptian servitude" and the wilderness sojourn.[1] Only this time, the psalm begins and ends on a note of festive joy. The intensity of the previous psalms gives way here to a respite of joy, a sober reminder, and a promise of God's protection and provision. The Asaph tradition grasps the life-transforming impact of the worship liturgy. We are not formed by information alone, but by the rhythms of grace and habits of the soul that shape daily life and the seasons of our lives. The command to obey the voice of God is embedded in resounding worship and in the preached remembrance of God's merciful deliverance.

Psalm 81 has been associated with the fall festival, the Feast of Tabernacles, coming five days after the Day of Atonement. The people of God were instructed "to take branches from luxuriant trees—from palms, willows and other leafy trees—and rejoice before the LORD your God for seven days. Celebrate this as a festival to the LORD for seven days each year." The Lord commanded the Israelites to "live in temporary shelters for seven days . . . so your descendants will know that I had the Israelites live in temporary shelters when I brought them out of Egypt. I am the LORD your God" (Lev. 23:40–43). The festival was designed to celebrate three great blessings: the "ingathering" of the firstfruits of the wheat harvest (Exod. 34:22), the Lord's saving redemption signified in an elaborate sacrificial liturgy for each of the seven days (Num. 29:12–40), and the prophetic expectation that God will fulfill all of his promises. Through Moses, the Lord commanded the people: "Be joyful

---

1   Reardon, *Christ in the Psalms*, 159.

at your festival—you, your sons and daughters, your male and female servants, and the Levites, the foreigners, the fatherless and the widows who live in your towns" (Deut. 16:14). This inclusive family celebration of the people of God included daily sacrifices and a special emphasis on the public reading of the law of God in the hearing of everyone (Deut. 31:9–13). The prophet Zechariah envisioned a climactic eschatological Festival of Tabernacles that gathered the peoples of the earth to worship the King, the Lord Almighty (Zech. 14:16–17).

CALL TO WORSHIP

> Sing for joy to God our strength;
> shout aloud to the God of Jacob!
> Begin the music, strike the timbrel,
> play the melodious harp and lyre.
> Sound the ram's horn at the New Moon,
> and when the moon is full, on the day of our festival;
> this is a decree for Israel,
> an ordinance of the God of Jacob.
> When God went out against Egypt,
> he established it a statute for Joseph.
> —Psalm 81:1–5b

Exuberant, jubilant praise is the first order of worship. The sound of the shofar (ram's horn) gathers the great assembly of the people of God for worship (Lev. 23:23). The procession begins with a dance. "Strike the timbrel" signals lively music set to a rhythmic beat. The shaking and striking of the tambourine is joined by stringed instruments, which are more like a guitar than a modern-day harp. Music and dance set a celebratory tone for this command performance instituted by God himself when the Israelites were redeemed from Egyptian bondage. This bold expression of embodied, expressive worship is in response to the Lord's command. Loving God takes practice, much like a musical instrument does, and the more we do it, the better we get at it and the more we love it. We are more than thinking beings and even more than believing beings. We are loving beings. We are defined by who or what we love.[2] We are embodied agents of desire or

---

2   Smith, *Desiring the Kingdom*, 37–52.

love, and when we enter into worship—body, mind, and soul—we show that love takes practice in worship practices.

Psalm 81 begins with a "just-do-it" imperative: "Sing for joy to God our strength." This command was not meant to impose worship on an unwilling people. The decree, "Shout aloud to the God of Jacob!" is a revelatory blessing countering the idolatry of everything else. The New Testament "makes no statute about feasts or fasts" because there is no need to.[3] The apostle Paul called these cultural liturgies and special days "a shadow of the things that were to come; the reality, however, is found in Christ" (Col. 2:17; see also Rom. 14:5). The will of God and human desire converge in the new creation. "The old has gone, the new is here!" (2 Cor. 5:17). The Lord puts his will in our minds and writes it on our hearts (Jer. 31:33), and we bind ourselves to the Lord and his everlasting promise (Jer. 50:5).

The worship liturgies of the people of God in the Old Testament are transposed in fresh and freeing ways in the New Testament. The author of Hebrews exhorted brothers and sisters in Christ to draw near to God in the full assurance that faith brings, that they may hold unswervingly to the hope they professed in Christ, and to consider how to spur one another on to love and good deeds. He challenged them not to give up meeting together (Heb. 10:19–25). The inspiration for worship is found in the filling of the Holy Spirit and the indwelling of the word of Christ with no separation between the Spirit and the word. We are challenged to embrace liturgies that let the peace of Christ rule and the word of Christ dwell in us richly, liturgies that involve teaching and admonishing one another "with all wisdom through psalms, hymns, and songs from the Spirit" in gratitude to the Lord (Col. 3:15–16).

CALL TO REMEMBER

I heard an unknown voice say:
"I removed the burden from their shoulders;
their hands were set free from the basket.
In your distress you called and I rescued you,
I answered you out of a thundercloud;
I tested you at the waters of Meribah.

---

3   Kidner, *Psalms 73–150*, 293.

Hear me, my people, and I will warn you—
if you would only listen to me, Israel!
You shall have no foreign god among you;
you shall not worship any god other than me.
I am the LORD your God,
who brought you up out of Egypt.
Open wide your mouth and I will fill it."
                                        —Psalm 81:5c–10

The psalmist faithfully declares the word of God. Like the apostle John who turned around to see the voice that was speaking to him and saw someone like a son of man (Rev. 1:12–13), the psalmist is neither vague nor generic, but rather humble and submissive. Neither the psalmist nor the apostle can exhaust the mystery. They cannot contain, control, package, or manipulate the voice. All they can do is humbly convey the message.

The psalmist deftly sketches the history of redemption by painting a picture of slave labor set free. The burden has been lifted from their shoulders, and the endless, oppressive, back-breaking labor of lifting heavy loads has ceased. Yahweh is their savior: "I removed the burden. . . . I rescued you. . . . I answered you. . . . I tested you." The substance of the redemptive message is straightforward; the Lord heard their cry of distress and saved them. But now the Lord insists, "Hear me, my people, and I will warn you—if you would only listen to me, Israel!" (Ps. 81:8; see Deut. 6:4). Salvation is not a point in time but a whole new way of living.

Only the first command, "I am the LORD your God. . . . You shall have no other gods before me" (Deut. 5:6–7), needs to be preached in order to include all the commands. Yet the force of the message is not the costly demand of obedience as much as God's gracious bounty freely given to those who hear and obey.[4] The climax of the preached word is all grace: "I am the LORD your God, who brought you up out of Egypt. Open wide your mouth and I will fill it" (Ps. 81:10). The analogy to eating and being satisfied covers a range of meaning from daily manna to daily dependence on the will and word of God. The psalmist alludes to Moses's warning: "When you have eaten and are satisfied, praise the

---

4   Kidner, *Psalms 73–150*, 295.

LORD your God. . . . Be careful that you do not forget the LORD your God, failing to observe his commands, his laws and his decrees that I am giving you this day" (Deut. 8:10–11).

The analogy of opening our mouth to consume the physical and spiritual bread of life runs through Scripture. Manna symbolizes God's complete provision. God meets our physical needs and our spiritual needs. From the temporal to the eternal, God's provision is complete. It covers the range of God's blessing from the Israelites' daily bread in the wilderness to the gift of salvation through our crucified and risen Lord. Every time we break bread together, we remember that it is God who strengthens our bodies and souls. There is an inseparable connection between the manna in the wilderness, our daily bread, and the bread of the Eucharist. When the Lord gave the Israelites manna and insisted that they keep a portion of it in the ark of the covenant as a testimony (Exod. 16:33; Heb. 9:4), he created a biblical image that pointed forward to the Bread of Life. Jesus summed it up this way: "Your ancestors ate the manna in the wilderness, yet they died. But here is the bread that comes down from heaven, which anyone may eat and not die. I am the living bread that came down from heaven. Whoever eats this bread will live forever" (John 6:49–51). Therefore whenever we "eat this bread and drink this cup, [we] proclaim the Lord's death until he comes" (1 Cor. 11:26). We remember Christ's broken body, his sacrifice for our sin, and his provision for our eternal salvation. God's provision is complete in Christ and meets all of our needs, body, mind, and soul. "For the bread of God is he who comes down from heaven and gives life to the world" (John 6:33 ESV).

CALL TO OBEY

"But my people would not listen to me;
Israel would not submit to me.
So I gave them over to their stubborn hearts
to follow their own devices.
If my people would only listen to me,
if Israel would only follow my ways,
how quickly I would subdue their enemies
and turn my hand against their foes!
Those who hate the LORD would cringe before him,

and their punishment would last forever.
But you would be fed with the finest of wheat;
with honey from the rock I would satisfy you."
—Psalm 81:11–16

The negative example of the rebellious Israelites in the wilderness was not only used by the psalmist in his generation, but by the apostles in the early church. Reardon observes, "Israel's infidelity . . . remains the Bible's perpetual admonition to the Church."[5] The author of Hebrews sums it up: "For we also have had the good news proclaimed to us, just as they did; but the message they heard was of no value to them, because they did not share the faith of those who obeyed" (Heb. 4:2). The apostle makes a similar case when he writes to the believers at Corinth: "These things happened to them as examples and were written down as warnings for us, on whom the culmination of the ages has come. So, if you think you are standing firm, be careful that you don't fall!" (1 Cor. 10:11–12).

Jesus's repeated emphasis on love made real in obedience may surprise some believers who think that the emphasis should be more on grace than works.[6] Some Christians have a habit of pitting works righteousness against the work of righteousness. They think that since Christ paid it all, nothing much is expected of them. Life goes along merrily with all of its worldly distractions and pursuits until death happens or Christ comes again. Grace is their spiritual life insurance policy. From Sunday to Sunday preachers assuage the guilty consciences of their worldly believers by quoting Romans as their signature benediction, "There is now no condemnation for those who are in Christ Jesus" (Rom. 8:1). They send believers into the world armed with grace as an excuse to pursue their selfish dreams without the dire warning that "if your right eye causes you to stumble, gouge it out and throw it away" or the clear prohibition, "You cannot serve both God and money" (Matt. 5:29; 6:24).

Dietrich Bonhoeffer exposed this cheap-grace mentality as the deadly enemy of the church.[7] He insisted that the New Testament marries the call

---

5   Reardon, *Christ in the Psalms*, 160.
6   Webster, *God Who Comforts*, 51–52.
7   Bonhoeffer, *Cost of Discipleship*, 47.

to obedience and the gift of grace. To believe is to obey and to obey is to believe. Belief without obedience is cheap grace and obedience without belief is works righteousness.[8] "Grace is costly," writes Bonhoeffer,

> because it calls us to follow, and it is grace because it calls us to follow Jesus Christ. It is costly because it costs a man his life, and it is grace because it gives a man the only true life. It is costly because it condemns sin, and grace because it justifies the sinner. Above all, it is costly because it cost God the life of his Son: "ye were bought at a price," and what has cost God much cannot be cheap for us. Above all, it is grace because God did not reckon his Son too dear a price to pay for our life, but delivered him up for us. Costly grace is the Incarnation of God.[9]

Put another way, "Costly grace and sacrificial obedience are woven into the tapestry of God's love for us. One cannot be separated from the other without destroying the whole tapestry."[10]

Psalm 81 concludes "with a strong reminder of God's grace and resource."[11] Renewal is more than a real possibility; it is the expectation. All the people of God must do is hear and obey. The prerequisite for God's gracious protection and provision is simple and straightforward: "If my people would *only* listen to me, if Israel would *only* follow my ways . . ." (Ps. 81:13, emphasis added). Goodness is not nearly as complicated as we make it out to be. Simple obedience invites God's quick response and enduring salvation. Enemies will cringe, and judgment will be final and lasting. The psalmist draws on the Song of Moses (Deut. 32:13) to emphasize the miracle of God's grace. God can bring sweet honey from rocks and even raise up the children of Abraham from stones (Matt. 3:9).

---

8   Bonhoeffer, *Cost of Discipleship*, 69, 74.
9   Bonhoeffer, *Cost of Discipleship*, 47–48.
10   Jim Eschenbrenner, personal correspondence, used with permission.
11   Kidner, *Psalms 73–150*, 296.

THE WILL OF GOD VERSUS THE WILL TO POWER

Psalm 82 declares that, in the end, there is no contest between the will of God and the will to power—God wins. Ultimately, God's justice will prevail against every form of injustice and oppression—human and demonic. But in the meantime, "our struggle is not against flesh and blood, but against the rulers, against the authorities, against the powers of this dark world and against the spiritual forces of evil in the heavenly realms" (Eph. 6:12). Psalm 82 is in the Asaph tradition, and it offers a big-picture vision of the just judgment of God.

The ambiguity over the identity of the "gods" mentioned in this psalm may be viewed positively. Instead of having to choose between the wicked officials of Israel or the rulers of other nations or demonic evil rulers and angels, the psalmist lumps them all together (see Revelation 13). The continuum of multiple evil sources makes sense with respect to the psalm and the political reality that confronts the world. The human and demonic will to power is set over and against the will of God. The weak and the fatherless, the poor and the oppressed, suffer injustice and oppression, even as the wicked are favored and empowered. In our analysis of the complexity of evil, it does little good to isolate either the human or demonic elements. Evil forms an inclusive whole that is anti-God and anti-Christ.

THE GREAT ASSEMBLY

> God presides in the great assembly;
> he renders judgment among the "gods";

"How long will you defend the unjust
and show partiality to the wicked?
Defend the weak and the fatherless;
uphold the cause of the poor and the oppressed.
Rescue the weak and the needy;
deliver them from the hand of the wicked.
The 'gods' know nothing, they understand nothing.
They walk about in darkness;
all the foundations of the earth are shaken."
—Psalm 82:1–5

The German philosopher Friedrich Nietzsche (1844–1900) mocked the notion that there was a God presiding over the great assembly. He despised salvation and judgment and claimed that hope in anything other than the will to power was an illusion. Nietzsche argued that humanity is falsely educated to believe in something other than the hard fact of exploitation and self-mastery.[1] Belief in God is an illusion created to avoid a deep-down, unteachable, unyielding spiritual fate that "life itself is the will to power."[2] "The cardinal instinct of an organic being," Nietzsche argued, is self-preservation. All talk of motive, purpose, freedom, and morality is meaningless. If humans were true to their animal instincts, they would reverence superior rank and the hardness of heart born of unfavorable circumstances. "Egoism belongs to the nature of a noble soul."[3] And "the noble soul [only] has reverence for itself."[4] For Nietzsche there were only two kinds of people, the exalted and the exploited, the proud and the humble, the powerful and the petty, the hardened and "the doglike people who allow themselves to be maltreated."[5] For Nietzsche humility was unbecoming of the noble soul. To exploit and dominate was a worthy goal for the human of superior rank and self-made self-worth. Nietzsche wanted a megaphone to shout from the housetops, "There is no God. There is no Incarnate One." There is only the human being who "will have to be an incarnate will to power," the person who "will strive to grow, spread, seize, become predominant."[6]

---

1 Nietzsche, *Beyond Good and Evil*, §56, 258.
2 Nietzsche, *Beyond Good and Evil*, §13, 211.
3 Nietzsche, *Beyond Good and Evil*, §265, 405.
4 Nietzsche, *Beyond Good and Evil*, §287, 418.
5 Nietzsche, *Beyond Good and Evil*, §260, 395.
6 Nietzsche, *Beyond Good and Evil*, §259, 393.

Even if Nietzsche had shouted in the psalmist's ear, the psalmist would not have flinched. The fool can say in his heart or cry from the rooftop that there is no God, but that does not change the fact. The psalmist declares, "God presides in the great assembly; he renders judgment among the 'gods.'" It is God who questions the "gods," and not the other way around. God is not in question. Humans are. Thus it is against all reason and compassion that the will to power seeks to overrule the will of God. The gods violate the moral order and do the unthinkable. They defend the unjust, favor the wicked, and oppress the poor. These gods are narcissistic. They lay claim to heaven and earth and strut around like masters of the universe. Earlier in the Psalms, Asaph described them this way: "They have no struggles; their bodies are healthy and strong. They are free from common human burdens; they are not plagued by human ills. Therefore pride is their necklace; they clothe themselves with violence. From their callous hearts comes iniquity; their evil imaginations have no limits. They scoff, and speak with malice; with arrogance they threaten oppression" (Ps. 73:4–8).

The moral order is inscribed on the human conscience and written in the heart (Rom. 2:15). God's requirements are as simple as they are beautiful: "He has shown you, O mortal, what is good. And what does the LORD require of you? To act justly and to love mercy and to walk humbly with your God" (Mic. 6:8). What could be more obvious: "Rescue the weak and the needy; deliver them from the hand of the wicked" (Ps. 82:4)? But the "gods" rebel and usurp God's moral authority. They exchange the will of God for the will to power. They undermine justice and deprive the people of their freedom. God renders his verdict against Israel's corrupt judges and their demonic allies. All forms of authority that attack the justice and righteousness of God, whether human or demonic, are condemned. "The 'gods' know nothing," declares the Lord. "They understand nothing." They are walking around in the dark, and the foundations of the earth are shaking.

THE DEATH SENTENCE

"I said, 'You are "gods";
you are all sons of the Most High.'
But you will die like mere mortals;
you will fall like every other ruler."
—Psalm 82:6–7

87

The living God is not intimidated by the human and demonic forces of evil. In the great assembly, God "renders judgment" and sentences all the "sons of the Most High" to death (vv. 1, 6). No matter how powerful and famous the "gods" may become, they fall like mere mortals. The apostle John's description of "the great supper of God" (Rev. 19:11–21) is commentary on Psalm 2: "Why do the nations conspire and the peoples plot in vain? The kings of the earth rise up and the rulers band together against the Lord and against his anointed, saying, 'Let us break their chains, and throw off their shackles.' The One enthroned in heaven laughs; the Lord scoffs at them. He rebukes them in his anger and terrifies them in his wrath, saying, 'I have installed my king on Zion, my holy mountain'" (Ps. 2:1–6).

Jesus's quote from Psalm 82 sheds light on its original meaning and thus on its meaning for us today. When Jesus claimed, "I and the Father are one," his opponents picked up rocks to stone him. "I have shown you many good works from the Father," Jesus said. "For which of these do you stone me?" His angry opponents replied, "We are not stoning you for any good work . . . but for blasphemy, because you, a mere man, claim to be God" (John 10:30–33). Jesus's line of defense was provocative. He essentially made a case for the divine endowment of all humanity. "Is it not written in your Law, 'I have said you are "gods"'"? (John 10:34; quoting Ps. 82:6). His statement echoes Psalm 8. When humanity is compared to the cosmos, humanity is minuscule and insignificant, but paradoxically when we are compared to God, our significance grows.

[W]hat is mankind that you are mindful of them, human beings that you care for them? You have made them a little lower than the angels and crowned them with glory and honor. (Ps. 8:4–5)

Craigie writes, "Many of the earliest versions took the [Hebrew word for 'God' or 'gods'] to mean 'angels.' . . . The translation 'angels' may have been prompted by modesty, for it may have seemed rather extravagant to claim that mankind was only a little less than God. Nevertheless, the translation 'God' is almost certainly correct, and the words probably contain an allusion to the image of God in mankind . . . within the created order."[7] Martens writes, "If one were to imagine a scale of 1 to 10, with

---

7   Craigie, *Psalms 1–50*, 108.

living creatures such as beasts as 1 and God as 10, then so high is the writer's estimation of humanity, he should have put him at 8 or 9. It is God, and not animals, who is man's closest relative."[8] Human significance is a gift bestowed by the grace of God. We are designated and endowed by God with privileges and responsibilities that we have not earned or merited. We are crowned with splendor and honor. We are not animals subject to the law of the jungle. We are God's image-bearers, mandated to "rule over the fish in the sea and the birds in the sky, over the livestock and all the wild animals, and over all the creatures that move along the ground" (Gen. 1:26). God blessed humanity and said, "Be fruitful and increase in number; fill the earth and subdue it. Rule over the fish in the sea and the birds in the sky and over every living creature that moves on the ground" (Gen. 1:28).

Jesus takes this revealed truth and argues from the lesser to the greater. If God spoke of people as "gods," then Jesus reasons it is not wrong for him to say, "I am God's Son." Surely, the way Jesus used Psalm 82 to link the reference to the "gods" to himself must have struck the religious leaders as provocative. Bruner sums it up well:

> Jesus is asking: If *powerful persons* are called "gods" in the Psalm because of the Word of God coming *to* them, then what should we call the person most especially sent *from* God to them? Indeed, what should we call *the Messiah* when he comes? Doesn't this absolutely unique emissary of God deserve the title *"God's Son"* as much as any earthly potentate? And doesn't Scripture often call the Messiah "God's Son"? (See esp. 2 Sam. 7:14; Ps. 2:7 . . .). Jesus is arguing "from the lesser to the greater," *a fortiori*, in his reading of Psalm 82: If Scripture calls addressed *mortals* gods, please tell me an appropriate title for God's addressing *Messiah*, his ambassador to the planet?[9]

It is ironic that Jesus used Psalm 82, a psalm that singles out corrupt rulers who deserved to be judged, to defend his messianic identity. The "gods" are under indictment and destined to die like the mere mortals they are, but in Jesus, his sent one, God intervenes to reverse the course of judgment and provide for redemption. "For God did not send his Son

---

8   Martens, *God's Design*, 202–3.
9   Bruner, *John*, 646–47 (emphasis his).

into the world to condemn the world, but to save the world through him" (John 3:17). But the irony goes deeper. The bad religious leaders are in cahoots with Rome. They have compromised and colluded with the devil to stay in power. And Jesus condemns them: "You belong to your father, the devil, and you want to carry out your father's desires" (John 8:44). Their only hope for redemption is in "the one whom the Father set apart as his very own and sent into the world" (John 10:36). The verdict is clear: "Whoever believes in him is not condemned, but whoever does not believe stands condemned already because they have not believed in the name of God's one and only Son" (John 3:18).

RISE UP

Rise up, O God, judge the earth,
for all the nations are your inheritance.
—Psalm 82:8

The psalmist has the final word. He calls for God to rise up and set things right. The nations belong to God, not the devil (Luke 4:5–8), and the psalmist believes that "only when the Lord comes to judge will there be a kingdom where justice and righteousness prevail."[10] But there is an amazing intervention. God determined that before he would rise up to judge, he would descend to deliver. Lewis describes the grand miracle of the Incarnate One this way: "In the Christian story God descends to re-ascend. He comes down; down from the heights of absolute being into time and space, down into humanity. . . . But He goes down to come up again and bring the whole ruined world up with Him."[11] "For God so loved the world that he gave his one and only Son, that whoever believes in him shall not perish but have eternal life" (John 3:16).

---

10   Ross, *Psalms*, 2:725.
11   Lewis, *Miracles*, 115.

JUST JUDGMENT

Psalm 83 ends the Asaph sequence of psalms with the international perspective of the prophets and God's judgment of the nations. Worship leaders in the Asaph tradition have acknowledged Israel's apostasy. They have not been blind to Israel's disobedience and unbelief. But now the focus is on the world. The psalmist prays for God's name to be upheld and revered. The global vision of Psalm 83 calls for judgment against all the nations that threaten to annihilate the people of God. But this judgment is not for the sake of vengeance. Its purpose is redemptive, "that they will seek your name" (Ps. 83:16).

Psalm 83 is an imprecatory psalm that begins by laying out an international conspiracy of intimidation, bullying, and plotting aimed at destroying the people of God.[1] This is followed by naming the nations that are involved and united in their shared hatred for Israel. The psalmist invokes the past and draws on history to establish a precedent for divine action against Israel's enemies. The psalm's "ruling thought is of God's vindication rather than man's conversion."[2] Nevertheless, the psalmist does not lose sight of the possibility of transformation and prays that God's judgment will cause hardened enemies to "seek your name" and "know that you, whose name is the Lord—that you alone are the Most High over all the earth" (vv. 16, 18).

NAMING THE ENEMY

> O God, do not remain silent;
> do not turn a deaf ear,
> do not stand aloof, O God.

---

1 Other imprecatory Psalms include Psalms 5, 10, 17, 35, 58, 59, 69, 70, 79, 109, 129, 137, 140.
2 Kidner, *Psalms 73–150*, 302.

See how your enemies growl,
how your foes rear their heads.
With cunning they conspire against your people;
they plot against those you cherish.
"Come," they say, "let us destroy them as a nation,
so that Israel's name is remembered no more."
With one mind they plot together;
they form an alliance against you—
the tents of Edom and the Ishmaelites,
of Moab and the Hagrites,
Byblos, Ammon and Amalek,
Philistia, with the people of Tyre.
Even Assyria has joined them
to reinforce Lot's descendants.
                                    —Psalm 83:1–8

The psalmist inspires believers in every age to turn to God when "enemies growl" and "foes rear their heads." God has promised to be with us always, even "to the very end of the age" (Matt. 28:20). God invites us to bring to him our laments and our inward groans, knowing that "the Spirit himself intercedes for us through wordless groans" (Rom. 8:26). The Spirit who helps us in our weakness uses the Psalms as an instrument to guide our understanding and shape our perspectives. Praying the Psalms is one way "the Spirit intercedes for God's people in accordance with the will of God" (Rom. 8:27). The saints who have gone before are pictured in the Revelation calling out in a loud voice, "How long, Sovereign Lord, holy and true, until you judge the inhabitants of the earth and avenge our blood?" (Rev. 6:10).

The antidote to fear is prayer. When we call on God to pay attention to our plight, we enter into the spiritual struggle with fresh awareness and deeper insight. Christ's followers know that their hope is not found in the approval of the surrounding cultural elite and power brokers. We cannot afford to think and talk as if our identity is wrapped up in "Canaanite" politics or "Philistine" strategies. Psalm 83 reminds us that our hope is in God and the work of the gospel exclusively. The Christian before the world is like Jesus before Pilate, and we need to hear Jesus's words over and over again to stay on mission: "My kingdom is not of this world. If it were, my servants would fight to prevent my arrest by the Jewish leaders. But now my kingdom is from another place" (John 18:36).

Psalm 83 is an antidote to the pervasive ideologies that threaten to dominate the "big picture" of our lives. Sociologist James Davison Hunter challenges believers "to disentangle the life and identity of the church from the life and identity of American society." He argues that the church has "uncritically assimilated to the dominant ways of life in a manner" that threatens to "compromise the fundamental integrity of its witness to the world."[3] Psalm 83 reinforces the apostolic conviction that the gospel of Jesus Christ is a countercultural movement that will remain a voice crying in the wilderness of an evil and broken culture. The people of God should not expect to be a controlling voice of culture, but they should aim to impress the world with Christ's goodness.

The psalmist is not naive as to the cunning strategies and the behind-the-scenes plots that aim to destroy the people of God. Nor is he unaware of the members of this conspiracy. He names them, all ten of them—ten being a symbolic number for completeness. In Revelation the number ten and its multiples signify a complete quota of tribulation or power, such as "ten days" of persecution or an army numbering "twice ten thousand times ten thousand" or a beast with "ten horns."[4] At the top of the enemies' list is long-time adversary Edom, Esau's ancestors (Gen. 36; Ps. 137:7; Jer. 49:7–22), followed by the descendants of Ishmael, the Ishmaelites (Gen. 16:15, 16; 25:12–18). Moab and Ammon trace their family roots to Lot (Gen. 19:36–38; Num. 22–24). The Hagrites are thought to come from Hagar (1 Chron. 5:10, 19, 20). Five more enemies are listed: Byblos (Gebal), Amalek, Philistia, Tyre, and Assyria. "All of these people attacked Israel off and on through the centuries; and they all had the same intention—the annihilation of Israel."[5] This psalm does not suggest that these ten nations were good friends. They were enemies of each other, and in the eighth and seventh centuries Assyria dominated the region. But what it does suggest is that when the Assyrians conquered these nations, they "reinforced Lot's descendants" in their historic quest for the annihilation of Israel.

---

3   Hunter, *To Change the World*, 184–85.
4   Rev. 2:10; 9:16; 12:3; 13:1; 17:7, 12, 16.
5   Ross, *Psalms*, 2:736.

CALLING DOWN JUDGMENT

Do to them as you did to Midian,
as you did to Sisera and Jabin at the river Kishon,
who perished at Endor
and became like dung on the ground.
Make their nobles like Oreb and Zeeb,
all their princes like Zebah and Zalmunna,
who said, "Let us take possession
of the pasturelands of God."
Make them like tumbleweed, my God,
like chaff before the wind.
As fire consumes the forest
or a flame sets the mountains ablaze,
so pursue them with the tempest
and terrify them with your storm.
Cover their faces with shame, LORD,
so that they will seek your name.
May they ever be ashamed and dismayed;
may they perish in disgrace.
Let them know that you, whose name is the LORD—
that you alone are the Most High over all the earth.
—Psalm 83:9–18

The psalmist establishes the precedent for God's just judgment by recalling the victory of Gideon over Midian (Judges 6–8), and Deborah and Barak's defeat of the Canaanite commander Sisera and King Jabin at the brook of Kishon (Judges 4–5). He wants all Israel's enemies to be defeated the way the Midianite leaders Oreb and Zeeb were defeated (Judges 7:25). All those who plot to take possession of "the pasturelands of God" deserve to come to the same end as the kings of Midian, Zebah, and Zalmunna, who were killed by Gideon himself (Judg. 8:21). The psalmist uses a litany of wasteland images to describe the judgment of God. He prays to God to reduce his enemies to tumbleweed and wind-blown chaff, the remains of a ravaging forest fire, and refuse bobbing in a tempest-tossed sea.

Prayer is the psalmist's defense against cunning enemies who seek to annihilate the people of God. God is the ultimate just judge who will right the wrongs and punish those who have hated Israel. But how does this psalm work today for believers who have been told by the Lord Jesus to love their enemies and pray for their persecutors (Matt. 5:44)? First, prayer is the place where believers can bring their anger and bitterness against evil to God. Prayer gives vent to the raw emotions of pain and suffering received at the hands of the wicked.

Second, Jesus spoke of hell often. He repeatedly promised that on the day of judgment, those who rejected the gospel would suffer a worse fate than Sodom and Gomorrah (Matt. 10:15; 11:21–24; Luke 10:12–15). Jesus stated it plainly, "There is a judge for the one who rejects me and does not accept my words; the very words I have spoken will condemn them at the last day" (John 12:48). "Repent or perish" was a refrain that ran through his ministry (Luke 13:2–5). Any generation that rejects the gospel is guilty of the blood of all the prophets (Luke 11:50–51). Jesus lashed out, "You snakes! You brood of vipers! How will you escape being condemned to hell?" (Matt. 23:33). To be ashamed of Jesus and his gospel was to identify with an "adulterous and sinful generation" and to invite a reciprocal response: "the Son of Man will be ashamed of you when he comes in his Father's glory with the holy angels" (Mark 8:36–38; see also Luke 9:23–26). Jesus warned, "Do not be afraid of those who kill the body but cannot kill the soul. Rather, be afraid of the One who can destroy both soul and body in hell" (Matt. 10:28).

Third, like the psalmist, Jesus described judgment in graphic and violent language. Hell is outer darkness, a place of weeping and gnashing of teeth (Matt. 22:13; 24:51; 25:30; Luke 13:28).

Jesus warned, "Anyone who says, 'You fool!' will be in danger of the fire of hell" (Matt. 5:22). And again, "If your hand or your foot causes you to stumble, cut it off and throw it away. It is better for you to enter life maimed or crippled than to have two hands or two feet and be thrown into eternal fire" (Matt. 18:8). Jesus offers these words of condemnation at the final judgment: "Depart from me, you who are cursed, into the eternal fire prepared for the devil and his angels" (Matt. 25:41).

Fourth, the psalmist alludes to an emphasis that deserves to dominate the praying imagination of believers today. He prays, "Cover their faces with shame, LORD, *so that they will seek your name. . . . Let them know that you, whose name is the* LORD—*that you alone are the Most High over all the earth*" (Ps. 83:16, emphasis added). Hope of conversion is nearly buried in the language of vindication and judgment, but it is there.[6] The psalmist prays for the enemy "that when they see the power of God and realize the folly of their endeavor they will seek [desire] the name of the Lord . . . and pray to him for mercy."[7] Beyond the desire for deliverance and judgment is "the ultimate desire of the psalmist" that others—even the enemies of the people of God—"might come to know and obey the true God."[8]

Augustine believed that the psalmist never would have prayed "so that they will seek your name" (v. 16) if he was not convinced that there were members of the "company of the enemies of God's people" who would be granted to turn to God "before the last judgment." For now everyone is mixed together, but some will repent and believe. They will "seek the name of the Lord."[9]

If the psalmist hinted at this redemptive hope, how much more should we, knowing that "God demonstrates his own love for us in this: While we were still sinners, Christ died for us. Since we have now been justified by his blood, how much more shall we be saved from God's wrath through him! For if, while we were God's enemies, we were reconciled to him through the death of his Son, how much more, having been reconciled, shall we be saved through his life!" (Rom. 5:8–10).

---

6   Kidner, *Psalms 73–150*, 302. Calvin, *Psalms*, 5.3:349. Calvin disagrees with this hopeful prospect. He believes that the ungodly are "inflated with intolerable pride" and that it is impossible "to abate their pride until they are laid prostrate, confounded and shamefully disappointed. When he declares (v. 16) that, as the result of this, 'they will seek the name of God,' he is not to be understood as speaking of their being brought to true repentance, or of their genuine conversion. . . . What is here meant is nothing more than a forced and slavish submission like that of Pharaoh, king of Egypt."

7   Ross, *Psalms*, 2:740.

8   Boice, *Psalms*, 2:686.

9   Augustine, *Expositions of the Psalms*, 8:399.

THE HOUSEHOLD OF FAITH

The prophetic intensity of the Asaph psalms yields to the longing for spiritual renewal found in Psalms 84–85. These psalms are attributed to the sons of Korah from the tribe of Levi (Psalms 42–49, 84, 85, 87, 88). King David made the descendants of Kohath worship leaders "in the house of the LORD after the ark came to rest there" (1 Chron. 6:31; see also vv. 22, 38). Their calling as worship leaders and the evidence of these psalms proves that the Korah family history is a beautiful redemption story. In the wilderness, the Korah clan rebelled against Moses and Aaron and suffered a devastating judgment (Numbers 16). The family was nearly wiped out, but at least one son survived and his descendants eventually became temple worship leaders in Israel.

The psalmist expresses his heartfelt longing for the real presence of the living God. There is an ecstatic intensity about his language: "how lovely!" "my soul yearns, even faints," "my heart and my flesh cry out" (Ps. 84:1–2).[1] Ecological images of nesting birds and springs in the desert capture our imagination. Deep emotion and satisfaction is conveyed by communal praise invoked by God's loving presence. Yahweh anoints his leaders and withholds no good thing from "those whose walk is blameless" (v. 11). The psalmist's soulful yearning is inspired not by ritual habit but by an abiding relationship with the Lord Almighty, his King and his God. While his pilgrimage is deeply personal, the psalmist shares his

---

1   Spurgeon, "Psalm 84," *Treasury of David*. Spurgeon writes, "This sacred ode is one of the choicest of the collection; it has a mild radiance about it, entitling it to be called *The Pearl of Psalms*. If the twenty-third be the most popular, the one-hundred-and-third the most joyful, the one-hundred-and-nineteenth the most deeply experimental, the fifty-first the most plaintive, this is one of the most sweet of the Psalms of peace."

quest and enters into worship with "those whose strength" is in God. He is in the company of like-minded pilgrims who find their happiness and fulfillment in the presence of God. This psalm is prayed by people who "decide to leave an ego-centered world and enter a God-centered world."[2]

THE HOUSE OF THE LORD

How lovely is your dwelling place,
LORD Almighty!
My soul yearns, even faints,
for the courts of the LORD;
my heart and my flesh cry out
for the living God.
Even the sparrow has found a home,
and the swallow a nest for herself,
where she may have her young—
a place near your altar,
LORD Almighty, my King and my God.
Blessed are those who dwell in your house;
they are ever praising you.
            —Psalm 84:1–4

The positive tenor of this psalm encourages today's believers to embrace life together in Christ as a joyful privilege. As Reardon explains, the progressive revelation of God transposes the psalmist's "passion for the sanctuary" into the believer's passion for Christ. Everything the temple stood for is fulfilled in him. Jesus is "God's true temple" (John 2:21; Rev. 21:22). "And because He is God's temple, God abides in Jesus. Jesus is the one place where we meet God, and we too abide in Jesus, being united to God in Him."[3] The psalmist's "language of love poetry" finds its true significance in Christ and in the body of Christ (1 Cor. 3:16; 6:19).[4] "We belong to one another only through and in Jesus Christ," writes Bonhoeffer, adding, "in Jesus Christ we have been chosen from eternity, accepted in time, and united for eternity."[5]

2   Peterson, *Answering God*, 23.
3   Reardon, *Christ in the Psalms*, 165.
4   Kidner, *Psalms 73–150*, 303.
5   Bonhoeffer, *Life Together*, 21.

We are invited by Jesus to make our home in him: "Remain in me, as I also remain in you" (John 15:4). The homemaking word (*meinai*) is used again when Jesus says, "Whoever eats my flesh and drinks my blood remains in me, and I in them" (John 6:56). Jesus used the word again when he said, "If you hold to my teaching [or, if you make your home in my word], you are really my disciples. Then you will know the truth, and the truth will set you free" (John 8:31–32).

When Jesus walked out of the temple for the last time, the old sacrificial, Levitical priestly temple system was basically rendered obsolete (Matt. 24:1). "The temple worship of the ancient people of God is all over and the way to God's holy presence has been opened up for all by means of this one sacrifice for the sin of the whole world."[6] Jesus is "the stone the builders rejected [which] has become the cornerstone" (Ps. 118:22).

Peter's Pentecost message confirmed that Jesus replaced the temple. The gospel eclipsed the temple. Zambian theologian Joe Kapolyo calls attention to the significance of Jesus abandoning institutional Judaism and the whole sacrificial system.[7] Only Christ fulfills the human need for salvation and the longing of the soul. If the temple is done away with, how much more will all religious traditions be eclipsed by the presence of Jesus? Jesus is Lord. He is the one who is greater than Judaism, Islam, Hinduism, Confucianism, ancestral worship, tribal animism, existential selfism, and all forms of Christ-less Christianity.[8]

The original band of disciples made an amazing adjustment to the physical departure of Jesus. They could no longer walk with Jesus or enjoy table fellowship. They could not see him heal the sick or hear him preach. He was no longer there for them in a literal sense, and they had to adjust. The New Testament is a testimony to the fact that the disciples made this adjustment amazingly well with the help of the Spirit of the risen and ascended Lord.[9]

The absence of a literal, physical Jesus is as relevant for us as it was for the original band of disciples. The disciples had to learn how to follow Jesus without his physical presence. This is true for today's disciples as

---

6   Bruner, *Matthew*, 2:757.
7   Kapolyo, "Matthew," 1161.
8   Webster, *Preaching Hebrews*, 112.
9   Webster, *God Who Kneels*, 119–21.

well. The danger of a "false literal" confronts the church today as it always has. Given the absence of Jesus, we are given to substitutes that stand in the place of a physical Jesus. The literal concreteness of a pre-Easter Jesus becomes transposed into the "false literal" experience of spiritual leaders who focus attention on themselves or other things. It may be powerful personalities or church bureaucracies or buildings or cherished rituals that stand in the place of Jesus. Instead of the church dependent on the fruit and gifts of the Spirit of Christ, we can give ourselves to "Christian" idols that stand in the place of a literal Jesus.

The longing expressed in Psalm 84 is for the living God made real in Jesus. It is not for a false literal (an idol) that attempts to substitute for God. This yearning for the presence of God runs counter to the wisdom of the age that says the church must adapt to the rise of consumerism.

Psalm 84 celebrates the inefficient irrelevance of the counterculture household of faith. We cannot prove the societal worth of the church to a secular world. Nor can we promote the gospel as a product—designed to meet our emotional and spiritual felt needs. It is not our aim to create brand loyalty in a highly competitive marketplace. What we can do is love people and call them to repentance and to new life in Christ. We can offer sinners like ourselves the gospel of grace. We can invite them into the body of Christ through baptism and communion. Worship is our highest priority and greatest passion, but as Calvin warned, we are not to be "sedulously attentive to the observance of outward ceremonies, but destitute of genuine heart godliness."[10] The psalmist's passion for the presence of God is exactly what we want today in every aspect of the life of the church.

The passion of Psalm 84 corresponds to the church of Acts' devotion to "the apostles' teaching and to fellowship, to the breaking of the bread and to prayer" (Acts 2:42). In Acts 2, description and prescription merge to form the nexus between God's work and our work, rendering everything else superfluous and extraneous. Psalm 84 deepens our understanding of what it means to be devoted to these four disciplines as the way to seek God's presence. The heartfelt yearning of Psalm 84 is transposed into practical spiritual disciplines or devotions that give the church authentic focus, identity, growth, and fellowship. The blessing

10   Calvin, *Psalms*, 5.3:357.

of the real presence of Christ means that we are at home with God. It is as natural and normal as songbirds nesting in the temple eaves. Beatitude-based believers have humbled themselves and acknowledged their utter dependence upon the mercy of God.

THE JOURNEY OF DESIRE

> Blessed are those whose strength is in you,
> whose hearts are set on pilgrimage.
> As they pass through the Valley of Baka,
> they make it a place of springs;
> the autumn rains also cover it with pools.
> They go from strength to strength,
> till each appears before God in Zion.
> Hear my prayer, LORD God Almighty;
> listen to me, God of Jacob.
> Look on our shield, O God;
> look with favor on your anointed one.
> —Psalm 84:5–9

The psalmist's journey may be a literal, physical pilgrimage to Jerusalem, or it may be an inward, meditative, spiritual journey to the presence of God.[11] Either way, the psalm gives voice to those who merge desire, devotion, and discipline. They put one step in front of the other in their faith journey. The line "whose hearts are set on pilgrimage" is literally "highways in their hearts." It means that the journey to God travels over and through a rocky heart and resistant mind. Even when the journey passes through the arid wilderness, the valley of Baka, the sojourners have "set their hearts on pilgrimage." God provides pools of fresh water in a dry and weary land. What might have been "a place of dry adversity" becomes "a place of springs."[12] Instead of growing weaker as they journey on, they become stronger. Hope in the Lord renews their strength; they "soar on wings like eagles," "run and not grow weary," and "walk and not be faint" (Isa. 40:31).

The psalmist focuses on the Lord God Almighty. Hear my prayer, "GOD-of-the-Angel-Armies! King! God!" (Ps. 84:4 MSG). He seeks a

---

11   Ross, *Psalms*, 2:753.
12   Ross, *Psalms*, 2:754.

direct response from the God of Jacob. He prays for the king, God's anointed one, who is strengthened by God to defend the people of God. He prays on the basis of God's promises to the house of David (2 Sam. 7:16). The psalmist prays to the one and only personal God, not to a vague generic deity who is free of any "intellectualized understanding."[13] "Modern spiritual consciousness is predicated upon the fact that God is gone," writes poet Christian Wiman, "and spiritual experience, for many of us, amounts mostly to an essential, deeply felt and necessary, but ultimately inchoate and transitory feeling of oneness or unity with existence. It is mystical and valuable, but distant."[14] This way of thinking is an invention of late modernity and is antithetical to the understanding of the psalmist who depends upon the God who has made himself known, the God of Jacob.

The winsome skeptic's disdain for empty religious jargon meets in the Psalms the power of God's personal revelation. "By sheer grace," writes Bonhoeffer, "God will not permit us to live even for a brief period in a dream world. He does not abandon us to those rapturous experiences and lofty moods that come over us like a dream."[15] The revelation of God in Christ is alive and active, penetrating to the core. If you are tempted to "do a little linguistic dance around Christianity," it's time to grapple with the fact that God has revealed himself and this is not godtalk—this is revelation.[16] God has spoken and the "ever praising" worshiper believes in "the primacy of God's word in everything: in creation, in salvation, in judgment, in blessing, in mercy, and in grace."[17]

THE BLESSING OF GOD

> Better is one day in your courts
> than a thousand elsewhere;
> I would rather be a doorkeeper in the house of my God
> than dwell in the tents of the wicked.
> For the LORD God is a sun and shield;
> the LORD bestows favor and honor;

13   Wiman, *My Bright Abyss*, 18.
14   Wiman, *My Bright Abyss*, 18.
15   Bonhoeffer, *Life Together*, 27.
16   Bonhoeffer, *Life Together*, 142.
17   Peterson, *Answering God*, 86.

no good thing does he withhold
from those whose walk is blameless.
LORD Almighty,
blessed is the one who trusts in you.
—Psalm 84:10–12

The psalmist's deepest joy comes from being at home in the house of God (Ps. 27:4; 73:25; Phil. 3:8). He would rather be in the presence of God than anywhere else. Just one day in Christ is better than a thousand days apart from Christ. Posted up at the entranceway as an usher or a janitor is more fulfilling for the psalmist than being seated at the head table in the East Room of the White House or winning a Nobel Prize or receiving an Oscar. The psalmist's "theory of relativity" means that nothing compares to the presence of God. Our translation "doorkeeper" is a bit misleading, because the official at the gate of the temple was a highly respected figure (1 Chron. 26:1, 12) who played an important role in administering the liturgy at the gate (Psalm 15). But the psalmist does not use the term for "gatekeeper." He speaks of one who is "waiting at the threshold." The humble and lowly status of the worshiper is preferred over official status in the world. Or as one translation reads, "I'd rather scrub floors in the house of my God than be honored as a guest in the palace of sin" (Ps. 84:10 MSG).

The reason for his passion for God is no mystery. "God, like a sun, gives grace to his people; and like a shield, he gives them glory."[18] This means that "the Spirit of glory and of God rests" on all those in Christ (1 Peter 4:14). It means that "he who did not spare his own Son, but gave him up for us all—how will he not also, along with him, graciously give us all things?" (Rom. 8:32). It means that because of the foreknowledge of God the Father, through the sanctifying work of the Spirit, and through the obedience of Jesus Christ and his sprinkled blood, we have a living hope, a lasting inheritance, and a coming salvation (1 Peter 1:2–5). The promise of God's presence is transposed into an even higher key. "For the Lamb at the center of the throne will be their shepherd; 'he will lead them to springs of living water' [Isa. 49:10]. 'And God will wipe away every tear from their eyes' [Isa. 25:8]" (Rev. 7:17). This means that "the peace of God, which transcends all understanding, will guard your hearts and your minds in Christ Jesus" (Phil. 4:7).

---

18   Ross, *Psalms*, 2:758.

RIGHTEOUSNESS AND PEACE KISS

P salm 85 is a meditation on salvation and spiritual renewal. We pray this psalm along with Nehemiah when he returned to the land of Israel with the exiles to reestablish Jerusalem. We pray this psalm along with Mary, the mother of Jesus, who prepared her heart and mind for the coming of "the Son of the Most High" (Luke 1:32). We pray this psalm with Jesus who made our salvation possible by his obedient and atoning sacrifice on our behalf. We pray this psalm with all those who seek the salvation that only God can give.

Salvation is not a religious abstraction but the lived experience of the redeemed. Every goodness we can possibly imagine finds its source in God's saving grace. Salvation encompasses deliverance from sin and death, from despair of self and alienation from others, and from the pressures of the world and a meaningless life.[1] Salvation changes us in every way, giving us an abiding relationship with God and a deep sense of hope and confidence. In Christ we live into a new reality; the old creation is gone and the new creation has come (2 Cor. 5:17).

The psalmist remembers the exodus as the epicenter of redemption. It is the pivotal event in Israel's history when the Lord restored the fortunes of Jacob, forgave the people's iniquity, and covered all their sins. He remembers the Lord turning away his wrath (Ps. 85:1–3). But now he prays for a restoration of that "first love" experience of God's saving grace. The psalmist does not feel the need to review Israel's rebellion and apostasy. He assumes that the cause of God's displeasure is common knowledge and does not need to be rehearsed. What is important is that

---

1   White, "Salvation," 968.

the psalmist's plea for full restoration be heard. He entreats the Lord to put away his displeasure and "grant us your salvation" (vv. 4–7). In the final section, the psalmist highlights the shared experience of the fullness of salvation by elaborating on the attributes of the Lord: peace, purity, wisdom, righteousness, glory, love, and faithfulness (vv. 8–13).

FORGIVENESS REMEMBERED

> You, LORD, showed favor to your land;
> you restored the fortunes of Jacob.
> You forgave the iniquity of your people
> and covered all their sins.
> You set aside all your wrath
> and turned from your fierce anger.
> —Psalm 85:1–3

The historical background for this psalm is difficult to determine. It may have come after the Babylonian captivity in the days of Ezra and Nehemiah (450–440 BC), when the faithful remnant cried out to God for help to reclaim the land, rebuild Jerusalem and the temple, and restore the people of God to their past blessings. Psalm 85 is a postexilic appeal for revival based on remembering God's blessing at Sinai. The pattern of redemption, rebellion, and renewal makes the psalm relevant in many situations where the forgiven faithful seek the joy of their salvation. It is easy to imagine Nehemiah identifying with this psalm. His prayer expresses many of these same themes: the Lord's covenant faithfulness, the acknowledgment of previous sin, the purpose of God's judgment, and the promise of restoration if the people return to him (Neh. 1:5–11). Nor is it difficult to imagine Mary four hundred years later being drawn to this psalm when she sang in praise to the Lord, "He has helped his servant Israel, remembering to be merciful to Abraham and his descendants forever, just as he promised our ancestors" (Luke 1:54–55). The ebb and flow of faithful obedience has characterized the people of God from the days of Israel to the present age of the church, giving this psalm universal appeal.

The psalmist begins with the foundation of restoration: forgiveness. For the believer, the epicenter of redemption has shifted from the exodus to the cross of Jesus Christ. This is where our appeal for renewal begins.

Christ has covered all our sins. The blood of the Passover lamb was a type pointing forward to the sacrifice of Christ on the cross. We are redeemed by "the precious blood of Christ, a lamb without blemish or defect" (1 Peter 1:19). Through faith in his blood we are able to draw near to the holy God (Rom. 3:25; Eph. 2:13). In Christ, we are "justified" (Rom. 5:9), redeemed (Eph. 1:7), and have "peace through his blood, shed on the cross" (Col. 1:20). The apostles emphasize the cleansing power of Christ's blood. The blood of Christ cleanses our consciences (Heb. 9:14) and "purifies us from all sin" (1 John 1:7). The power of Christ's forgiveness in our lives inspires us to "love each other deeply, because love covers over a multitude of sins" (1 Peter 4:8; see James 5:20). This "covering" of sin, this community-building love, depends absolutely on the atoning, sacrificial love of Christ. The apostle Paul says, "Since we have now been justified by his blood, how much more shall we be saved from God's wrath through him!" (Rom. 5:9). The psalmist asks the Lord to "set aside" all his wrath and turn from his "fierce anger" (Ps. 85:3), and the apostles declare that Jesus "rescues us from the coming wrath" (1 Thess. 1:10).

RENEWAL

> Restore us again, God our Savior,
> and put away your displeasure toward us.
> Will you be angry with us forever?
> Will you prolong your anger through all generations?
> Will you not revive us again,
> that your people may rejoice in you?
> Show us your unfailing love [*hesed*], LORD,
> and grant us your salvation.
> —Psalm 85:4–7

There is an overriding communal cast to this renewal prayer that makes it hard for people steeped in Western individualism to appreciate. Westerners begin with the individual, but the psalmist begins with the people of God. When he says, "Restore us again, God our Savior," he includes the history of the people of God who stand together through time. They are not a collection of networked individuals but a faithful company who share a common salvation, even as they share together judgment, repentance, and restoration. Nehemiah is not a solitary figure who prays on behalf of himself. He is the Lord's servant praying for the people of Israel. He confesses his sins and the sins of his people (Neh. 1:6–7). Mary's prayer is deeply personal, "My soul glorifies the Lord" (Luke 1:46), but also powerfully communal. She is in solidarity with Abraham and his descendants. The psalmist refuses to make this prayer for renewal and restoration about himself. It is about us, the people of God, and not about "me."

The author of Hebrews says we have confidence to enter the Most Holy Place by the blood of Jesus (Heb. 10:19). But the psalmist is also bold, and his confidence stems from the same source. The reason the believer can boldly enter into the presence of God is the same reason the psalmist can pray the way he does. It is not about our self-confidence but God's self-consistency. The reason the prayer gradually gathers strength is because all the petitions depend upon the promises of God.[2] The psalmist dares to beseech God for his "unfailing love [*hesed*]," because he knows the character, promises, and actions of God his Savior.[3]

This boldness is not to the credit of the psalmist but the to the mercy of God. Whatever is good and praiseworthy flows from the mercy of God and not what we deserve. This leads to a humble boldness. Augustine expressed it this way: "Seeing that we are not proud means that we are not lifted up. And if we are not lifted up, we will not fall. And if we don't fall, we will stand. And in standing we will cling fast and abide. And when we abide we will rejoice in the Lord our God. This is the path to confidence. Everything we have, our father, our country, our inheritance, our salvation comes from the mercy of God."[4]

---

2   Kidner, *Psalms 73–150*, 308.

3   Regarding the term *hesed*, Jacobson writes, "Traditionally, a wide range of English terms have been employed in the attempt to capture the meaning of *hesed*: 'mercy,' 'loving-kindness,' 'steadfast love,' 'faithfulness,' 'covenantal love,' 'loving faithfulness,' and the like. We find that none of these words or phrases satisfactorily express the range and depth of *hesed*. . . . The relational nature of the term cannot be overemphasized. It describes the duties, benefits, and commitments that one party bears to another party as a result of the relationship between them. The Lord's *hesed* is the basis on which the psalmist dares to ask for deliverance and forgiveness. The Lord's *hesed* describes how and why the Lord created and sustains the good creation. The Lord's *hesed* is that to which the hymns of praise and songs of thanksgiving bear witness. The Lord's *hesed* is what the wisdom psalms teach. And *hesed* is the most important characteristic that God desires to see embodied both in individuals and in the communities that pray the psalms" (DeClaissé-Walford, Jacobson, and Tanner, *Book of Psalms*, 8).

4   Augustine, *Expositions on the Psalms*, 8:406.

CONVERGENCE

I will listen to what God the LORD says;
he promises peace to his people, his faithful servants—
but let them not turn to folly.
Surely his salvation is near those who fear him,
that his glory may dwell in our land.
Love and faithfulness meet together;
righteousness and peace kiss each other.
Faithfulness springs forth from the earth,
and righteousness looks down from heaven.
The LORD will indeed give what is good,
and our land will yield its harvest.
Righteousness goes before him
and prepares the way for his steps.
—Psalm 85:8–13

The convergence of all that is good creates a beautiful picture of salvation. The psalmist's confident hope comes from listening to the word of God. God promises an inner harmony and an ultimate convergence of righteousness and peace. The divine purpose—bringing unity to all things in heaven and on earth in Christ—overcomes the great divorce between our fallenness and our fulfillment. The psalmist envisions the end goal, and from our vantage point in salvation history we understand the means to that goal. Through the incarnation, God descends into our suffering humanity, joins us on the ash heap, takes up this mean battle with Satan, and goes to the cross. The Lord of Glory is crucified, but the cross is not the last word, and the resurrection is not a wild card played at the end. There is a beautiful coherence between the life, death, and resurrection of Jesus and the truth of the universe. The power of the resurrection fits with the wonder and meaning of life as we know it, from our understanding of the created order to the justice of the moral order.[5] Christ makes possible the promise of peace to God's faithful servants. Christ brings salvation near to those who fear him. In Christ, love and faithfulness meet and righteousness and peace kiss.

The Hebrew poet has paired the blessings of salvation: peace and faithfulness, salvation and glory, love and faithfulness, righteousness and

5   Webster, *Follow the Lamb*, 32.

peace. These are not opposites that require reconciliation, but blessings that prove reconciliation. Each attribute is a reflection of the Lord's goodness and character, like a musical variation in the symphony of salvation beautifully orchestrated by the Chief Musician. Love and faithfulness are friends united in Christ. Righteousness and peace kiss each other because Christ Jesus who is our peace has made us righteous in him. We cannot have peace without righteousness nor righteousness without peace. Only in Christ do they come together. Augustine reads the testimony of the Incarnate One in the faithfulness that springs from the earth, and the Father's acceptance of the atoning sacrifice in the righteousness that looks down from heaven.[6] When Jesus prayed Psalm 85 he must have identified himself and his ministry with the promise of the abundant life and the fruitful harvest (John 10:10; Luke 10:2). He united righteousness and peace and love and faithfulness like no one else, and who better than the Christ can it be said, "Righteousness goes before him and prepares the way for his steps" (Ps. 85:13).

---

6   Augustine, *Expositions on the Psalms* 8:408–9.

A HEART FOR THE LORD

The theme of this David psalm is complete dependence upon the Lord. Its placement in the middle of the Korah psalms gets our attention. Psalm 86 contradicts any notion of the autonomous individual self. David is passionately dependent upon the Lord, who is the subject of all his thoughts, pleas, prayers, and praise.[1] Every line reminds us that the Lord is sovereign over all.

The psalmist identifies God with three different names. Four times he uses the name *Yahweh*, which stands for the unique character of the covenant-keeping God who revealed himself by name to Moses (Ps. 86:1, 6, 11, 17; see Exod. 6:3). Five times he uses *Elohim* (vv. 2, 10, 12, 14, 15), a more general term for God that is derived from a plural of majesty and is used in the singular for the transcendent God of creation. *Adonai*, which means "Master" or "Sovereign," is the name for God that

---

1   Ross writes: "A number of commentators have rated this psalm somewhat second class because of its lack of originality. It seems to use standard expressions and motifs from earlier psalms" (*Psalms*, 2:778). Wilcock writes: "Nearly the whole of this one [Psalm 86] turns out to be a mosaic of fragments pieced together from others [psalms], and from related Old Testament scriptures." Wilcock refers to "recycled" passages and the fabric of Psalm 86 being a "patchwork," adding, "but David himself would have found that it fitted him well enough, and what he would own, we ought not to call common" (*The Message of Psalms*, 2:56–57). Goldingay writes: "Although practically every phrase in the psalm can be linked with some verse in the Psalms, it would be misleading to list these in such a way as to suggest that the psalmist was directly taking phrases from those sources. Its relationship with the other psalms is more like that of the Revelation of John with the Old Testament, where hardly a verse would survive without the scriptural phraseology that lies behind it, but the book comes into being because the visionary is soaked in the Scriptures rather than because he is directly sampling them at every point" (*Psalms*, 2:619).

the psalmist weaves throughout the psalm. It is translated "Lord" seven times in this psalm (vv. 3, 4, 5, 8, 9, 12, 15), and it is used as a reminder of the supplicant's submission and subservience to the Lord. We imagine Jesus praying Psalm 86 out of devotion to the Father's will. We hear echoes of the psalmist's prayer, "I will glorify your name forever" (v. 12) in Jesus's prayer of consecration (John 17:1–26). David's determination to remain resilient in spite of his enemies fits perfectly with Jesus's calm confidence before his sworn enemies.

HEAR ME OUT

Hear me, LORD [Yahweh], and answer me,
for I am poor and needy.
Guard my life, for I am faithful to you;
save your servant who trusts in you.
You are my God; have mercy on me, Lord [Adonai],
for I call to you all day long.
Bring joy to your servant, Lord [Adonai],
for I put my trust in you.
You, Lord [Adonai], are forgiving and good,
abounding in love to all who call to you.
Hear my prayer, LORD [Yahweh];
listen to my cry for mercy.
When I am in distress, I call to you,
because you answer me.
　　　　　　　　　—Psalm 86:1–7

The devotional passion expressed at the outset of this psalm helps sweep away spiritual apathy. Psalm 86 articulates what authentic dependence upon the Lord involves. This first section begins and ends with the psalmist entreating Yahweh to listen (vv. 1, 6). He offers five compelling personal reasons. God will hear him because, "I am poor and needy" (v. 1), "I am faithful to you" (v. 2), "I call to you all day long" (v. 3), "I put my trust in you" (v. 4), and "I call to you, because you answer me" (v. 7). Every one of these reasons can be traced back to the character of God who is "forgiving and good" (v. 5), "abounding in love" (v. 5), and responsive to distress (v. 7). The Lord will respond because of his great and marvelous deeds (v. 10), because of his great love toward him and his deliverance from death (v. 13), and because the Lord is "compassionate and gracious, slow to anger and abounding in love and faithfulness" (v. 15). The psalmist's appeal is predicated on the prior action of God's mercy: "for you, LORD [Yahweh], have helped me and comforted me" (v. 17).

ONLY YOU, LORD

Among the gods there is none like you, Lord [Adonai];
no deeds can compare with yours.
All the nations you have made
will come and worship before you, Lord [Adonai];
they will bring glory to your name.
For you are great and do marvelous deeds;
you alone are God.
Teach me your way, LORD [Yahweh],
that I may rely on your faithfulness;
give me an undivided heart,
that I may fear your name.
I will praise you, Lord [Adonai] my God, with all my heart;
I will glorify your name forever.
For great is your love toward me;
you have delivered me from the depths,
from the realm of the dead.
                              —Psalm 86:8–13

The appeal of the psalmist to be heard by God leads to an eruption of praise. Compared to the unreal gods of the pagan imagination, David declares emphatically there is no contest—the Lord wins. "There is none like you, no deeds compare with yours" (v. 8). Calvin comments that the psalmist has gathered courage and new strength for prayer. He commends the psalmist for holding in "contempt and derision all the false gods in whom the heathen world imagined some help was to be found."[2] The gods are a lost cause, but the nations are not. The psalmist credits the Lord with their existence and says that one day all the nations will recognize and worship the Lord. David's doxology is bold on two fronts—the theological and the political. The Lord rules over all. David declares, "You alone are God" (v. 10). There is no division in the psalmist's mind between personal devotion and social engagement. There is a largeness to David's world, and the Lord is at the center. He would agree

---

2   Calvin, *Psalms*, 5.3:384.

with Wells: "The self is a canvas too narrow, too cramped, to contain the largeness of Christian truth."[3]

David has yet to share with the Lord the besetting problem that lies behind his personal lament and his deep need to be heard. That will come in the final section (vv. 14–17), but he has prioritized his prayer in a beautiful way. Regardless of the vortex of threatening circumstances, he prays for wisdom. "Teach me your way, LORD, that I may rely on your faithfulness" (v. 11). The psalmist knows that to lead, he must be led. He seeks to be mastered by the Master. When Augustine came to this verse in his sermon on this psalm he immediately exclaimed, "Your way, Your truth, Your life is Christ. Therefore the Body [of Christ] belongs to Him, and Body is of Him." Then he quotes Jesus saying, "I am the Way, and the Truth, and the Life" (John 14:6), adding, "It is one thing to lead to the way, another to guide in the way." Believers, Augustine insists, "must be guided by Him in the way itself, lest they fall."[4]

This desire for wisdom goes beyond training and schooling. David longs for understanding and insight so he may remain faithful to the Lord even in stressful circumstances. He wants his intuition and visceral reaction to life's pressing problems to be governed and guided by the will of God. This wisdom is not primarily a matter of doctrine and discursive knowledge, although these play a vital role and should not be diminished. The focus of the psalmist is not so much on person-as-thinker or person-as-believer, as it is on person-as-lover.[5] Augustine assumes that the follower of Jesus Christ is an embodied agent who needs some precious hand-holding as she makes her way. He asks: How does the Lord lead us? To which he answers, "By always admonishing, always giving you His hand."[6]

His prayer for wisdom, "Teach me your way, LORD," moves immediately to his plea, "Give me an undivided heart that I may fear your name" (Ps. 86:11). The apostle's prayer echoes the psalmist's concerns (Phil. 1:9–11). The heart symbolizes who we are in the depth of our being. We are commanded to love the Lord our God with all our heart and with all our soul and with all our strength (Deut. 6:5). Yet we are

---

3   Wells, *No Place for Truth*, 183.
4   Augustine, *Expositions of the Psalms*, 8:415.
5   Smith, *Desiring the Kingdom*, 62.
6   Augustine, *Expositions of the Psalms*, 8:415.

told by the prophet Jeremiah that "the heart is deceitful above all things and beyond cure" (Jer. 17:9). Jesus said, "For out of the heart come evil thoughts—murder, adultery, sexual immorality, theft, false testimony, slander" (Matt. 15:19; see Luke 6:45). Yet it is with the heart that we believe and are justified, and it is with the mouth that we confess and are saved (Rom. 10:10). David had a heart after God's own heart (Acts 13:22), and the hardhearted Israelites were said to have a "heart of stone" (Ezek. 36:26). Real wisdom is trusting in the Lord with all your heart and leaning not on your own understanding (Prov. 3:5). Throughout the Old Testament the people of God are exhorted to serve the Lord with all their heart and soul (Deut. 10:12; Josh. 22:5). True communication means speaking the truth from the heart (Ps. 15:2), because the message has been taken to heart (Rev. 1:3), even as true counsel instructs the heart (Ps. 16:7). True repentance is "a broken and contrite heart" (Ps. 51:17; see Joel 2:13; Rom. 2:29). Real maturity is characterized by having "integrity of heart" (Ps. 78:72), "an undivided heart" (Ps. 86:11), "an upright heart" (Ps. 119:7), a "singleness of heart" (Jer. 32:39), a humble heart (Matt. 11:29), a "heart of wisdom" (Ps. 90:12), and a "sincere heart in full assurance of faith" (Heb. 10:22 NASB).

Only the Lord really knows the heart. The psalmist prays, "May the words of my mouth and the meditation of my heart be pleasing in your sight, O Lord, my rock and my redeemer" (Ps. 19:14 NLT). "Test me, Lord, and try me, examine my heart and my mind; for I have always been mindful of your unfailing love and have lived in reliance on your faithfulness" (Ps. 26:2–3). What we are like outwardly may be a charade. The real issue is a person's heart, which has a way of showing its true colors under the pressure of time and circumstance. As the psalmist prayed, "Surely you desire truth in the inner self; you teach wisdom in the inmost place" (Ps. 51:6).[7]

The psalmist sees the undivided heart as a gift that naturally leads to praise. When we have begun to grasp the Lord's great love for us, how can we keep from praising? "I had never noticed that all enjoyment spontaneously overflows into praise," wrote Lewis. "The world rings with praise." We praise spontaneously what we like—what we love. We do not have to be badgered or lectured in how to praise. Lewis continues,

---

7   Webster, *Soundtrack of the Soul*, 73–74.

"I had not noticed how the humblest, and at the same time the most balanced and capacious minds, praised most, while the cranks, misfits and malcontents praised least."[8]

The proof of the Lord's great love for David is found in his deliverance from death: "You have delivered me from the depths, from the realm of the dead" (Ps. 86:13). The word that David uses for death is *she'ol* (see also Ps. 6:5), which refers "to the underworld or the realm of the dead."[9] The psalmist seems to imply that he is grateful for "a future deliverance from the power of death."[10] It was not just that his life had been spared physically but that he was saved "from a still deeper abyss of death."[11] This kind of death is referred to in the book of Revelation as "the second death" (Rev. 2:11; 20:14), and those whose name are written in the Lamb's book of life need not fear the second death. The exuberance of the psalmist is shared by the New Testament believer who can say with Paul, "For to me, to live is Christ and to die is gain" (Phil. 1:21).

TURN TO ME

> Arrogant foes are attacking me, O God;
> ruthless people are trying to kill me—
> they have no regard for you.
> But you, Lord [Adonai], are a compassionate and gracious God,
> slow to anger, abounding in love and faithfulness.
> Turn to me and have mercy on me;
> show your strength in behalf of your servant;
> save me, because I serve you
> just as my mother did.
> Give me a sign of your goodness,
> that my enemies may see it and be put to shame,
> for you, LORD [Yahweh], have helped me and comforted me.
> —Psalm 86:14–17

Finally, we get to the presenting problem, but everything that has been said is fundamental to the supplicant's spiritual formation. David's

8 Lewis, *Reflections on the Psalms*, 93–94.
9 Ross, *Psalms*, 2:784.
10 Kidner, *Psalms 73–150*, 313.
11 Calvin, *Psalms*, 5.3:390.

description of "arrogant foes" and "ruthless people" recall Psalms 3–7 in Book 1. These psalms describe the Absalom conspiracy and the rebellious reaction of Saul's ancestors from the tribe of Benjamin (2 Samuel 13–20). These psalms, along with Psalm 86, must have resonated with Jesus, who faced the scorn and ridicule of the religious leaders who conspired against him and plotted his death. They gave Jesus the words to pray when confronted by "arrogant foes" and "ruthless people."

By this point in the psalm, we sense that David has almost lost interest in his enemies. They remain a serious threat, but his focus on the Lord is complete. We picture Jesus praying this way about his enemies. Instead of elaborating on how bad his enemies were, Jesus, like David, focused on how good God is. David quotes from the Lord's word to Moses, "But you, Lord, are a compassionate and gracious God, slow to anger and abounding in love and faithfulness" (Ps. 86:15; see Exod. 34:6). The issue for believers is not how bad the world is, but how good the Lord is. Instead of praying for the defeat of his enemies, David prays for a sign of the Lord's goodness so as to shame them into true recognition and submission to God. He asks the Lord for evidence of his mercy and strength. His plea is endearing, "Save me, because I serve you just as my mother did" (v. 16). His poignant bottom line underscores the absolute sufficiency he has found in the Lord: "for you, LORD, have helped me and comforted me" (v. 17).

BORN AGAIN

salm 86 has embedded in its personal plea for spiritual renewal a prophecy that anticipates the global reach of the gospel. The psalmist declares, "All the nations you have made will come and worship before you, Lord; they will bring glory to your name" (Ps. 86:9). In Psalm 87 the sons of Korah celebrate this amazing truth with a psalm dedicated to the city of God and the gathering of God's people from "every tribe and language and people and nation" (Rev. 5:9).

We cannot pray Psalm 87 without hearing the Lord's Great Commission to go and make disciples of all nations. We remember the magi who came from the east to worship the one who was born king of the Jews (Matt. 2:1–2). We recall the Samaritan woman (John 4:1–42), the Roman centurion (Luke 7:1–10), and the Syrophoenician woman (Mark 7:24–30), all of whom put their faith and trust in Jesus. The exclamation of the Roman soldier at the foot of the cross, "Surely he was the Son of God!" has become the testimony of many from every nation and people group. Psalm 87 anticipates the outpouring of the Holy Spirit at Pentecost and the worldwide impact of the gospel.

The terse, staccato style of Psalm 87 lends itself to a burst of praise. Exuberance describes this good news psalm. It deserves to be sung or shouted. The gates of Zion are flung open to the world so that all may enter into the city of God and the joy of the Lord. The inclusiveness of the kingdom is glorious and the songs of praise never cease.

THE CITY OF GOD

He has founded his city on the holy mountain.
The LORD loves the gates of Zion
more than all the other dwellings of Jacob.

> Glorious things are said of you,
> city of God:
> —Psalm 87:1–3

The psalm begins with an "abrupt and emphatic" statement of fact.[1] God "founded" this place. The meaning and purpose of this city on the holy mountain is established in the will of God. The place itself is not holy. God makes it holy. The "gates of Zion" stand for the whole city and represent the bustling human activity that brings energy and joy to the city. The Lord's love for the "gates" is a metaphor for his electing love that makes this place his home and the people his people. The psalm will go on to prove that the Lord's exclusive love for Zion, "more than all the dwellings of Jacob," is for the sake of inclusion. The reason "glorious things" are said about this city is because everybody is welcome—everybody can find their true home here.

We explored the meaning of Zion in our study of Psalm 14. Zion, the city of David, is the *place* from which salvation comes. When Jesus Christ came, *person* replaced *place*. The Incarnate One fulfilled and embodied everything about salvation. For "salvation is found in no one else, for there is no other name under heaven given to mankind by which we must be saved" (Acts 4:12).

In himself, Jesus summed up the meaning of Zion, and the meaning of the "land" was replaced by the meaning of the person. Wright explains, "The physical territory of Jewish Palestine is nowhere referred to with any theological significance in the New Testament. The land as a holy place has ceased to have relevance. . . . Furthermore, the geographical land of Israel has no place in New Testament teaching regarding the ultimate future of God's people."[2] Instead of the holiness of *place*, "Christianity has fundamentally . . . substituted the holiness of the *Person*: it has Christified holy space."[3]

Even before the coming of Jesus Christ, the meaning of Zion was always more spiritual than political and more universal in scope than ethnic. "Salvation was not a matter of making earthly Zion the center of

---

1   Kidner, *Psalms 73–150*, 314.
2   Wright, *Eye for an Eye*, 93.
3   Wright, *Eye for an Eye*, 93, quoting W. D. Davis, *The Gospel and the Land* (Berkeley: University of California Press, 1974), 368.

life; it was a matter of trusting in the Lord and being guaranteed a place in a more glorious city in his eternal kingdom."[4] Psalm 87 corresponds with the prophecy of Isaiah and the glory of Zion, when all the nations will gather to recognize what God has done:

> Your gates will always stand open. . . . The children of your oppressors will come bowing before you; all who despise you will bow down at your feet and will call you the City of the LORD, Zion of the Holy One of Israel. Although you have been forsaken and hated, with no one traveling through, I will make you the everlasting pride and the joy of all generations. . . . Then you will know that I, the LORD, am your Savior, your Redeemer, the Mighty One of Jacob. (Isa. 60:11, 14–16)

The author of Hebrews also envisions Mount Zion welcoming the people of God. "You have not come to a mountain that can be touched and that is burning with fire; to darkness, gloom and storm. . . . But you have come to Mount Zion, to the city of the living God" (Heb. 12:18, 22). All the identifying qualities of Mount Zion are relationally God-centered and culminate in Jesus the mediator of the new covenant, whose sprinkled, sacrificial blood is powerful to save.

> But you have come to Mount Zion, to the city of the living God, the heavenly Jerusalem. You have come to thousands upon thousands of angels in joyful assembly, to the church of the firstborn, whose names are written in heaven. You have come to God, the Judge of all, to the spirits of the righteous made perfect, to Jesus the mediator of a new covenant, and to the sprinkled blood that speaks a better word than the blood of Abel,. (Heb. 12:22–24).

The apostle John sees "the Holy City, the new Jerusalem, coming down out of heaven from God" (Rev. 21:2). This Holy City is home to the 144,000 who stand on Mount Zion (Rev. 14:1; Joel 2:32; Heb. 12:22; Gal. 4:26). They represent "the totality of God's people throughout the ages," as well as the militant last generation of believers fighting to the end.[5] John's reference to Mount Zion echoes the Lord's promise, "I have installed my king on Zion, my holy mountain" (Ps. 2:6).

---

4   Ross, *Psalms*, 2:798.
5   Beale, *Revelation*, 733; see Bauckham, *Climax of Prophecy*, 229–32.

THE CITIZENS OF ZION

"I will record Rahab and Babylon
among those who acknowledge me—
Philistia too, and Tyre, along with Cush
and will say, 'This one was born in Zion.'"
Indeed of Zion it will be said,
"This one and that one were born in her,
and the Most High himself will establish her."
The LORD will write in the register of the peoples:
"This one was born in Zion."
As they make music they will sing,
"All my fountains are in you."
                                        —Psalm 87:4–7

Without hesitation or prejudice the psalmist quotes the Lord's description of what is so glorious about Zion.[6] The citizens of Zion are drawn from everywhere, even Israel's enemies and rivals. The most unlikely candidates for conversion become the citizens of God's kingdom because they know him and worship him. Shockingly, archenemies and oppressors are suddenly fellow citizens with God's people, rejoicing side by side and singing their hearts out, in praise of Yahweh. The five nations listed, Egypt (Rahab), Babylon, Philistia, Tyre, and Cush (Nubia and parts of Ethiopia) all have a history of violence and hatred against Israel. But the tragic past is not remembered in the wake of this glorious news.

It is not just that these foreign nationalities have been accepted and assimilated into Israel. Miraculously, these Egyptians and Babylonians and Ethiopians have been reborn in the city of God. They are not second-class citizens. The Lord himself declares, "This one was born in Zion." And then he repeats it for emphasis: "Indeed of Zion it will be said, 'This one and that one were born in her.'" And then again for the third time: "The LORD will write in the register of the peoples: 'This one was born in Zion.'" The psalmist uses the language of birth to speak of conversion and in doing so "anticipates the later language of being 'born again' in the New Testament."[7] The new birth is not a matter of natural descent or of human enterprise. This is a work of the Holy Spirit. "Every conversion

---

6   Ross, *Psalms*, 2:795.
7   Ross, *Psalms*, 2:796.

is a virgin birth. 'With human beings this [new life] is impossible; but with God absolutely everything is possible' (Matt. 19:26). The Holy Spirit, in other words is the miraculous *how* of New Life."[8] The only way to become the children of God is to be born of God (John 1:13). The psalmist's expression "this one and that one" (Ps. 87:5) emphasizes one person at a time. One by one we enter the kingdom of God.

It is not difficult to imagine Jesus praying Psalm 87 when you consider him saying to Nicodemus, "Very truly I tell you, no one can see the kingdom of God unless they are born again" (John 3:3). Undoubtedly Nicodemus understood himself to be a solid citizen of the kingdom of God—the ultimate insider if there ever was one. He was a Pharisee who sat on the Jewish ruling council. But Jesus implied otherwise when he repeated, "Very truly I tell you, no one can enter the kingdom of God unless they are born of water and the Spirit. . . . You should not be surprised at my saying, 'You must be born again'" (John 3:5, 7). It must have been shocking to Nicodemus to realize that he had to be "born of the Spirit," just like God-fearing Gentiles from far-flung nations.

The meaning of Psalm 87 is played out throughout the Gospels. For Matthew, the magi represent the unexpected, but very welcome, citizens of the kingdom of God. They are like Rahab, the surprising recipient of God's grace when the Israelites entered the Promised Land. They are like Naaman the Syrian, trusting in God's word. They are like the Queen of Sheba, but they are bowing before the one greater than Solomon (Matt. 12:42). They are like the Samaritan woman in the gospel of John and the Roman centurion in Luke's gospel. Surely if God can raise up the children of Abraham from stones, as Jesus said, then he can extend his grace to Eastern magi and Mongolians and Latin Americans. If God's grace can overcome the distance between Babylon and Bethlehem, it can overcome all cultural and intellectual barriers. As Jesus said, "I have other sheep that are not of this sheep pen . . . there shall be one flock and one shepherd" (John 10:16). The impact of the gospel led the apostles to see the promise of Zion fulfilled in the heavenly Jerusalem. Paul wrote, "The Jerusalem that is above is free, and she is our mother" (Gal. 4:26).

The psalm ends on a note of joyful celebration, and "as they make music they will sing, 'All my fountains [or springs] are in you'" (Ps. 87:7).

---

8   Bruner, *John*, 24.

A similar theme is sung in Psalm 46:4: "There is a river whose streams make glad the city of God" (see Ezek. 47:1). In an arid land where water is scarce and a constant concern, there is nothing like an endless supply of fresh, running water to symbolize life. If the language of new birth invokes Jesus's conversation with Nicodemus, then, springs of fresh water make us think of Jesus's conversation with the woman at the well. "Whoever drinks the water I give them will never thirst. Indeed, the water I give them will become in them a spring of water welling up to eternal life" (John 4:14).

THE DEATH PRAYER

Psalm 88 may be the saddest prayer in the Psalter because no one wants to ever have to pray this prayer. Death and dying are tough subjects under any circumstances, but the conditions described in this psalm are the worst imaginable. The psalmist hits rock bottom in every way. He is already half dead with one foot in the grave. He is physically spent, emotionally crushed, utterly alone, and abandoned by friends. He feels utterly rejected by everyone, including the Lord. He is overwhelmed by his troubles and drowning under the breaking waves of God's wrath.

The lament psalms usually give some hint of hope or glimmer of praise, but there is nothing positive here. The whole psalm from beginning to end is more like a loud, painful wail from the hospice bed than anything else. Yet it is in Jesus's Prayer Book.

I shared with my friend who turned eighty this year that we were praying for my wife's ninety-four-year-old father. We prayed that he would remain alert and ambulatory right up until he died. We suspected that institutional care would break him, and we hoped he would be spared. My friend's response was, "We all pray for that, but it doesn't usually work out that way."

However, in my father-in-law's case it did. Our prayers were answered. On the weekend before he died, he went to the gym on his own and to the movies with his son. On Sunday he went to church and then to a concert at night with friends. Coming out of the concert, his walker got caught in a crack in the sidewalk and he fell. Two days later he died in the hospital from internal bleeding. An hour before he died, he quoted Proverbs 3:5–6 in four languages: Chiluba, French, Portuguese, and English. He had acquired these languages over a lifetime of missionary service. Shortly before he died he told my brother-in-law, "I'm homesick for heaven."

I would love to go that way. I imagine we all would. But for some of us, the dying process will be so extreme that we will end up praying Psalm 88. Dying can be very cruel, an unmitigated horror, even for those who take Jesus at his word: "I am the resurrection and the life. The one who believes in me will live, even though they die; and whoever lives by believing in me will never die" (John 11:25–26). Such is the frailty and weakness of the human condition that such a prayer needs to be in our prayer book, and we need to know it is there.

OVERWHELMED

> LORD [Yahweh], you are the God who saves me;
> day and night I cry out to you.
> May my prayer come before you;
> turn your ear to my cry.
> I am overwhelmed with troubles
> and my life draws near to death.
> I am counted among those who go down to the pit;
> I am like one without strength.
> I am set apart from the dead,
> like the slain who lie in the grave,
> whom you remember no more,
> who are cut off from your care.
> You have put me in the lowest pit,
> in the darkest depths.
> Your wrath lies heavily on me;
> you have overwhelmed me with all your waves.
> You have taken from me my closest friends
> and have made me repulsive to them.
> I am confined and cannot escape;
> my eyes are dim with grief.
> —Psalm 88:1–9a

The more we grasp the gritty faith of the psalmist, the more we understand why this sad psalm is in the Psalter. His resilient faith is evident in five ways: First, he is not silent; he prays—and that fact alone is no small feat. Second, he persists in calling out to God to save him. After all is said and done, God is his salvation. Third, he credits the sovereignty of God with everything, even his suffering. He lets God be God. Nothing that happens to him is blamed on secondary causes. Fourth, the psalmist believes that to live is to behold God's wonders and experience his love. He rests his case for deliverance on the faithfulness of God in the land of the living. Our mission is to praise God. Fifth, everything comes down to God and him. As far from God as he may feel, it is his relationship with God that matters most to him and upon which everything else depends.

Sometimes we complain of being "overwhelmed." I have used the word to describe the normal pressures of daily work. But that is not how the psalmist is using the word. He is overwhelmed because of the intensity of all his troubles and because he is on the verge of death. He is in a life and death situation, and death is winning. Prayer is his recourse. All of the ugly, disparaging groans and indictments he utters are safe to express in the supplicant's privileged communion with God. The reason Psalm 88 is in the Psalter is because God gives us permission to pray this way. Brokenhearted, soul-despairing prayers are redemptive, no matter how dark and tragic they may sound to those who overhear them. God invites these wrenching prayers and even promises to pray through them. "We do not know what we ought to pray for, but the Spirit himself intercedes for us through wordless groans" (Rom. 8:26).

Despair is found in an alternative discourse of silence and escape. The danger we dread is when the nursing home patient or the distraught widow or the addicted teen shuts down and withdraws into their private hell. For believers to refuse to vent their raw emotion in prayer or to cloak their prayers in pious clichés is the greater danger, because it turns the sufferer inward upon him- or herself. It is naive to think that believers are not tempted to turn to opium and its derivatives instead of prayer. Hydrocodone and oxycodone are the drugs of choice for people trying to escape the kind of pain described in Psalm 88. When these drugs are carefully administered to relieve pain, they serve a necessary purpose. Most of us have personally experienced the positive benefit of pain medications. It is when these drugs are overprescribed and abused that they end up doing more harm than good. Although hydrocodone and oxycodone were not available to the psalmist, the cultivation of the poppy plant goes back as far as six thousand years. Andrew Sullivan reports that Homer called it a "wondrous substance." The eighth-century-BC Greek poet marveled that those who consumed opium "did not shed a tear all day long, even if their mother or father had died, even if a brother or beloved son was killed before their own eyes." "For millennia," writes Sullivan, opium has "salved pain" and "suspended grief."[1] The psalmist boldly testifies to his need to pray, especially in the valley of the shadow of death. The dark night of the soul has no purpose other than prayer, and any retreat from prayer into drugs or despair rejects the honesty of Psalm 88.

The psalmist's lament is passionately God directed, even though his extreme pain and grief renders his plea self-centered. He defines himself in four disturbing "I am" statements: "I am overwhelmed with troubles. . . . I am on the verge of death. . . . I am without strength. . . . I am as good as dead" (Ps. 88:3–5).[2] But then he takes his lament a step further and credits God for his dire circumstances in four indictment statements: "You have put me in the lowest pit. . . . Your wrath lies heavily on me. . . . You have overwhelmed me. . . . You have taken from me my closest friends" (vv. 6–8). The psalmist has no patience for secondary causes. No mention is made of sickness and disease or enemies and foes. Implicit in his lament is his faith in the sovereignty of God and the conviction that nothing happens to him apart from the will of God. He does not waste his energy blaming others or bemoaning his actions. This is all between God and himself. His final "I am" statement brings this section to a close: "I am confined and cannot escape; my eyes are dim with grief" (vv. 8–9).

APPEALING FOR DELIVERANCE

I call to you, Lord, every day;
I spread out my hands to you.

---

1   Sullivan, "Opioid Epidemic in America."
2   Augustine, *Expositions of the Psalms*, 8:424. Augustine insists on a verse-by-verse messianic interpretation of Psalm 88. He hears "the voice of Christ" in every line of prophecy. In some cases it is easy to hear echoes of Psalm 88, for example, when Jesus in Gethsemane said, "My soul is overwhelmed with sorrow to the point of death" (Matt. 26:38; Ps. 88:3). In other cases it is more difficult. Augustine relates the meaning of v. 5, which he translates, "free among the dead," to Jesus's statement, "I have authority to lay it [my life] down and authority to take it up again" (John 10:18). Calvin bluntly refuted Augustine's "refined interpretation," saying, "That Christ is here described, and that he is said to be free among the dead, because he obtained victory over death . . . has no connection with the meaning of the passage" (*Psalms*, 5:409).

Do you show your wonders to the dead?
Do their spirits rise up and praise you?
Is your love declared in the grave,
your faithfulness in Destruction?
Are your wonders known in the place of darkness,
or your righteous deeds in the land of oblivion?
                                   —Psalm 88:9b–12

For a second time the psalmist makes a passionate plea for deliverance. His body language reflects his intensity. He is probably on
his knees or stretched out on the ground with his hands palms up
beseeching God. Implicit in his appeal is the chief end of man—to
glorify and praise God. He reasons that if he is dead, he can no
longer behold the wonders of God. If he dies, he cannot return as a
"shadow" to praise the Lord. If he goes down to the grave, he cannot
testify to the faithfulness of God. His appeal is God-honoring rather
than self-serving, and his reasoning reveals a child of the covenant
who thinks and acts according to the love and righteousness of God.
If God wants the testimony of his faithfulness to continue in the life
of the psalmist, then he will have to save him from "this unwarranted
and fast-approaching death."[3]
    We can imagine Jesus praying this psalm in the days leading up to
the crucifixion. He identified with the psalmist's sorrow and fear of imminent death, but unlike the psalmist, he understood that his death and
resurrection were crucial to the revelation of God's love and faithfulness.
He prayed to the Father, "I have brought you glory on earth by finishing
the work you gave me to do" (John 17:4). Instead of death ending his
testimony, death was the necessary fulfillment of his testimony. The author
of Hebrews describes Christ appearing "once for all at the culmination
of the ages to do away with sin by the sacrifice of himself" (Heb. 9:26).
This is why the apostle Paul said, "May I never boast except in the cross
of our Lord Jesus Christ, through which the world has been crucified to
me, and I to the world" (Gal. 6:14).

---

3   Ross, *Psalms*, 2:811.

UNRESOLVED LAMENT

But I cry to you for help, Lord;
in the morning my prayer comes before you.
Why, Lord, do you reject me
and hide your face from me?
From my youth I have suffered and been close to death;
I have borne your terrors and am in despair.
Your wrath has swept over me;
your terrors have destroyed me.
All day long they surround me like a flood;
they have completely engulfed me.
You have taken from me friend and neighbor—
darkness is my closest friend.

—Psalm 88:13–18

The lament psalms invariably reach resolution in praise, but this psalm is the exception that proves the rule. This last section repeats the difficult themes of the first: rejection, isolation, abandonment, and fear of death. The psalmist adds a depressing note: "From my youth I have suffered and been close to death" (v. 15). This is what someone who has suffered a lifelong debilitating and deadly illness might say. Not only is his lament intensive but extensive. Perpetual pain has been the story of this person's life. Psalm 88 gives voice to the many faithful believers who live with intense chronic pain and life-draining weakness. Anderson says the psalm "creates an impression of unrelieved gloom without a ray of light," which raises the question why this afflicted person prays at all.[4] The fact that his passionate cry for help is directed to the Lord and punctuates the psalm three times testifies to his utter dependence on the Lord. The psalmist is like Job who, at the point of his greatest bondage and fear, proved the depth of his faith precisely because he had no worldly reason to trust in God.

We want resolution for our pain and grief, and the degree to which we want it often corresponds to the intensity of our pain. Whether we plead with God three times or a thousand times, we may hear the Lord say, "My grace is sufficient for you, for my power is made perfect in weakness" (2 Cor. 12:9). Earlier I shared how our prayers

---

4   Anderson, *Psalms*, 2:623.

for my father-in-law were answered. He was physically, mentally, and spiritually active right up to his death at the age of ninety-four. This was not the case, however, with my mother-in-law, Mary. She was diagnosed with multiple myeloma twelve years before she died, and she suffered the ravages of both the disease and chemotherapy. The cancer spread throughout her body, resulting in extreme pain that never let up. Drugs and radiation of the brain caused a fundamental personality change that hollowed out this beautiful, fun-loving, God-fearing mother and grandmother. My father-in-law could say at the end, "I'm homesick for heaven," but I remember when Mary, who never swore, woke up one morning and said, "Oh, hell, I'm still here! I dreamed that I had died and gone to heaven."

PSALM 89

THE COVENANT PRAYER

Psalms 88 and 89 are extreme prayers. Together they form a provocative sequence to bring Book 3 to a sober and unsettling end. Psalm 88 is a deeply personal lament on death and dying, and Psalm 89 is a passionate public lament on God's covenant love and the future of faithfulness. If Friedrich Nietzsche had considered these psalms, he might have thought twice about his charge that believers were naive. The intensity of the psalmist's quest for answers in the face of death and silence echo Job on the ash heap crying out, "The LORD gave, and the LORD has taken away; blessed be the name of the LORD" (Job 1:21 NRSV). These psalms recall Jacob's all-night wrestling match as he clung to God, saying, "I will not let you go unless you bless me" (Gen. 32:26). These two psalms explore the sharp edge between hope and hopelessness with a resilient faith that is not afraid to speak to God boldly. They invoke the memory of Jesus in Gethsemane, praying, "Father, if you are willing, take this cup from me; yet not my will, but yours be done" (Luke 22:42). Implicit in the Spirit's inspiration is a messianic yearning for the new life that is beyond death and for the new covenant that lasts forever.

Psalm 89 seems long, given the singularity of the tension running through the psalm. Two-thirds of the psalm establishes the great faithfulness of the Lord whose steadfast covenant love establishes creation and the Davidic covenant *forever* (Ps. 89:1–37). The final third laments the undoing of everything promised by the Lord. The people of God and the anointed one are rejected, defiled, plundered, scorned, and ashamed (vv. 38–51). The sharp contrast in the same psalm between faithfulness and futility is shocking. The psalm closes with the people of God taunted by all the nations and mocked by their enemies. The psalm is long, but it is impossible to break it up and still deliver its intended message. The tension in the text leads to the passion of the passage. The tension in Psalm 89 between the everlasting promise of the Lord's love and faithfulness and the painful present experience of futility and shame cannot be ignored. If the psalm is divided up into positive and negative sermons, the meaning is lost.

CREATION AND COVENANT

I will sing of the LORD's great love [*hesed*] forever;
with my mouth I will make your faithfulness known
through all generations.
I will declare that your love [*hesed*] stands firm forever,
that you have established your faithfulness in heaven itself.
You said, "I have made a covenant with my chosen one,
I have sworn to David my servant,
'I will establish your line forever
and make your throne firm through all generations.'"
The heavens praise your wonders, LORD,
your faithfulness too, in the assembly of the holy ones.
For who in the skies above can compare with the LORD?
Who is like the LORD among the heavenly beings?
In the council of the holy ones God is greatly feared;
he is more awesome than all who surround him.
Who is like you, LORD God Almighty?
You, LORD, are mighty, and your faithfulness surrounds you.
You rule over the surging sea;
when its waves mount up, you still them.
You crushed Rahab like one of the slain;
with your strong arm you scattered your enemies.
The heavens are yours, and yours also the earth;
you founded the world and all that is in it.
You created the north and the south;
Tabor and Hermon sing for joy at your name.
Your arm is endowed with power;
your hand is strong, your right hand exalted.
—Psalm 89:1–13

There is no hint in the first section that a powerful lament is coming. Ethan the Ezrahite sets the story of the Lord's great love to music.[1] Everything is positive, from the highest heavens to the smallest child. He is eager to sing praise and to declare truth in concert with creation and the heavenly hosts. These opening verses inspired James Fillmore to write the popular twentieth-century hymn "I Will Sing of the Mercies of the Lord Forever," but it was the Lord's covenant promises to David (2 Sam. 7:5–16) that inspired the psalmist to see God's great faithfulness to creation and the house of David. He stresses the "foreverness" of God's covenant promises to David whose throne is established "firm through all generations" (Ps. 89:4). The privilege of relationship ("my chosen one") and the purpose of responsibility ("my servant") are united in a single everlasting calling.

The psalmist focuses on the Lord's "truthfulness" or "faithfulness" (vv. 1, 2, 5, 8, 14, 24, 33, 49). Goldingay translates 'ĕmûnâ as "truthfulness," whereas the NIV and ESV use "faithfulness."[2] Hesed is also repeated seven times and is translated "commitment," "steadfast love," "great love," or "faithful love" (vv. 1, 2, 14, 24, 28, 33, 49). In each of these references it is the Lord's truthfulness, faithfulness, great love, and commitment that is being praised. These powerful attributes cannot be defined any further than the perfection of truth, faithfulness, love, and commitment. This highly relational understanding of the Lord is what the psalmist praises. The attributes are on full display in the heavens above and on the earth below. No one compares to the Lord. God is sovereign over creation and David's throne. The heavens praise the Lord's wonders and "the assembly of the holy ones" praise his faithfulness (see Job 1–2). All of creation, including the hosts of angels, offer reverent and exuberant praise to God.[3]

---

1   In 1 Kings 4:31, Solomon is said to be wiser than Ethan the Ezrahite and Heman (Psalm 88). Both names are referenced in 1 Chron. 2:6 as sons of Zerah from the tribe of Judah and identified as temple musicians in 1 Chron. 15:17, 19.

2   Goldingay, Psalms, 2:668.

3   The Bible consistently refers to angels not as flighty, cherub-like creatures, but as behind-the-scenes messengers on a mission. They worship God, reveal his will, and do his bidding. The basic assumption that angels play a strategic role in the drama of salvation history is undebatable. Distinguished scientist Edward O. Wilson stretches credulity when he encourages belief in extraterrestrial beings. He writes, "The meaning of human existence is best understood in perspective, by comparing our species with other conceivable life-forms and, by deduction, even

Next, the psalmist features the chaos of nature and nations. The "surging sea" is ruled by God and brought under control, and enemies like Rahab, a nickname for Egypt (Isa. 51:9–10), are crushed and scattered. The whole cosmos belongs to the Lord. The heavens are his; the earth is his. He founded the world and created north, south, east, and west. "You own the cosmos—you made everything in it, everything from atom to archangel. You positioned the North and South Poles; the mountains Tabor and Hermon sing duets to you" (Ps. 89:11–12 MSG). The psalmist's praise is on the same page as the apostle's praise, when Paul says, "For in him all things were created: things in heaven and on earth, visible and invisible, whether thrones or powers or rulers or authorities; all things have been created through him and for him. He is before all things, and in him all things hold together" (Col. 1:16–17).

RIGHTEOUSNESS AND JUSTICE

Righteousness and justice are the foundation of your throne;
love [hesed] and faithfulness go before you.
Blessed are those who have learned to acclaim you,
who walk in the light of your presence, LORD.
They rejoice in your name all day long;
they celebrate your righteousness.
For you are their glory and strength,
and by your favor you exalt our horn.
Indeed, our shield belongs to the LORD,
our king to the Holy One of Israel.
                                        —Psalm 89:14–18

This five-verse bridge between the celebration of the Lord's power in creation and the Lord's covenant faithfulness to his anointed one David is especially significant in the light of Jesus's teaching. The psalmist revels in the moral character revealed in and through the Lord's rule: righteousness, justice, love, and faithfulness. These life-giving, life-transforming, divine

---

those that might exist outside the Solar System." Wilson believes that God is an "idol of the mind" and faith is a product of "the biological evolution of human instinct," but he also believes in the plausible existence of aliens. If one of the world's most distinguished evolutionary biologists can write convincingly about aliens, perhaps Christians should believe confidently in what the Bible says about angels.

attributes correspond beautifully to Jesus's teaching on the Sermon on the Mount. Jesus may have had in mind the psalmist's blessing (v. 15) as he began his sermon with the Beatitudes.

"Righteousness" is not a stodgy, stuffy religious word, but a comprehensive, powerful word that embraces justification by faith in Christ, personal holiness, the gift of sanctification, and the pursuit of social justice in every sphere of life. "It would be a mistake to suppose," writes John Stott,

> that the biblical word "righteousness" means only a right relationship with God on the one hand and a moral righteousness of character and conduct on the other. For biblical righteousness is more than a private and personal affair; it includes social righteousness as well. And social righteousness, as we learn from the law and the prophets, is concerned with seeking man's liberation from oppression, together with the promotion of civil rights, justice in the law courts, integrity in business dealings and honor in home and family affairs. Thus Christians are committed to hunger for righteousness in the whole human community as something pleasing to a righteous God.[4]

The way of righteousness, justice, love, and faithfulness resonates with Jesus's understanding of heart righteousness. Believers learn to acclaim the Lord, walk in his light, and rejoice in his righteousness. Jesus taught that true righteousness was not an imposed obligation but a joyful privilege flowing out of a covenant relationship. The joyful description of the believer walking in the light of the Lord's presence, rejoicing in his name all day long, and celebrating his righteousness is for God's great glory and our great good. The psalmist closes out this bridge by referencing the king and the promise of God's favor. Righteousness exalts the king and strengthens his "horn," a symbol of power and might. Justice, love, and faithfulness establish the king as the people's "shield," a symbol of sovereignty, and demonstrate tangibly that the king belongs to the Lord, the Holy One of Israel.

FAITHFULNESS FOREVER

Once you spoke in a vision,
to your faithful people you said:

---

4   Stott, *Christian Counter-Culture*, 45.

"I have bestowed strength on a warrior;
I have raised up a young man among the people.
I have found David my servant;
with my sacred oil I have anointed him.
My hand will sustain him;
surely my arm will strengthen him.
The enemy will not get the better of him;
the wicked will not oppress him.
I will crush his foes before him
and strike down his adversaries.
My faithful love [*hesed*] will be with him,
and through my name his horn will be exalted.
I will set his hand over the sea,
his right hand over the rivers.
He will call out to me, 'You are my Father,
my God, the Rock my Savior.'
And I will appoint him to be my firstborn,
the most exalted of the kings of the earth.
I will maintain my love [*hesed*] to him forever,
and my covenant with him will never fail.
I will establish his line forever,
his throne as long as the heavens endure.
If his sons forsake my law
and do not follow my statutes,
if they violate my decrees
and fail to keep my commands,
I will punish their sin with the rod,
their iniquity with flogging;
but I will not take my love [*hesed*] from him,
nor will I ever betray my faithfulness.
I will not violate my covenant
or alter what my lips have uttered.
Once for all, I have sworn by my holiness—
and I will not lie to David—
that his line will continue forever
and his throne endure before me like the sun;
it will be established forever like the moon,
the faithful witness in the sky."
                    —Psalm 89:19–37

The question addressed decisively in this section is not what David can do for the Lord, but what the Lord has done and will do for David. Life is not measured by what is achieved for God but by what is received from God. The Lord uses fourteen first-person "I" statements in Psalm 89:13–37 to describe his actions on behalf of his anointed one. The same number of "I" statements is used in 2 Samuel 7:8–16 to explain what the Lord will do for his beloved people and for David. The thrust of the prophet's message is the same as the psalmist's. David is not a self-made man. The Lord made David who he is and gave him everything he has. The Lord gave him strength, raised him up, anointed him, and crushed his foes. The Lord established David's reign over the sea and over the rivers and promised that his covenant with David would never fail. Even when David's sons and future generations are disobedient and faithless, the Lord declares, "I will not take my love from him, nor will I ever betray my faithfulness. . . . I will not lie to David" (Ps. 89:33, 35).

The relationship between the Lord and David is so special that it goes beyond David to the future Son of David, of whom David said, "The Lord says to my lord: 'Sit at my right hand until I make your enemies a footstool for your feet'" (Ps. 110:1). David calls on the Lord, saying, "You are my Father, my God, the Rock my Savior," and David is designated as the Lord's "firstborn," one who is exalted above all the kings of the earth (Ps. 89:26–27; see also 2:7). For hundreds of years it appeared that these glowing promises of the eternal reign to David and his heirs were hyperbole. Israel was an oppressed and beleaguered people who returned from exile to repopulate and rebuild their land under threat from the world's superpowers. It looked like the line of David had reached its end and that these glorious prophecies were only faint hints of past glory. But then something miraculous happened that changed the course of history: "God sent the angel Gabriel to Nazareth, a town in Galilee, to a virgin pledged to be married to a man named Joseph, a descendant of David" (Luke 1:26–27). God picked up the thin thread of salvation history and made good on his promises to the house of David. Gabriel said to Mary, "You will conceive and give birth to a son, and you are to call him Jesus. He will be great and will be called the Son of the Most High. The Lord God will give him the throne of his father David, and he will reign over Jacob's descendants forever; his kingdom will never end" (Luke 1:31–33).

HOW LONG?

But you have rejected, you have spurned,
you have been very angry with your anointed one.
You have renounced the covenant with your servant
and have defiled his crown in the dust.
You have broken through all his walls
and reduced his strongholds to ruins.
All who pass by have plundered him;
he has become the scorn of his neighbors.
You have exalted the right hand of his foes;
you have made all his enemies rejoice.
Indeed, you have turned back the edge of his sword
and have not supported him in battle.
You have put an end to his splendor
and cast his throne to the ground.
You have cut short the days of his youth;
you have covered him with a mantle of shame.
How long, LORD? Will you hide yourself forever?
How long will your wrath burn like fire?
Remember how fleeting is my life.
For what futility you have created all humanity!
Who can live and not see death,
or who can escape the power of the grave?
Lord, where is your former great love [hesed],
which in your faithfulness you swore to David?
Remember, Lord, how your servant has been mocked,
how I bear in my heart the taunts of all the nations,
the taunts with which your enemies, LORD, have mocked,
with which they have mocked every step of your anointed one.
—Psalm 89:38–51

The lengthy description of God's great faithfulness, his enduring
truthfulness, and his everlasting covenant love is suddenly and without
warning countered in a stark description of utter rejection. Like a bolt of
lightning coming out of nowhere, the psalmist paints a picture of total
disaster and devastation. Kidner writes, "Either the unclouded praise of
verses 1–37 was a miracle of self-discipline, if it was composed in this
situation, or else it was drawn from an existing psalm to strike a positive
note (by a different exercise of self-discipline) before the unburdening of

grief which now ensues."[5] Now we begin to see why Psalm 88, the somber psalm on death, is linked to Psalm 89, the sober psalm of rejection. The psalmist refused to spend any time on secondary causes. The cause of this devastation is not credited to the apostasy of the northern kingdom or to the idol-worshiping kings of Judah. Babylon's king Nebuchadnezzar is not blamed for the fall of Jerusalem (2 Kings 24). To be sure, enemies and foes and the power of the sword are factors in this tragic lament, but the psalmist insists that it is the Lord who bears primary responsibility. "But you," the psalmist cries. "You have rejected, you have spurned, you have been very angry with your anointed one" (Ps. 89:38). The verbs of judgment and rejection pile up on one another: You have renounced the covenant, defiled the crown, broken down your anointed one's defenses, reduced the city to ruins, exalted the enemy, made the enemy rejoice, supported the enemy in battle, put an end to your anointed one's splendor, cut short the days of his youth, and covered him with shame. The celebration of God's great faithfulness is turned into an intense, painful lament of God's great faithlessness. But the psalmist does not blame God for his apparent faithlessness and abandonment. He does not judge God's absence nihilistically. He does not give himself over to despair. Implicit in the psalmist's lament is an earnest and lively commitment to the sovereignty of God over all creation, over all history, over the people of God, and over everyone. This lament is not an accusation of despair as much as an expectation of deliverance. There are no grounds for optimism, but every reason to hope.

The psalmist does not ask, "Why?" He does not ask why, precisely because of the message of the prophets and conviction of the psalmists. He has a firm grip on Israel's history of apostasy and idolatry. He knows why divine judgment has fallen on the people of God, why the crown has been defiled, and why Israel's enemies have had the upper hand. Instead of asking why, he asks, "How long, Lord? Will you hide yourself forever?" It is not a question of whether God will fulfill his covenant but of when. The psalmist appeals to the Lord for action because of the brevity and futility of life. Unless the Lord shows his great love and faithfulness, there is no reason for hope. As the Lord's anointed one, he asks the Lord to remember how fleeting is his life. He pleads with the Lord to

---

5   Kidner, *Psalms 73–150*, 324.

be mindful of his persecution. He has been mocked and taunted by his enemies. "They have mocked every step of your anointed one" (v. 51). The trajectory of salvation history leads downward to the manger. The descent of the Messiah was preceded by the descent of the people of God. It is not difficult to imagine Jesus, the Son of David, the Anointed One, praying these words as he suffered the taunts and mockery of religious and political powerbrokers. The people of God were living in the state of rejection described by the psalmist, and their only hope was in a deliverer who took up their pain and bore their suffering. "He was despised and rejected by mankind, a man of suffering, and familiar with pain" (Isa. 53:3). The power of the psalm to capture the movement of history that led to the cross cannot be credited to authorial intent, but it can be credited to the inspiration of the Holy Spirit. The psalmist did not know how the covenant-keeping Lord of truthfulness and faithfulness would keep his promises to the house of David. He did not know how the rejection and humiliation of the Son of David would establish God's faithfulness. Who ever imagined that the Lord of Glory would become the Crucified God? The Anointed One "made himself nothing by taking the very nature of a servant, being made in human likeness. And being found in appearance as a man, he humbled himself by becoming obedient to death—even death on a cross!" (Phil. 2:7–8).

DOXOLOGY

> Praise be to the LORD forever!
> Amen and Amen.
> —Psalm 89:52

Book 3 of Jesus's prayer book ends in doxology (see also Pss. 41:13; 72:19; 106:48; 150:6). If the psalmist here praised the Lord for his truthfulness, faithfulness, steadfast love, and commitment, how much more should we? When we sing of the mercies of the Lord, we cannot help but think of Jesus Christ and praise the Lord.

BOOK 4

PSALMS 90–106

TEACH US TO NUMBER OUR DAYS

We begin Book 4 (Psalms 90–106) mindful of the searching notes of Psalms 88 and 89. Far from ignoring the threat of the second death or the despair of a world void of God's saving grace, the Psalms confront these issues head-on. The truth that emerges is twofold. First, there is deep confidence in the Lord who saves and demonstrates his great love and mercy. Second, there is a yearning expectation for the Messiah that is unfulfilled and in need of completion. The Psalms emphasize both truths: the gift of God's covenant love and the consummation of God's great faithfulness in the coming Anointed One.

Psalm 90, like the two previous psalms, begins with a strong affirmation of an enduring and abiding relationship: "Lord, you have been our dwelling place throughout all generations" (Ps. 90:1). Everything that follows in the psalm flows from this covenant relationship. This conviction grounds the discussion on the frailty, brevity, and depravity of life and inspires the believer's sincere search for wisdom. It is out of physical and spiritual weakness that the people of God humbly pray for the Lord's favor in their lives. To be able to greet the morning with joy is a gift from God. To leave a testimony for the people of God and future generations is a blessing from God. Only the Lord our God can establish the work of our hands.

The superscription credits Moses, the man of God, with this psalm.[1] This gives credibility to the possibility that the psalm's backstory may be the rebellion at Kadesh, when the Israelites refused to enter the Promised

---

[1] Tanner notes that the dedication of Psalm 90 to Moses begins Book 4, and a reference to Moses and Exodus 32 ends it (Ps. 106:23) (DeClaissé-Walford, Jacobson, and Tanner, *Book of Psalms*, 685).

Land and the whole assembly talked about stoning Moses and Aaron. The Lord responded by judging all the Israelites who were twenty years and older to a lifetime of wilderness wandering. Caleb and Joshua were the exception, but every other adult was destined to die in the wilderness (Num. 14:1–43). Later, Moses and Aaron were judged for their own act of disobedience. They were told, "you will not bring this community into the land I give them" (Num. 20:12). These tragic events in the wilderness may lie behind Moses's plea for compassion and his passion for the eternal and holy God. Moses knew something of the power of God's anger.

Spurgeon reminds believers that they stand on higher ground than Moses.[2] The power of God's indwelling presence, made real through the Incarnation of God and the presence of the Spirit of Christ, enables believers to draw near to God with a sincere heart and with the full assurance that faith brings (Heb. 10:22). Nevertheless, Moses in Psalm 90 exudes a confidence in God and a grip on reality that is free from despair or bitterness. Even though Moses belonged to the generation that was passing away in the wilderness, his Spirit-inspired psalm leads believers today through the challenges of this transitory life.

GOD'S ETERNITY, HUMANITY'S BREVITY

> Lord, you have been our dwelling place
> throughout all generations.
> Before the mountains were born
> or you brought forth the whole world,
> from everlasting to everlasting you are God.
> You turn people back to dust,
> saying, "Return to dust, you mortals."
> A thousand years in your sight
> are like a day that has just gone by,
> or like a watch in the night.
> Yet you sweep people away in the sleep of death—
> they are like the new grass of the morning:
> In the morning it springs up new,
> but by evening it is dry and withered.
> —Psalm 90:1–6

---

2   Spurgeon, "Psalm 90," *Treasury of David.*

Shortly before he died, Moses pronounced a blessing: "The eternal God is your refuge, and underneath are the everlasting arms" (Deut. 33:27). The theme of eternal refuge sets the tone for Psalm 90. The psalmist opens with the overarching truth upon which everything else depends: "Lord, you have been our dwelling place throughout all generations." This is not a platitude, but a profound recognition of God's loving care and eternal protection. There is no hint of despair or lament; "his spirit is one of humble submission and trust."[3] When we pray this psalm today we acknowledge that all of our weaknesses and all of our hopes are subsumed under this great truth. The sovereign and majestic Lord is our refuge (Ps. 91:9). When Jesus spoke of the vine and the branches on the night he was betrayed, he embraced the truth of God's everlasting protection and provision. He made the eternal refuge of God personal: "As the Father has loved me, so have I loved you. Now remain in my love" (John 15:9).

Time and space are God's creation. God lives outside of time. "His life is not dribbled out moment by moment like ours," writes Lewis. "If you picture Time as a straight line along which we have to travel, then you must picture God as the whole page on which the line is drawn."[4] Before anything ever was, God is. The mountains were birthed and the world conceived by the word of the eternal God, prompting the psalmist to declare, "From everlasting to everlasting you are God" (Ps. 90:2). The author of Hebrews writes, "By faith we understand that the universe was formed at God's command, so that what is seen was not made out of what was visible" (Heb. 11:3). Mortals, by contrast, are mere dust. The Hebrew word for "dust" used here is not the same one used in Genesis 3:19, but the idea of returning back to it alludes to the curse of Adam and uses the same verb.[5]

Not only are we mortal, "earth to earth, dust to dust," but the psalmist is impressed with the brevity of life. We are such frail creatures that life passes by like a dream. One minute we are awake, and the next minute we are asleep (a metaphor the psalmist uses for death). The newborn child makes us acutely aware of how fragile life is. To

3   Stott, *Favorite Psalms*, 77.
4   Lewis, *Mere Christianity*, 168.
5   Kidner, *Psalms 73–150*, 328.

God a whole millennium is equivalent to a single day (2 Peter 3:8) or even a four-hour night watch (Ps. 90:4). When compared to God, our life span is like grass that springs up in the morning and by evening is dried up and withered. "It is like water spilt on the ground, like a shadow which passes when the sun comes out, and like smoke or mist dispersed by the wind."[6] With a few choice phrases the psalmist cuts humanity down to size.

To grasp the brevity of life does not mean we accept the futility of life. This short life span is framed by God's sovereign purposes and infused with God's eternal meaning. The psalmist's realism runs contrary to what medical doctor Samuel Harrington describes as "a uniquely American persona filled with hopefulness, optimism, anticipation, and expectation." Harrington sees "our society's emphasis on youth, celebrity, and consumerism coupled with the successful marketing of medical advances, health care products, and political promises" as contributing to unrealistic expectations of longevity. Remarkably, life expectancy between seventy years and eighty has remained fairly constant. Harrington uses the concept of "compression morbidity" to refer to the fact that we are "living longer, healthier lives and dying quickly with less disability." Life expectancy is still about seventy-nine, with the maximum improvements in health occurring between ages fifty and seventy. In other words, "if seventy is the new fifty, then eighty-six is the new eighty-five."[7] We are living healthier longer but still dying at about the same age.

We may like to think of ourselves as the zenith of evolutionary development, but the psalmist thinks of us as a wispy dream or a blade of grass. The psalmist did not use these metaphors to disparage humanity. He is simply being honest about our humanity. Our value lies neither in our chemical constitution nor in our longevity. The meaning of the person lies in our unique and wonderful relationship with our Creator, in whose image we are made. We are recipients of his wisdom, compassion, unfailing love, and favor. Before the psalmist is through, he will move us from dust to destiny and from ashes to glory. But first we must reckon with God's anger.

---

6   Stott, *Favorite Psalms*, 78.
7   Harrington, *At Peace*, 30.

GOD'S WRATH, HUMANITY'S DEPRAVITY

> We are consumed by your anger
> and terrified by your indignation.
> You have set our iniquities before you,
> our secret sins in the light of your presence.
> All our days pass away under your wrath;
> we finish our years with a moan.
> Our days may come to seventy years,
> or eighty, if our strength endures;
> yet the best of them are but trouble and sorrow,
> for they quickly pass, and we fly away.
> If only we knew the power of your anger!
> Your wrath is as great as the fear that is your due.
> —Psalm 90:7–11

If our lives are frail and transitory in the physical universe, they are weak and corrupt in the moral universe. We live under a curse that strikes the body and the soul. As the psalmist says, "Surely I was sinful at birth, sinful from the time my mother conceived me" (Ps. 51:5). There is no escaping the verdict that "all have sinned and fall short of the glory of God" (Rom. 3:23). We are in fact already "dead in [our] transgressions and sins" (Eph. 2:1). We are all miserable sinners subject to the wrath of God.

The psalmist's description of God's anger is devastating personally. The language is graphic. We are consumed by God's anger and terrified by his indignation. Our secret sins are exposed. It is like sitting across from the oncologist and being told you have stage four pancreatic cancer. Our sinful state impacts each and every one of us in deeply personal and practical ways. This is not some abstract assessment that can be brushed aside. Being a sinner, no matter how good we think we are, is not some neutral propositional fact that can be duly noted and then forgotten. This is far worse than a jury handing down a guilty verdict and sentencing us to prison. Facing God's wrath is far more terrifying. Judgment has eternal consequences. The psalmist describes an existential crisis that ought to scare the hell out of us. All of our days are spent under the burden of the fall and the weight of our sinful choices. Trace the cause of our mortality, weakness, brokenness, and brevity back to its source, and it is sin.

It is not difficult to imagine Moses penning these words and feeling their sorrow deeply. Nor is it difficult to imagine the editors and compilers of the Psalms drawing a connection between the wilderness experience of the Israelites in Exodus 32 and the exiled Israelites in Babylon. The psalmist holds two realities in tension: God's righteous anger and God's redeeming mercy. Moses lived to be one hundred and twenty years (Deut. 34:7), and at the end of his life he was denied entrance into the Promised Land because he struck the rock. I'm sure Moses wished he had that moment back, when reverence for the Lord might have replaced his anger against the people. "If only we knew the power of your anger!" laments Moses, as if to say, "If I had only taken your word more seriously, I never would have violated your explicit command. I would have spoken to the rock." Moses learned the hard way that the Lord means business, but don't we all? We struggle to learn: "Your wrath is as great as the fear that is your due" (Ps. 90:11). Suffering and conflict dogged Moses's whole life. Even the best years were filled with trouble and sorrow (v. 10). Moses rightly observed that "we finish our years with a moan" (v. 9). As we pray this psalm we sense that Moses was not bitter or angry. He knew he had no cause to be disappointed with God. Disappointed with himself, yes, but not with God.

GOD'S STEADFAST LOVE, HUMANITY'S HOPE
Teach us to number our days,
that we may gain a heart of wisdom.
Relent, LORD! How long will it be?
Have compassion on your servants.
Satisfy us in the morning with your unfailing love,
that we may sing for joy and be glad all our days.
Make us glad for as many days as you have afflicted us,
for as many years as we have seen trouble.
May your deeds be shown to your servants,
your splendor to their children.
May the favor of the Lord our God rest on us;
establish the work of our hands for us—
yes, establish the work of our hands.
—Psalm 90:12–17

With sober realism and straightforward honesty, the first two sections lead to a communal prayer for wisdom. The psalmist enters a corporate plea for the Lord's compassion, steadfast love, empowerment, and favor.

He gives voice to the holy ambition of the people of God. Having grappled with a biblical view of mortality and immorality, the psalmist prays boldly for an outpouring of God's grace. He prays for God's imperative action: teach us wisdom, turn back to us in mercy, satisfy us with your love, make us glad for the opportunity to serve, make your action in our lives real and glorious to our children, and establish the work of our hands. Instead of receiving what their fallen status deserves, the psalmist prays for a great reversal. Instead of turning people back to dust, he prays for compassion and strength to serve the Lord.

Teach us wisdom (v. 12). If we do the math according to Psalm 90, we will use whatever time we have left for God's kingdom purposes. We don't know whether we are going to die young or live long, but we desire to make "the most of every opportunity, because the days are evil" (Eph. 5:16).

Turn back to us in mercy (Ps. 90:13). The great truth of the gospel is this: "While we were still sinners, Christ died for us" (Rom. 5:8). On our own merit we are but dust, and the apostle agrees with the psalmist that "the wages of sin is death." But because of God's great mercy, "the gift of God is eternal life in Christ Jesus our Lord" (Rom. 6:23).

Satisfy us in the morning with your unfailing love (v. 14). Dietrich Bonhoeffer, the well-known German pastor and martyr, was a strong advocate for morning meditation and prayer. He reasoned that since Jesus rose "very early in the morning" and "went off to a solitary place" to pray (Mark 1:35), so should we. Bonhoeffer insisted that our first thoughts should not be "for our own plans and worries, not even for our zeal to accomplish our own work, but for God's liberating grace, God's sanctifying presence."[8] Bonhoeffer's lyrical description of the value of meeting with God in the morning is a beautiful meditation on Psalm 90:14.

Make us glad for whatever time we have left to serve (Ps. 90:15, 17). In the limited time we have left on this side of eternity, we greet the challenge to serve as a joy and privilege, not a burden and duty. In a moment the psalmist will conclude with a double emphasis, requesting the Lord to "establish the work of our hands" (v. 17). We aspire for the apostle's commendation: "We remember before our God and Father your work produced by faith, your labor prompted by love, and your endurance

---

8   Bonhoeffer, *Meditating on the Word*, 32.

inspired by hope in our Lord Jesus Christ" (1 Thess. 1:3). Paul was the
best example of this. He embraced the mission of the gospel of grace with
a palpable sense of privilege and passion. He made no attempt to cajole,
berate, or browbeat people into the work of the gospel. What he sought
to do was compel believers by his infectious joy, his profound gratitude,
and his sense of great honor. He was truly grateful for the responsibility
of administering the gospel of grace.

Make your actions in our lives real and glorious to our children (Ps.
90:16). We hold the treasure of the gospel in jars of clay for a purpose,
"to show that this all-surpassing power is from God and not from us"
(2 Cor. 4:7). We embrace the responsibility "to contend for the faith
that was once for all entrusted to God's holy people" (Jude 3). For we
are called "because Christ suffered for [us], leaving [us] an example, that
[we] should follow in his steps" (1 Peter 2:21). We say with the apostle
Paul, "I have been crucified with Christ and I no longer live, but Christ
lives in me. The life I now live in the body, I live by faith in the Son of
God, who loved me and gave himself for me" (Gal. 2:20).

Establish the work of our hands (Ps. 90:17). Psalm 90 is often read
at funerals, but it is always meant for the living. Life is short and we are
sinners, but by the grace of God we have the promise of an abundant life
on this side of eternity and an everlasting life when we die (John 3:16;
10:10). To that end, the apostle Paul concludes his powerful message
on the resurrection with these words: "Therefore, my dear brothers and
sisters, stand firm. Let nothing move you. Always give yourselves fully
to the work of the Lord, because you know that your labor in the Lord
is not in vain" (1 Cor. 15:58).

At the age of forty-five, Isaac Watts (1674–1748), often called the
father of English hymnody, published a hymnal titled *The Psalms of
David in the Language of the New Testament* (1719). At the time, congre-
gational worship was limited to singing ponderous metrical psalms with
the words strictly limited to the actual text of the Bible. Watts sought
to change that by putting the theology of the Psalms to a musical style
that was more inspiring and expressive. Watts argued that hymns could
be "free expressions of Christian truth in poetical form."[9] He based his
first hymnal on a paraphrase of the Psalms, and after two hundred and

---

9   Colquhoun, *Hymns That Live*, 69.

fifty years we are still singing what God gifted and inspired him to write. "O God, Our Help in Ages Past" comes from Psalm 90.

> O God, our help in ages past, our hope for years to come,
> Our shelter from the stormy blast, and our eternal home!
> Under the shadow of thy throne thy saints have dwelt secure;
> Sufficient is thine arm alone, and our defense is sure.
> Before the hills in order stood, or earth received her frame,
> From everlasting thou art God, to endless years the same.
> A thousand ages in thy sight are like an evening gone;
> Short as the watch that ends the night, before the rising sun.
> Time, like an ever-rolling stream, bears all its sons away;
> They fly, forgotten, as a dream dies at the opening day.
> O God, our help in ages past, our hope for years to come,
> Be thou our guide while life shall last, and our eternal home!

THE LORD IS MY REFUGE

Psalms 90 and 91 open Book 4 (Psalms 90–106) with a vivid description of the existential threat facing the people of God. First there is the reality of the human condition: our frailty and depravity, followed by a fearful vulnerability to a host of life-threatening dangers. Yet the overarching reality is faith, not fear—the faith of those who place their trust in the Lord.

The two psalms run parallel in some key ways. The Lord is our dwelling place (Ps. 90:1) and we dwell "in the shelter of the Most High" (Ps. 91:1). Wisdom teaches us to number our days (Ps. 90:12) and confession inspires us to declare, "The LORD is my refuge" (Ps. 91:9). The holy boldness of Psalm 90 belongs to those who are able "to enter the Most Holy Place by the blood of Jesus" (Heb. 10:19). Seven imperatives satisfy the redemptive revolution and invoke the full range of blessing: teach, turn back, satisfy, make us glad, reveal, bless, and "establish the work of our hands" (Ps. 90:17). Only the Lord, who became human and "made his dwelling with us," fulfills the sevenfold pledge: "I will rescue him; I will protect him. . . . I will answer him; I will be with him in trouble, I will deliver him and honor him. . . . I will satisfy him" and "[I will] show him my salvation" (Ps. 91:14–16).

The reality of fear and the conditions that produce it are *not* ignored by the psalmist, but neither are they given first place. The psalmist opens with a faith-filled declaration. Praying the Psalms invariably places human matters in the context of God's sovereign power and purposes. We begin here with an affirmation of confidence in God rather than an account of our troubles. The psalmist's spiritual direction corresponds with the apostle's encouragement: "Do not be anxious about anything, but in every situation, by prayer and petition, with thanksgiving, present your requests to God" (Phil. 4:6). Begin with God and prayerfully work through the problems. This is what the psalmist does. Before he details the dangers, he devotes his attention to the truth. He begins with four metaphors for security and four names for God.

THE PROMISE
Whoever dwells in the shelter of the Most High
will rest in the shadow of the Almighty.
I will say of the LORD, "He is my refuge and my fortress,
my God, in whom I trust."

—Psalm 91:1–2

Psalm 91 is a psalm about fear, faith, and fellowship with God. The psalmist begins with a powerful faith statement, followed by a vow of trust. This eloquent opening is "enriched not only by the four metaphors for security ['shelter,' 'shadow,' 'refuge,' 'fortress'] but by the four divine names ['Most High,' 'Almighty,' 'the LORD,' 'my God']."[1] This is not the kind of counsel that comes to mind when someone says, "Think happy thoughts!" There is not an escapist syllable in the psalm. Nothing is spiritualized and no short-term, quick-fix solutions are suggested. The psalmist insists on a peace that we cannot give to ourselves, no matter how hard we try, whether it be through mind control, mood-altering substances, entertainment, or fun company. There is no humanistic solution to the deepest fears we feel and no diversion strong enough to give us peace. The psalm is not a prescription for stress management, but a description of trusting in God. Psalm 91 is about the peace of God, which transcends all understanding. It helps us embrace the peace that will guard our hearts and minds in Christ Jesus (Phil. 4:7). Jesus said, "Peace I leave with you; my peace I give you. I do not give to you as the world gives. Do not let your hearts be troubled and do not be afraid" (John 14:27). Psalm 91 helps Christians explore what Jesus meant when he offered a peace that the world cannot give. It is the peace that transcends our understanding that we seek to know and experience.

The opening statement of Psalm 91 propels the believer's praying imagination forward to Jesus's invitation to "remain in me" (John 15:5).

---

1   Kidner, *Psalms 73–150*, 332.

The word to *remain* or *abide* or *make our home* with Jesus is used eleven times to emphasize the importance of making our home with Jesus (John 15:4–10).[2] To make our home with Jesus is to persist in the life of faith. It is a loyal steadfastness to Christ characterized by a continuous openness to all that God in Christ offers us. To remain in Jesus is a deeply personal experience, but it is far more practical than it is mystical. The disciple's life is expressed in loving obedience and obedient love. *Abiding* does not mean fleeing the world or disengaging from the world, but rather being like Jesus in the world: faithful to the Father's will, compassionate to those in need, boldly prophetic to those who seek to manipulate the truth to their sinful advantage, and resting in the salvation that is by God's grace through faith and that is not of ourselves but the gift of God. Being fruitful is a simple matter of hearing and obeying: "see that what you have heard from the beginning remains in you. If it does, you also will remain in the Son and in the Father. And this is what he promised us—eternal life" (1 John 2:24–25).[3]

Shadow of the Almighty is the title Elizabeth Elliot chose for her biography of her husband Jim Elliot. What would cause a widow whose missionary husband died, along with four other men, in the jungle of Ecuador, to choose a title that celebrates the protection of God? Only the peace that passes all understanding, and only the peace that the world cannot give, explains such confidence in God. On the afternoon of January 8, 1956, Jim Elliot, Nate Saint, Ed McCully, Pete Fleming, and Roger Youdarian sang the hymn together, "We Rest on Thee, Our Shield and Our Defender." Later that day they were killed by the very people they had come to help. "Mission accomplished," wrote Elizabeth Elliot. "The world called it 'a nightmare of tragedy.' The world did not recognize the truth of the second clause in Jim Elliot's credo: 'He is no fool who gives what he cannot keep to gain what he cannot lose.'"[4]

THE PERIL

Surely he will save you
from the fowler's snare

2   In our English translations of John 15:4 the second occurrence of "remain" is
     implicit in the Greek: "Remain in me, as I also remain in you."
3   Webster, *God Who Comforts*, 96.
4   Elliot, *Shadow of the Almighty*, 19.

and from the deadly pestilence.
He will cover you with his feathers,
and under his wings you will find refuge;
his faithfulness will be your shield and rampart.
You will not fear the terror of night,
nor the arrow that flies by day,
nor the pestilence that stalks in the darkness,
nor the plague that destroys at midday.
A thousand may fall at your side,
ten thousand at your right hand,
but it will not come near you.
You will only observe with your eyes
and see the punishment of the wicked.
If you say, "The LORD is my refuge,"
and you make the Most High your dwelling,
no harm will overtake you,
no disaster will come near your tent.
For he will command his angels concerning you
to guard you in all your ways;
they will lift you up in their hands,
so that you will not strike your foot against a stone.
You will tread on the lion and the cobra;
you will trample the great lion and the serpent.
                              —Psalm 91:3–13

The psalmist exposes our fears and names them: the fowler's snare, the deadly pestilence, the night terror, the arrow that flies by day, the pestilence that stalks in the darkness, the plague that destroys at midday. We are subject to a frightening array of hidden traps and deadly hazards, but the psalmist delivers an unqualified message of hope, "Surely he will save you" (Ps. 90:3). Danger lurks in the unseen trap laid by the enemy and in the infectious germs of a deadly disease. We are under attack by terrorists at night and by armies during the day. Disease stalks the darkness at midnight and plagues destroy at midday. The dangers are many: deception and disease, hidden evils and public calamities, personal traumas and shared fears. Evil works around the clock. Night serves to heighten fear and intensify terror, and daylight only gives our attackers a better target. We have real fears that attack the soul. Yet no matter how perilous the situation may be, the psalmist boldly preaches a no-fear gospel. Although faced by pervasive, persistent, and pernicious evil, we are challenged to trust in the Lord.

Throughout the section the reader is addressed personally. "You" singular marks the object of the Lord's affection and protection. The psalmist uses a full range of images, from a mother hen collecting her chicks under her wings to a strong military defense that protects with everything in its arsenal, from the soldier's shield to ramparts surrounding the fortress. The scale of the protection is unprecedented: "a thousand may fall at your side, ten thousand at your right hand, but it will not come near you" (v. 7). The promise and the peril could not be greater. The people of God form a minority that is threatened by all types of evil, but they can afford to be calm because the Lord is their protection. They are not asked to fight but to "observe with your eyes" the punishment of the wicked (v. 8).

The counsel of the psalmist corresponds to the spiritual direction of the apostles: "Do not be overcome by evil, but overcome evil with good" (Rom. 12:21). "'Do not fear their threats; do not be frightened.' But in your hearts revere Christ as Lord" (1 Peter 3:14–15). "Do not be afraid of what you are about to suffer. I tell you, the devil will put some of you in prison to test you, and you will suffer persecution. . . . Be faithful, even to the point of death, and I will give you life as your victor's crown" (Rev. 2:10). It is good for Christians to be shocked by evil and to feel the acute jabs of moral pain. If we are Creator-less, a mere product of time and chance in an evolutionary process, then pain and suffering must be accepted as part of nature. Lewis writes, "In a sense, [Christianity] creates, rather than solves, the problem of pain, for pain would be no problem unless, side by side with our daily experience of this painful world, we had received what we think a good assurance that ultimate reality is righteous and loving."[5]

We recognize what is ugly, because we compare it to what is beautiful. No matter how twisted and deficient it may be, humankind still has the knowledge of right and wrong. The wisdom and beauty of God's order stands in stark contrast to Adam's fallen world. Diseases and illnesses are defined in relationship to health and wholeness. Everything that might be lost through pain and evil is what God designed and desired for human-kind: physical health, emotional well-being, a loving family life, national

---

5   Lewis, *Problem of Pain*, 24.

peace and security, compassion for those in need, spiritual strength, and love for one's neighbor. The problem of sin and evil is not ignored in the Bible, nor by God today. It remains the burden of the gospel.

You ask, "Where is God in all this pain and suffering and evil?" God's answer is very straightforward: it is climactically expressed in the incarnation, the crucifixion, and the resurrection of Jesus Christ. God put himself into the battle against evil, fighting for our salvation—not as we might expect, swooping down and destroying all opposition, because that would have meant destroying us in the process, but by taking upon himself the judgment for our sin. God himself died on the cross for our sins, paying the ultimate price for humanity's sinful rebellion. Thus, the world's worst case of terrorism occurred when Jesus was nailed to the cross, because the worst case is not determined by the number of lives lost, but by the magnitude of the injustice. Christ's cross is the world's only hope for salvation.

We imagine Jesus praying Psalm 91 when he was led by the Spirit into the wilderness to be tempted by the devil (Luke 4:1–13). In the midst of evil and in the throes of severe trial, the psalmist boldly proclaims, "If you say, 'The Lord is my refuge,' and you make the Most High your dwelling, no harm will overtake you" (Ps. 91:9–10). The promise is strikingly absolute! The assurance is categorical! "No disaster will come near your tent" (v. 10). It was precisely this absolute promise that the devil sought to use against Jesus. The devil followed Jesus's "it is written" strategy and quoted from Psalm 91 (vv. 11–12): "For it is written: 'He will command his angels concerning you, and they will lift you up in their hands, so that you will not strike your foot against a stone'" (Matt. 4:6). This was a strange text for the devil to choose, because it has to do with God commanding the angels to be our guardians. One would think that this must have been one of the devil's least favorite psalms, because it stands as an indictment against everything the devil stood for. In his role as the great accuser, he covertly used this psalm of protection to conceal his demonic purpose. Truth be known, he must have hated this psalm. What God inspired for our confidence, the devil twisted for our contempt. The devil quoted the psalm word perfectly. He knew *what* he was reading, but he didn't know *how* to read it. God intended the promise of deliverance for our confidence and assurance, but it was just like the devil "to read this promise as an invitation to arrogance."[6] We misunderstand the Lord's promise of protection if we conclude that believers will never suffer harm, that they will never be attacked by a lion or bitten by a poisonous snake. Believers have been delivered from lions (Dan. 6:16) and saved from snakebites (Acts 28:5), but Christians suffer the ravages of war and violence, death and disease, scarcity and famine right alongside non-Christians. Okorocha writes, "The word of the Lord is not 'I will save them from all trouble,' but 'I will be with him in trouble' (Ps. 91:15)."[7] The promise is not an easy life but deliverance. Hebrews 11 is the story of faith and courage in the midst of struggle. It is a testimony against a prosperity gospel that promises health and wealth. There's not the slightest hint in Psalm 91 of a trouble-free existence, but there is the profoundest hope of eternal security. This psalm says so much about fear that no one could ever surmise that Christ's followers will have it easy. On the contrary, we encounter trouble from every side, and that is why we turn to the Lord to save, cover, protect, shield, rescue, deliver, and satisfy.

THE PLEDGE

"Because he loves me," says the LORD, "I will rescue him;
I will protect him, for he acknowledges my name.
He will call on me, and I will answer him;
I will be with him in trouble,
I will deliver him and honor him.
With long life I will satisfy him
and show him my salvation."
        —Psalm 91:14–16

Psalm 91 concludes in much the same way that Psalm 90 concludes. The Lord is our dwelling place, and the mortality and depravity of the human condition teach us to number our days that we may gain a heart of wisdom. We need the Lord to turn to us, to show us his compassion, and to satisfy us with his unfailing love. Only the Lord can establish the witness of our lives and the work of our hands (Ps. 90:16–17). Psalm 91

6   Kidner, *Psalms 73–150*, 333.
7   Okorocha and Foulkes, "Psalms," 699.

begins with a personal declaration of faith in God and then proceeds to challenge the people of God to trust the Lord. The weight of the psalm stresses God's commitment to us, asking only that we dwell in the shelter of the Most High. Our work is to let God protect us, deliver us, and save us. All that is left for us to do is observe with our eyes the judgment of the wicked and the justice of God. The psalmist does not minimize the hardships that believers will encounter. The dangers described in the psalm cover the full range of fear, but we cannot save ourselves; only God can, and he promises to do so.

What does the Lord ask in return? Only that we might love him, honor him, and call upon him.

> "Because he loves me," says the LORD,
> "I will rescue him;
> I will protect him, for he acknowledges my name. He will call upon me,
> and I will answer him;
> I will be with him in trouble,
> I will deliver him and honor him.
> With long life will I satisfy him
> and show him my salvation." (vv. 14–16)

This sevenfold promise places the entire responsibility of our salvation upon the Lord. Our place is to love the Lord our God and dwell under the shelter of the Most High. Only God can provide our eternal security. The apostle Paul writes, "If God is for us, who can be against us? . . . Who shall separate us from the love of Christ? Shall trouble or hardship or persecution or famine or nakedness or danger or sword?" Paul's answer is emphatic, "No, in all these things we are more than conquerors through him who loved us" (Rom. 8:31, 35–37). Therefore, we let the peace of Christ rule in our hearts (Col. 3:15). There is no better place to be than in the shelter of the Most High and to rest under the shadow of the Almighty.

RHYTHMS OF PRAISE

Psalm 92 breaks out the instruments and tunes up the soul. The intensity of Psalms 90 and 91 gives way to a Sabbath song of praise. The psalmist covers the *why*, *when*, and *how* of worship. We praise the Lord for who he is and what he has done. In the morning we proclaim his love, and in the evening we praise his faithfulness. By bookending the day with praise, the psalmist covers all points in between (a figure of speech known as a "merism"). Praise comes in many forms, from graphic design and poetry to fasting and prayer, but here the psalmist calls for a ten-stringed lyre, a harp, and the human voice.

The seven-part chiastic structure gives a memorable flow to the psalm. The why, when, and how of worship begins the psalm (Ps. 92:1–3) and a picture of the true worshiper concludes the psalm (vv. 12–15). The Lord, the Most High, opens the psalm, and the Lord, my Rock, concludes the psalm. The second (vv. 4–5) and sixth sections (vv. 10–11) celebrate the great benefits experienced by those who worship the Lord. The third (vv. 6–7) and fifth sections (v. 9) describe the fate of senseless people who flourish for a brief time before the Lord destroys them forever. At the very center of the psalm is the truth upon which everything depends: "But you, LORD, are forever exalted" (v. 8). As Wilcock explains, the progression of the psalm "is as natural as going for a walk and returning by the same route."[1]

SABBATH/SUNDAY WORSHIP

It is good to praise the LORD
and make music to your name, O Most High,

---

1   Wilcock, *The Message of Psalms*, 2:82.

proclaiming your love in the morning
and your faithfulness at night,
to the music of the ten-stringed lyre
and the melody of the harp.
For you make me glad by your deeds, LORD;
I sing for joy at what your hands have done.
How great are your works, LORD,
how profound your thoughts!
Senseless people do not know,
fools do not understand,
that though the wicked spring up like grass
and all evildoers flourish,
they will be destroyed forever.
—Psalm 92:1–7

Music is a flexible and fluid medium for praise that tends to mirror the local culture. There should be no such thing as churchy music or music labeled "religious" or "sacred." Music, like speech, often has a telltale dialect or accent, but the medium itself is neutral. The overriding concern is always the same: does the music serve the message? In the case of Psalm 92, the message is stated clearly twice, once at the beginning and then again at the end. Music that serves the message well proclaims the Lord's love and faithfulness. Music that accompanies the gospel will proclaim that the Lord is upright, "he is my Rock" and in him "there is no wickedness" (v. 15). Whatever musical style serves the gospel message is always the right kind of music. If the music gives rhythm and melody, voice and expression to exuberant praise, then it is the right kind of music. Based on Psalm 92 Isaac Watts begins one of his hymns, "Sweet is the work, my God, my King, / to praise thy name, give thanks and sing, / to show thy love by morning light, / and talk of all thy truth at night."

The Psalms call us into worship with vigorous songs of praise: "Come, let us sing for joy to the LORD; let us shout aloud to the Rock of our salvation. Let us come before him with thanksgiving and extol him with music and song" (Ps. 95:1–2). Worship is exuberant: "Shout for joy to the LORD, all the earth. Worship the LORD with gladness; come before him with joyful songs" (Ps. 100:1–2). It is fresh and vital: "Sing to the LORD a new song; sing to the LORD, all the earth. Sing to the LORD, praise his name; proclaim his salvation day after day. Declare

his glory among the nations, his marvelous deeds among all peoples"
(Ps. 96:1–3). We have a song to be sung to the nations that will turn
their hearts to the Lord.[2]

The inspiration for this music is not found in a musical tradition
or in the talent of the musician, but in the full range of what the Lord
has done. The psalmist says, "You make me glad by your deeds, LORD;
I sing for joy at what your hands have done" (v. 4). The joyous good
news of God's action inspires the musician to lead the people in praise.
The musician plays, the choir leads, and the congregation sings because
the Lord has given his people reason to rejoice.[3] The reason for praise
remains constant; the Lord's great works and the Lord's deep thoughts
inspire a full range of musical creativity that draws in every instrument,
every genre, every style of musical expression and submits it all to the
sacred purpose of glorifying God. The psalmist and the apostle are on
the same page as to what inspires the music:

> Oh, the depth of the riches of the wisdom and knowledge of God!
> How unsearchable his judgments,
> and his paths beyond tracing out!
> "Who has known the mind of the Lord?
> Or who has been his counselor?"
> "Who has ever given to God,
> that God should repay them?"
> For from him and through him and for him are all things.
> To him be the glory forever! Amen.
> (Rom. 11:33–36; quoting Isa. 40:13 and Job 41:11)

Worship that is set to lively and expressive music is never meant to
soften, obscure, or compete with the proclamation of the gospel. Real
worship exalts the gospel message over the musical medium. Calvin
opposed "instrumental music" in worship because he claimed it aped
the practice of God's ancient people "in a senseless and absurd manner,
exhibiting a silly delight in that worship of the Old Testament which was
figurative, and terminated with the Gospel."[4] Sadly, Calvin got it wrong.

---

2   Webster, *Living Word*, 108.
3   Ross, *Psalms*, 3:68.
4   Calvin, *Psalms*, 5.3:495.

His opinion against musical instruments in worship fostered a guilty conscience where God intended Spirit-filled inspiration. The Psalms teach the people of God to use every musical means available to praise the Lord. Thankfully, many churches throughout the world participate in lively and joyous worship every Sunday.[5]

THE BENEFITS OF WORSHIP

> But you, LORD, are forever exalted.
> For surely your enemies, LORD,
> surely your enemies will perish;
> all evildoers will be scattered.
> You have exalted my horn like that of a wild ox;
> fine oils have been poured on me.
> My eyes have seen the defeat of my adversaries;
> my ears have heard the rout of my wicked foes.
> The righteous will flourish like a palm tree,
> they will grow like a cedar of Lebanon;
> planted in the house of the LORD,
> they will flourish in the courts of our God.
> They will still bear fruit in old age,
> they will stay fresh and green,
> proclaiming, "The LORD is upright;
> he is my Rock, and there is no wickedness in him."
> —Psalm 92:8–15

A simple, one-sentence statement of faith centers the psalm and signals our return journey through now familiar themes: the judgment of evildoers, the empowering of the anointed one, the flourishing of the righteous, and the proclamation of praise to the Lord. The psalmist sets up a striking contrast between the Lord who is exalted forever and the wicked who only flourish briefly before their destruction. The Lord's enemies perish. The righteous are empowered. Evildoers are uprooted and scattered. The people of God are anointed, consecrated, and planted

---

5   Ross states that the essence of Psalm 92 worship is to proclaim God's righteousness to the world. He adds, "Unfortunately, believers today have all but abandoned individual and corporate praise of this kind. When this happens, the basic witness of the church is seriously weakened" (*Psalms*, 3:72). My sense is that this pessimistic conclusion is unwarranted.

in the house of the Lord. Like the towering palm tree, the righteous are erect and dignified. They have the strength of the cedar, and they still bear fruit into old age. "They will stay fresh and green" (v. 14). The metaphors pile up to a crescendo that climaxes in the psalmist's proclamation, "The LORD is upright; he is my Rock, and there is no wickedness in him" (v. 15).

The Lord is revered for bringing an end to evil, but there is no joy in seeing the wicked defeated, only relief that one day all things will be set right. We remember the word of the apostle: "The Lord is not slow in keeping his promise, as some understand slowness. Instead he is patient with you, not wanting anyone to perish, but everyone to come to repentance" (2 Peter 3:9). Senseless people need not remain senseless. Fools can forsake their foolishness and become wise. The Lord does not make enemies; they make themselves. Evildoers are self-made and self-destructive. They run against the grain of the universe and become their own worst enemy.

Calvin is surely right when he says that the ignorance and blindness alluded to in this psalm apply to "all without exception, whose understandings have not been illuminated by Divine grace." "It ought to be our prayer to God," writes Calvin, "that he would purge our sight, and qualify us for meditation upon his works."[6] The evidence of grace is found in the unique blessing that only God can give. The flourishing of the wicked and the flourishing of the righteous are radically different. The psalmist compares the short-lived success of senseless people who are destined for judgment to the enduring fruitfulness of an empowered and anointed people who are "planted in the house of the LORD" (Ps. 92:13). The psalmist does not sell the aged short. He envisions a fruitful vitality that remains fresh. Hans Urs von Balthasar observes that "Christian childlikeness and Christian maturity are not in tension with one another. Even at an advanced age, the saints enjoy a marvelous youthfulness."[7]

---

6   Calvin, *Psalms*, 5.3:498.
7   Urs von Balthasar, *Unless You Become*, 41.

YAHWEH REIGNS!

Psalm 93 builds on the theme of praise announced in Psalm 92 by boldly proclaiming, "Yahweh reigns!" In this brief psalm the Lord is acknowledged as exalted over all time and eternity, over all nature and creation, and over all human law and conscience. The psalm heralds the news as an obvious and incontestable fact. Psalm 93 takes the centerpiece of Psalm 92, "You, LORD, are forever exalted," and expands on the theme of Yahweh's rule. This psalm is in the company of other psalms that proclaim the Lord's sovereignty over all.[1]

It is impossible to pray this countercultural truth without experiencing dissonance with the prevailing scientific, social, and political ideologies. We are immersed in a culture that prides itself on nature alone and the imperial self. Everywhere we look, whether in the family or the university or the workplace or in pop culture, the messaging is the same. Self-rule in a sphere of random naturalness is the prevailing ideology. The American dream and the ideologies of the West are in sharp conflict with Jesus's gospel and the kingdom of God.

To pray Psalm 93 is to proclaim that Yahweh is king, that he is robed in majesty, and that he is sovereign over all. The revolutionary reality of this psalm must not be prayed naively, lest we unwittingly evade the radical and subversive truth of the gospel. We need to learn to laugh with the One enthroned in heaven (Ps. 2:1–4) and to ask "how much our nationalistic pride in self-government subverts our Christian commitment to God's sovereignty."[2]

---

1   This group of psalms is known as the enthronement psalms (Psalms 29, 47, 93, 94, 95, 96, 97, 98, 99) because these psalms celebrate the reign of the Lord over all. Yahweh is King over creation and the nations. Waltke writes in *An Old Testament Theology*, 886, "I AM is king! He has been Israel's refuge in the past, long before monarchy existed; he will continue to be Israel's refuge now that monarchy is gone; and blessed are they that trust in him. His kingdom comes."

2   Peterson, *Earth and Altar*, 54.

For many Christians around the world, Psalm 93 is a powerful statement declaring that the Lord is sovereign over the political regimes that exploit and oppress them. Early Christians prayed Psalm 93 when the Caesars ruled with an iron fist and demanded to be worshiped on penalty of death. To pray Psalm 93 was an act of subversion requiring courage. Emperor Domitian filled Rome with statues of himself and required officials to address him as "Our Lord and God." Domitian executed Christians in 93 AD, including his nephew Flavius Clemens, for refusing to offer sacrifices to his image. Psalm 93 was not a rhetorical flourish designed to give color commentary to Christian worship but a declaration of praise to the King of Kings and Lord of Lords in defiance of the Roman imperial cult.

As followers of King Jesus we are meant to pray this psalm in a new light: "In putting everything under them, God left nothing that is not subject to them. Yet at present we do not see everything subject to them. But we do see Jesus, who was made lower than the angels for a little while, now crowned with glory and honor because he suffered death, so that by the grace of God he might taste death for everyone" (Heb. 2:8–9). The proclamation that "the LORD reigns" is a bold political truth that runs counter to every sphere of our pluralistic culture—intellectual, social, political, racial, and tribal.

ROBED IN MAJESTY

> The LORD reigns, he is robed in majesty;
> the LORD is robed in majesty and armed with strength;
> indeed, the world is established, firm and secure.
> Your throne was established long ago;
> you are from all eternity.
> —Psalm 93:1–2

"Yahweh reigns!" is an exclamatory shout announcing the rule of God. Although we wait for the final consummation of the kingdom of God, the psalmist's focus is on the present reality of God's sovereignty. The Lord is robed in majesty and armed with strength. We are his subjects.

The psalmist begins, not with an expectation, but with a conviction. Whatever we long for in the future has already begun in the present. Believers consciously live under the Lord's rule, and in some significant ways. They live above politics, not only at the end of time, but now, in time. Their destiny is not in the hands of presidents, dictators, rebels, and terrorists. The sovereignty of God over all creation has always been true, but how we think about that rule has changed since the coming of Jesus Christ. The early church proclaimed, "For in him all things were created: things in heaven and on earth, visible and invisible, whether thrones or powers or rulers or authorities; all things have been created through him and for him. He is before all things, and in him all things hold together" (Col. 1:16–17). In Christ, history has reached its defining moment, and the crucified, risen, and ascended Lord has bound the devil for a thousand years and released the gospel to every tribe, nation, and people group.

In God's merciful and missional millennium, Satan is bound and unable to deceive the nations for a thousand years (Rev. 20:1–6). One thousand years symbolizes the perfection of God's mercy and the completeness of the church from Pentecost to the second coming of Christ. Martyred and witnessing saints in heaven and on earth continue to seek first Christ's kingdom in the fellowship of his suffering and in the power of his resurrection. At the end of the church age all the images of final judgment, including the battle of Armageddon and the great supper of God, come to fulfillment. The impact of the Lord's rule and reign from the ascension to the second coming of Christ frees the nations to hear the gospel. As the apostle Paul said to the people of Lystra, "We are bringing you good news, telling you to turn from these worthless things to the living God, who made the heavens and the earth and the sea and everything in them. In the past, he let all nations go their own way. Yet he has not left himself without testimony" (Acts 14:15–17).

The psalmist uses three quick metaphors to describe the character and nature of God. The Lord is robed in majesty, armed with strength, and enthroned for all eternity. The psalmist repeats for emphasis that the Lord is robed in majesty. "Not with emblems of majesty," wrote Surgeon, "but with majesty itself: everything which surrounds him is majestic. His is not the semblance but the reality of sovereignty. In nature, providence, and salvation the Lord is infinite in majesty."[3] To be clothed in majesty and armed with strength corresponds to the apostle John's vision of

---

3   Spurgeon, "Psalm 93," *Treasury of David*.

"someone like a son of man, dressed in a robe reaching down to his feet and with a golden sash around his chest" (Rev. 1:13). His eyes were like blazing fire; his feet were like bronze glowing in a furnace; his voice was like the sound of rushing waters (Rev. 1:14–15). The apostle and the psalmist invoke meaning through metaphor by using royal and priestly images to shape and inspire our understanding of the Lord's majesty. To worship the King is to remember that he established the world firm and immovable and his throne is forever, from all eternity.

MIGHTIER THAN BREAKERS OF THE SEA

The seas have lifted up, LORD,
the seas have lifted up their voice;
the seas have lifted up their pounding waves.
Mightier than the thunder of the great waters,
mightier than the breakers of the sea—
the LORD on high is mighty.
Your statutes, LORD, stand firm;
holiness adorns your house
for endless days.
—Psalm 93:3–5

The churning, tumultuous, raging seas represent the unleashed powers of chaos. The psalmist takes this single image, the pounding waves of the seas, to symbolize all that threatens the sovereignty of God. The Hebrew people found in the raging sea an apt metaphor for natural disaster, social upheaval, and political chaos. All that threatens to overwhelm the world is captured in "this master metaphor for anarchy."[4] The prophet Isaiah writes, "Woe to the many nations that rage—they rage like the raging sea! Woe to the peoples who roar—they roar like the roaring of great waters!" Nevertheless, the Lord is able to quell the storm with a simple rebuke: "Although the peoples roar like the roar of surging waters, when he rebukes them they flee far away" (Isa. 17:12–13). Jeremiah likened the sound of an advancing army to the sound of the roaring sea (Jer. 6:23; 50:42).

The meaning of the metaphor persists in our own reference to the storms of life, when the waves come crashing down and we are powerless

---

4   Peterson, *Earth and Altar*, 59.

PSALM 93   YAHWEH REIGNS!

before forces beyond our control. If God is not sovereign, then we do in fact live in chaos. If "randomness and chance permeate the universe," then we are all caught in life's rip currents. We are paddling desperately to stay afloat as we drift out to sea.[5] The psalmist here reminds us that the Lord is "mightier than the thunder of the great waters, mightier than the breakers of the sea—the LORD on high is mighty" (v. 4).

In the new heaven and the new earth, the apostle John announces that there will no longer be any sea. But if you are an ocean lifeguard who loves to surf and can't imagine living away from the beach, it is important to understand what the metaphor meant to ancient Israel and to the early church. What is missing in the new order is any hint of evil or drownings, storms, and shark attacks. What remains in the new heaven and the new earth are beautiful ocean vistas, great swells, and a sea teaming with God's creation. We can hardly imagine what life will be like without the threat of chaos.

The abrupt transition from the thunder of great waves to the statutes of the Lord remind the worshiper that the forces of nature have met their match in the word of the Lord. Kidner writes, "Here is God's true glory, not of mere strength but of character: wholly reassuring, wholly demanding."[6] Genesis begins with the earth "formless and empty": "darkness was over the surface of the deep, and the Spirit of God was hovering over the waters" (Gen. 1:2). And then God spoke creation into existence, and his powerful word sustains creation (Heb. 1:3). While Job was still on the ash heap, the Lord spoke to him out of the storm and said, "Listen now, and I will speak; I will question you, and you shall answer me" (Job 42:4). When Jesus and the disciples were crossing the Sea of Galilee, a sudden squall swept down on the lake and threatened to swamp the boat. In a panic, the disciples woke Jesus, saying, "Master, Master, we're going to drown!" But the one who is "mightier than the thunder of the great waters" (Ps. 93:4) simply "got up and rebuked the wind and the raging waters; the storm subsided, and all was calm." Luke adds, "In fear and amazement they asked one another, 'Who is this? He commands even the winds and the water, and they obey him'" (Luke 8:24–25). We know this person to be King Jesus. Yahweh reigns!

---

5   Peterson, *Earth and Altar*, 60.
6   Kidner, *Psalms 73–150*, 339.

RETRIBUTIVE JUSTICE

Two thrones vie for control, the eternal throne of the Lord (Ps. 93:2) and the corrupt throne of the wicked (Ps. 94:20). Psalm 93 celebrates Yahweh's reign. He is robed in majesty, he is mightier than the chaos, and his commands stand firm forever. Psalm 94 laments the power of the wicked to crush the people of God, to slay the widow, to kill the foreigner, and to murder the fatherless. The psalmist calls for the Lord "to pay back to the proud what they deserve" (Ps. 94:2). This juxtaposition of psalms and the clash of thrones, one sovereign and just, the other pretentious and evil, is celebrated and lamented *in worship*.

The reason these two psalms are back to back and set in the sequence of Psalms 90–99 is because they explore the already-and-not-yet reality of the reign of God. God's rule has begun, salvation history is unfolding, but the final judgment and the consummation of salvation has not yet taken place. Meanwhile, the throne of destruction continues to produce misery and wreak havoc. The people of God announce, "Yahweh reigns!" even as they wait for God to set things right and bring about his judgment of the wicked. The certainty of the Lord's sovereignty is held in tension with the certainty of the Lord's retributive justice.

If we are guilty of a rote recital of the exuberance of Psalm 93, we are probably guilty of ignoring altogether the painful plea for justice in Psalm 94. We know neither the agony nor the ecstasy of real worship. We have trimmed reality to consumer satisfaction and left the real issues outside the scope of worship. We edit out the psalms that don't fit our upbeat worship service, and we cut out subjects that people might find awkward or difficult. Psalm 94 takes us out of our comfort zone and places us in the mess and muddle of a sin-twisted, broken world. Who wants to be reminded *in worship* of evildoers who oppress the poor and gang up on the innocent? Acting as a faithful worship pastor, the psalmist boldly says, "We do!"

Psalm 94 begins with a plea for justice, asking God to rise up and judge the wicked, followed by a description of the hateful actions and arrogant attitudes of the wicked (vv. 1–7). The "senseless" and "foolish" among the people are put on notice that the Lord knows the futility of their plans and lives. On the contrary, those who trust in the Lord and put their confidence in the law will be remembered and vindicated (vv. 8–15). Yet this still leaves the psalmist feeling alone and vulnerable until he consoles himself with the Lord's unfailing love and future vindication (vv. 16–23).

JUDGE OF THE EARTH

The LORD is a God who avenges.
O God who avenges, shine forth.
Rise up, Judge of the earth;
pay back to the proud what they deserve.
How long, LORD, will the wicked,
how long will the wicked be jubilant?
They pour out arrogant words;
all the evildoers are full of boasting.
They crush your people, LORD;
they oppress your inheritance.
They slay the widow and the foreigner;
they murder the fatherless.
They say, "The LORD does not see;
the God of Jacob takes no notice."
—Psalm 94:1–7

The psalmist is eager for retributive justice, but only the Lord who is robed in majesty and whose statutes are holy can "shine forth" and vindicate the righteous. Only he can retaliate against the wicked and set things right. To be indifferent to these fundamental concerns or squeamish in their articulation, *especially in worship*, is to turn a deaf ear and a blind eye to the pressing social justice concerns of the people of God. The apostle echoes the psalmist's conviction when he writes, "Do not repay anyone evil for evil. Be careful to do what is right in the eyes of everyone. If it is possible, as far as it depends on you, live at peace with everyone. Do not take revenge, my dear friends, but leave room for God's wrath, for it is written: 'It is mine to avenge; I will repay,' says the Lord" (Rom. 12:17–19; quoting Deut. 32:35).

The psalmist's plea not only belongs to an earlier dispensation, but to the shared passion of God's people throughout salvation history. The gospel echoes the psalmist's cry for justice, even as it proclaims the good news of salvation. We are all sinners in need of salvation by grace through faith in the one who gave his own life as an atoning sacrifice for our redemption. We include ourselves among those who are guilty of pouring out arrogant words and oppressing others. We may not have pulled the trigger on the widow or murdered the orphan, but through our indifference and apathy the helpless have suffered. The social justice implications of our wealth and power, of our voting record, of our hoarding of wealth, and of our business decisions will be reckoned with in God's judgment. A couple who has been denied health insurance coverage for an essential operation for their newborn baby may sit in the same pew with an executive from the insurance company who made that decision. Every day we make costly decisions that value the "bottom line" over the just and righteous treatment of the person. Christ's followers are called to make a kingdom-of-God difference in such situations, or else they will say, "The LORD does not see; the God of Jacob takes no notice" (v. 7).

To argue that the wrath of God is obsolete is to argue against the teaching of the Bible, the nature of God, and even the moral sensibilities of what it means to be human.[1] If there is no divine accountability for sin and evil, it is impossible to live out the gospel of Christ. To deny the wrath of God often means that one has not experienced the horrors of war and the tragedy of evil.[2] The wrath of God does not mean "the intemperate outburst of an uncontrolled character. It is rather the temperature of God's love, the manifestation of his will and power to resist, to overcome, to burn away all that contradicts his counsels of love."[3] The wrath of God is not an embarrassment but a blessing. It is a moral necessity inherent in God's holiness and love and essential for human flourishing.

The psalmist paints a particularly colorful and damning picture of the wicked. The question "How long?" is repeated twice for emphasis, implying that this evil has gone on unchecked for some time. The wicked are described as jubilant and unashamed. They are proud of their evil

---

1   Webster, *Follow the Lamb*, 231.
2   Volf, *Exclusion and Embrace*, 304.
3   Barth, *Ephesians*, 231–32.

accomplishments. They crush, oppress, slay, and murder the weak and defenseless among the people of God, boasting all the while of their personal gain and corporate profit. It is an "inside job" orchestrated by Israelites against the people of God—their own people. They project their own moral indifference and ambiguity onto God, reasoning that the Lord does not see or care.

Through the centuries believers have asked this same question, "How long?" In the book of Revelation martyred saints cry out, "O Sovereign Lord, holy and true, how long before you will judge and avenge our blood on those who dwell on the earth?" (Rev. 6:10 ESV). This fifth-seal revelation honors the eighth beatitude: "Blessed are those who are persecuted because of righteousness, for theirs is the kingdom of heaven" (Matt. 5:10). The apostle and the psalmist alike look forward to the judgment of God. But until then, patience, vigilance, and courage are required.

WISDOM PREVAILS

> Take notice, you senseless ones among the people;
> you fools, when will you become wise?
> Does he who fashioned the ear not hear?
> Does he who formed the eye not see?
> Does he who disciplines nations not punish?
> Does he who teaches mankind lack knowledge?
> The Lord knows all human plans;
> he knows that they are futile.
> Blessed is the one you discipline, Lord,
> the one you teach from your law;
> you grant them relief from the days of trouble,
> till a pit is dug for the wicked.
> For the Lord will not reject his people;
> he will never forsake his inheritance.
> Judgment will again be founded on righteousness,
> and all the upright in heart will follow it.
> —Psalm 94:8–15

Two groups of people are addressed. First, senseless fools are warned to become wise, because the one who created hearing, hears, and the one who created seeing, sees. In a series of rhetorical questions the psalmist seeks to convict and sober the Israelites who think that somehow they can get away with disobeying God's law and abusing God's people. They may conceive of a moralistic, therapeutic deity that is satisfied with temple worship and is distant and detached when it comes to the daily affairs of life. The first question is incredulous: "When will you become wise?" The implication is that there is no excuse. The obvious answer lies in knowing that God knows and cares: "Does he who fashioned the ear not hear? Does he who formed the eye not see?" Of course he does!

The psalmist exposes two false dichotomies. Since we are prone to sin, we like to think that God weighs in on the big issues and ignores our "small crimes and misdemeanors." The psalmist asks, "Does he who disciplines nations not punish?" The question implies that the fool thinks he can get by with his shady deals because God is preoccupied with larger issues. The second question is "Does he who teaches mankind lack knowledge?" The implication is that there is a big gap between theory and practice. The fool thinks to himself, God is too important to be concerned about my shenanigans. If the "little people" get crushed in my success plan, that's their problem. The psalmist weighs in against every effort to evade the moral imperative by stating the truth: "The LORD knows all human plans; he knows that they are futile" (v. 11). The apostle Paul quoted this verse when he warned the believers in Corinth not to be deceived by the wisdom of the age, "For the wisdom of this world is foolishness in God's sight. As it is written: 'He catches the wise in their craftiness' [Job 5:13]; and again, 'The Lord knows that the thoughts of the wise are futile' [Ps. 94:11]" (1 Cor. 3:19–20).

The second group of people addressed are the faithful who seek to please the Lord. They are not warned; they are blessed. These sincere believers are given reassurance that the hardships they have endured will serve to strengthen their faith. What the evildoer intends for harm, the Lord intends for our good (Gen. 50:20). The psalmist believes it is to our advantage to be tried and tested, because a true understanding of practical obedience doesn't happen automatically. This is a powerful New Testament theme. Christians are called to "work out your salvation with fear and trembling, for it is God who works in you to will and to act in order to fulfill his good purpose" (Phil. 2:12–13). James said, "Consider it pure joy, my brothers and sisters, whenever you face trials of many kinds, because you know that the testing of your faith produces perseverance. Let perseverance finish its work so that you may be mature and complete, not lacking anything" (James 1:2–4). The author of Hebrews believed that suffering provided resistance training, strengthening the believer's moral and ethical actions. We were meant to become like Jesus, learning obedience by what we suffer (Heb. 5:8). We face a constant choice. We either take "the path of least resistance—going along with the values, norms, and practices" acceptable to society—or we obey the will of God and suffer "the consequences of criticism and condemnation by unbelieving family and friends."[4]

The blessing of the Lord's discipline is followed by the reassurance that the Lord will grant relief "till a pit is dug for the wicked" (Ps. 94:13; see Pss. 7:15; 9:15; 35:7–8). The promise continues to be affirmed that the Lord will set things right and hold evildoers accountable. The Lord will not abandon his people; he will not forsake his inheritance. When the psalmist says, "Judgment will again be founded on righteousness, and all the upright in heart will follow it" (Ps. 94:15), he is not placing the burden of good works on sin-prone individuals. He is not challenging the faithful to try harder to prove themselves. On the contrary, his message of reassurance is based on Yahweh's covenant commitment to his people. Righteousness rests on the covenant of grace and the upright in heart rejoice.

THE THRONE OF DESTRUCTION

> Who will rise up for me against the wicked?
> Who will take a stand for me against evildoers?
> Unless the LORD had given me help,
> I would soon have dwelt in the silence of death.
> When I said, "My foot is slipping,"
> your unfailing love, LORD, supported me.
> When anxiety was great within me,
> your consolation brought me joy.
> Can a corrupt throne be allied with you—
> a throne that brings on misery by its decrees?
> The wicked band together against the righteous
> and condemn the innocent to death.
> But the LORD has become my fortress,
> and my God the rock in whom I take refuge.

---

4   Jobes, *1 Peter*, 265.

He will repay them for their sins
and destroy them for their wickedness;
the LORD our God will destroy them.
—Psalm 94:16–23

The dilemma of belonging to God in a perverse world is keenly felt by the psalmist. He feels alone and powerless in his desire to remain faithful. He is at the end of his rope. A lonely "me" cries out for help and quickly adds, "If GOD hadn't been there for me, I never would have made it" (v. 17 MSG). If the Lord in his unfailing love had not held him fast, he would have fallen (see Ps. 73:2). When he was upset and beside himself, the Lord calmed him down and cheered him up. Each problem identified by the psalmist, his vulnerability, his defenselessness, his weakness, and his anxiety, is matched by the Lord's help: his unfailing love, his presence, his support, and his joy. In the chaos of a fallen and broken world, the psalmist feels like a "comrade in arms" with the Lord.

The psalmist asks a question that demands an emphatic "no." The corrupt throne that brings on misery cannot exist alongside the righteous throne of the Lord whose holy statutes adorn the household of faith. Calvin recognized the danger of a similar "emergency" when "the wicked may be permitted, in the providence of God, to mount the seat of judgment, and launch destruction upon the upright and the righteous, under color of law." He goes on to say that "we must learn to bear submissively not only with unrighteous violence, but with charges most injurious to our character, and most undeserved."[5] Along these same lines, Spurgeon feared the tyrannical rule of a national church with its synagogue of ritualism and its popish idols and pompous priests. He envisioned an immoral morality that reinforced sectarian dogma at the expense of faithfulness and obedience.[6]

No matter how powerful the wicked may become by banding together against the righteous and condemning the innocent to death, the psalmist declares that the Lord, who is "my fortress," my "rock," and my "refuge," will repay evildoers for their sins and destroy them for their wickedness. At the beginning, the psalmist repeated twice for emphasis that God alone avenges, and now at the end, he repeats twice for emphasis that God alone will destroy the wicked.

---

5   Calvin, *Psalms*, 6.4:30.
6   Spurgeon, "Psalm 94," *Treasury of David*.

WORSHIP AND WARNING

I n keeping with the theme of the enthronement psalms (Psalms 93–100), Psalm 95 extols "the great King above all gods" and leads the people of God in exuberant worship to the Lord, "the Rock of our salvation." To this vibrant call to worship, the psalm adds an equally poignant challenge to obedience. The psalmist reaches back to when the Israelites were in the wilderness and rebelled against the Lord God. He draws on this dark experience in the past to inspire a different response *today*. Some have argued that Psalm 95 is composed of two unrelated fragments, but there is nothing unusual about combining an invitation to heartfelt worship and a warning against hardness of heart.[1] The honest believer recognizes the need for both witness and warning, inspiration and exhortation. Psalm 95 unites devotion and discipline.

CALL TO WORSHIP

Come, let us sing for joy to the Lord;
let us shout aloud to the Rock of our salvation.
Let us come before him with thanksgiving
and extol him with music and song.
For the Lord is the great God,
the great King above all gods.
In his hand are the depths of the earth,
and the mountain peaks belong to him.
The sea is his, for he made it,
and his hands formed the dry land.

---

1 Kidner, *Psalms 73–150*, 343.

Come, let us bow down in worship,
let us kneel before the LORD our Maker;
for he is our God
and we are the people of his pasture,
the flock under his care.

—Psalm 95:1–7c

The call to worship is a simple invitation: "Come, let us sing for joy to the LORD." There is little doubt as to its meaning and no reason for confusion. This call to worship is preceded by the gospel invitation, "Come, follow me" (Matt. 4:19). Church attendance is not what the psalmist had in mind. His twice repeated "let us" envisions real worship. The welcoming imperative "come" challenges us to sing for joy, to shout aloud, to bow down, and to kneel before the Lord our Maker. There is nothing complicated about the verb "come," except to say that worship is all encompassing. Worship is personal and participatory at its core, never passive. The psalmist describes a body language that engages the mind and heart and awakens the soul. Exuberant worship calls for hearts and minds devoted to the Lord. Jesus invited people to himself: "Come to me, all you who are weary and burdened, and I will give you rest. Take my yoke upon you and learn from me, for I am gentle and humble in heart, and you will find rest for your souls. For my yoke is easy and my burden is light" (Matt. 11:28–30). The call to worship is grounded in the invitation of the gospel.

The psalmist offers the rationale for exuberant worship. The Lord is described as the Rock of our salvation, the great God, the great King above all gods, the Lord our Maker, and the shepherd of God's flock. The clear focus is on *who* God is rather than what he has done. Yet, implicit in these descriptive titles is the understanding that God has done it all. The Lord creates, redeems, rules, and shepherds. He holds everything together from the deepest depths to the highest heavens. "The sea is his, for he made it, and his hands formed the dry land" (Ps. 95:5). There is no polytheistic or pluralistic competition. Either the Lord is "the great King above all gods" or Israel's God is no god at all. Far from a liability, exclusivity inspires worship's exuberance.

Celebrities may express their opinions, and their opinions may be popular, but that doesn't make them true. Oprah Winfrey counters the psalmist when she says, "One of the biggest mistakes humans make is to believe there is only one way. Actually, there are many diverse paths leading to what you call God."[2] Twentieth-century hero Mahatma Gandhi summed up his opinion in an essay entitled "All Religions Are True": "Religions are different roads converging to the same point. What does it matter if we take different roads so long as we reach the same goal? Wherein is the cause for quarreling?" For Gandhi and many others the Eternal One is perceived differently in different cultures, because whatever we mean by "God" exceeds the scope of human thought and experience. The global village shares different religious perceptions of the one transcendent reality.[3]

The psalmist boldly identifies the one and only living God, who is Lord over creation and redemption. The force of his exclusive truth claim stands against pagan tribal deities and the gods of nature. His call to worship is not an innocuous religious claim, but a powerful absolute truth that shatters pagan idolatries and secular ideologies. The apostles echo the conviction of the psalmist and make the absolute claim that salvation is found in the Incarnate One, Jesus Christ (Acts 4:12). The early church was convinced that Jesus was the revelation of God, the culmination of a long history of revelation. The exclusive truth of the gospel is consistent with God's promise from the beginning: God chose a small, weak, insignificant nation through which to make himself known and bless the world. The exclusiveness of the gospel is consistent with the character of revelation and the nature of God's own self-disclosure.

CHALLENGE TO OBEY

Today, if only you would hear his voice,
"Do not harden your hearts as you did at Meribah,
as you did that day at Massah in the wilderness,
where your ancestors tested me;
they tried me, though they had seen what I did.
For forty years I was angry with that generation;
I said, 'They are a people whose hearts go astray,
and they have not known my ways.'
So I declared on oath in my anger,
'They shall never enter my rest.'"
—Psalm 95:7d–11

---

2   Taylor, "Church of O," 45.
3   Quoted in Burch, *Alternative Goals in Religion*, 111.

Exuberant worship, with its joyful singing and body language of praise and devotion, comes down to a singular exhortation: "Today, if only you would hear his voice." "Today," like the word "Come," has a sense of immediacy and urgency. Surely, "the people of his pasture, and the flock under his care" (v. 7) listen to the voice of the Shepherd. Jesus declared, "I am the good shepherd," and explaining, "his sheep follow [the shepherd] because they know his voice" (John 10:11, 4). He even spoke of having other sheep that are not of this sheep pen, adding, "They too will listen to my voice, and there shall be one flock and one shepherd" (John 10:16).

Psalm 95 takes us back to Israel's failure in the wilderness, when the beneficiaries of the exodus quarreled with Moses over water at Rephidim (Exod. 17:7) and then rebelled against the Lord at Kadesh (Numbers 14). Moses gave nicknames to these notorious places: *Meribah* means "quarreling," and *Massah* means "testing." He gave these names because "the Israelites quarreled and because they tested the LORD, saying, 'Is the LORD among us or not?'" (Exod. 17:7). The people's refusal to go into the Promised Land summed up their chronic contempt for God. "Kadesh became the symbol of Israel's disobedience, the place where God's past redemption was forgotten and where divine promise no longer impelled the people to obedience."[4]

Psalm 95 is more concerned with the persistent pattern of stubborn rebellion and hard-hearted resistance to God's will than with specific instances of sin. The psalmist draws on hundreds of years of history and exhorts believers, "Do not harden your hearts as you did at Meribah, as you did that day at Massah in the wilderness" (Ps. 95:8). Israel's waywardness is captured in the Lord's verdict: "Their hearts are always going astray, and they have not known my ways" (Heb. 3:10).

The author of Hebrews "makes these verses [8–11] an urgent message for Christians today."[5] His exposition of Psalm 95 supports his warning against hard-hearted unbelief and inspires his vision for firm-to-the-end faithfulness. He presses home the urgency of his warning and the immediacy of his challenge by repeating *today* five times. The pastor's confidence is not in his personal powers of persuasion but in the word

---

4   Lane, *Hebrews*, 1:85.
5   Stott, *Favorite Psalms*, 86.

of God, which he describes as living and active, sharper than any dou-
ble-edged surgical knife. "Everything is uncovered and laid bare before
the eyes of him to whom we must give account" (Heb. 4:12–13). The
exhortation in Hebrews follows God's precedent-setting judgment against
the Israelites in the wilderness. The author is concerned that believers
were in danger of drifting away (Heb. 2:1) and turning "away from the
living God" (Heb. 3:12).

Hebrews links Psalm 95 and the exodus typology to the church.
Bruce explains,

> The death of Christ is itself called an "exodus" [Luke 9:31]; he is the true
> passover, sacrificed for his people, "a lamb without blemish and spot"
> [1 Peter 1:19]. They, like Israel in early days, are "the church in the wilder-
> ness" [Acts 7:38]; their baptism into Christ is the antitype of Israel's passage
> through the Red Sea [1 Cor. 10:1–11]; their sacramental feeding on him
> by faith is the antitype of Israel's nourishment with manna and the water
> from the rock. Christ, the living Rock, is their guide through the wilderness
> [1 Cor. 10:4b]; the heavenly rest which lies before them is the counterpart
> to the earthly Canaan which is the goal of the Israelites.[6]

The pressing importance of the Hebrews' exhortation is expressed
in the repetition of the word *today* five times and *rest* thirteen times.
These two words, *today* and *rest*, form a dynamic *already, not yet* tension.
Daily faithfulness and everlasting rest are inseparably linked. When the
next generation of Israelites finally entered God's Promised Land, they
experienced rest from their enemies (Deut. 12:10; Josh. 23:1), but that
rest was only a type of the everlasting rest promised in Christ.

Rest as understood by the psalmist goes beyond the experience of
Joshua. "For if Joshua had given them rest, God would not have spoken
later about another day" (Heb. 4:8). Hebrews sees the ground for this
everlasting rest at the beginning of time in creation's seventh day. "There
remains, then, a Sabbath-rest for the people of God; for anyone who
enters God's rest also rests from their works, just as God did from his"
(Heb. 4:9–10). Taken together, these two types—Israel in the Promised
Land and God resting on the seventh day—point forward to God's everlasting rest (Rev. 14:13). In Hebrews we see the significance of Christ's

---

6   Bruce, *Hebrews*, 96–97; see Jude 5.

high priestly work in achieving the ultimate rest for the people of God by fulfilling the Day of Atonement ("a day of sabbath rest," Lev. 16:31), and we see that "the imagery of rest is best understood as a complex symbol for the whole soteriological process."[7]

Psalm 95 gave Hebrews a redemptive trajectory to work with. The meaning of *rest* is now best understood in the light of Christ and what he achieved as our sacerdotal priest.[8] The call to worship and the challenge to obey converges in Christian discipleship. The preacher and the psalmist agree, "Let us, therefore, make every effort to enter that rest, so that no one will perish by following their example of disobedience" (Heb. 4:11). The English translation, "make every effort," hardly does justice to the intensity of the Greek phrase. It means "take pains," "spare no effort," "give it all you've got." "This blissful rest in unbroken fellowship with God is the goal to which his people are urged to press forward."[9]

---

7   Guthrie, "Hebrews," 959.
8   Calvin, *Psalms*, 6.4:46. Calvin minimizes the relationship between Hebrews and Psalm 95. Calvin writes, "We might stop a moment here to compare what the Apostle states in the third and fourth chapters of his Epistle to the Hebrews, with the passage now before us. That the Apostle follows the Greek version, need occasion no surprise. Neither is he to be considered as undertaking professedly to treat this passage. He only insists upon the adverb *Today*, and upon the word *Rest*. And first, he states that the expression *today*, is not to be confined to the time when the Law was given, but properly applies to the Gospel, when God began to speak openly. The fuller and more perfect declaration of doctrine demanded the greater share of attention." The author of Hebrews may take issue with Calvin's assertion that he is not interpreting or treating Psalm 95, but rather pulling out two words, "today" and "rest." On the contrary, the apostolic hermeneutic depends on the whole of Psalm 95.
9   Bruce, *Hebrews*, 110.

EVANGELISTIC WORSHIP

Aseries of enthronement psalms (Psalms 93–100) lead the people of God in celebration of the Lord's reign. These songs may have had their liturgical origin at the fall Feast of Tabernacles, but they work just as well today when Christians gather to worship the triune God and celebrate the rule and reign of Jesus Christ. Psalm 96 draws on other psalms (Psalms 29, 93) and is echoed in the book of Isaiah (v. 11 in Isa. 44:23; 49:13; v. 12 in Isa. 44:23; 55:12; v. 13 in Isa. 40:10, 50:19, 20, 60:1; 62:11).[1] While it may be debated who came first, the psalmist or the prophet, what is certain is the resounding call to worship. Through the centuries the people of God have been called to sing to the Lord a new song and to ascribe to the Lord the glory due his name (Ps. 96:1, 8). The global reach of this call to worship is anticipated in Psalm 96, so we should not be surprised that believers all around the world use this psalm to worship the Lord "in the splendor of his holiness" (v. 9).

The historical background and inspiration for this "new song" may have been when King David brought the ark of God into Jerusalem (1 Chron. 16:23–33; 2 Sam. 6:12–19). As the processional approached the city of David, those who carried the ark of the covenant stopped every six steps to make sacrifices. We are told that all of Israel was in on the special occasion. The people were shouting praise; musicians were blaring trumpets; and David, dressed like a servant, wearing only a linen ephod, danced with all his might. The king threw caution to the wind and abandoned royal decorum as he leaped and danced before the Lord.

---

1 Ross, *Psalms*, 3:133.

The occasion was marked by joy and generosity as the people celebrated the testimony of the Lord's covenant promises.

The narrative behind the liturgy of Psalm 96 highlights several significant truths about worship. David's dancing before the Lord with all his might delivered a never-to-be-forgotten witness to the glory and majesty of Israel's covenant-keeping God, Yahweh. Consider the difference between David *lecturing* about the greatness of God and David's freedom to leap and dance before the Lord. All of Israel, from the lowest servants to the ranking members of his royal cabinet, witnessed the king's visible and visceral response to the truth of God. Smoke and the scent of sacrifices filled the air. The king humbled himself like a servant. He took off his royal robes and put on a servant's tunic and danced with all his might. In that total sensory experience David embodied worship. He used his body to say, "Worship the Lord in the splendor of his holiness" (v. 9). He proved it by his actions. Physicality and spirituality merged in a dramatic embodied expression of lived truth. By reading between the lines of this story, we begin to understand the adrenaline-pumping passion of the psalmist.

Ironically, Uzzah's shocking death earlier may have played a part in provoking David's passion. The seemingly innocuous efficiency of an ox-drawn cart and Uzzah's innocent reaching out and taking hold of the ark of God when the oxen stumbled proved deadly and disastrous. "David was afraid of the LORD that day" (2 Sam. 6:9), and the whole "we-can-manage-this" processional ended right there on the spot. Three months later, when the processional resumed, nothing was taken for granted; every step forward was celebrated by king, priests, people, and musicians in a choreographed liturgy of praise. Uzzah's death humbled David, filled him with the fear of the Lord, and undoubtedly led to David's passionate worship.

Added to this experience was the exchange between David and his wife Michal. She was embarrassed by her husband's emotional display. She didn't understand her husband's devotion to the Lord. Her sense of shame and disgust can be heard in her sarcastic rebuke, "How the king of Israel has distinguished himself today, going around half-naked in full view of the slave girls of his servants as any vulgar fellow would!" David's response was spoken like a king, like an unashamed passionate worshiper. He declared, "I will celebrate before the LORD," adding, "I will become even more undignified than this, and I will be humiliated in my own eyes. But by these slave girls you spoke of, I will be held in honor" (2 Sam. 6:20–22).

SING!

Sing to the LORD a new song;
sing to the LORD, all the earth.
Sing to the LORD, praise his name;
proclaim his salvation day after day.
Declare his glory among the nations,
his marvelous deeds among all peoples.
For great is the LORD and most worthy of praise;
he is to be feared above all gods.
For all the gods of the nations are idols,
but the LORD made the heavens.
Splendor and majesty are before him;
strength and glory are in his sanctuary.
—Psalm 96:1–6

Six imperatives launch this all-out call to worship: Sing! Sing! Sing! Praise! Proclaim! Declare! Every imperative is a call to action. Every one a vocal, vibrant, joyful exclamation, emphatically responding to who the Lord is and what he has done. "Nothing listless or introverted, nothing stale, befits the praise of God."[2] In the Spirit, the psalmist calls all believers to submit their traditions, habits, and liturgies to this flat-out, no-holds-barred, exuberant worship. Four imperatives focus worship Godward, followed by two imperatives, "proclaim" and "declare," that propel the message outward. In the Greek version (LXX), the verb "to proclaim" gives us the word "evangelize." Derek Kidner writes, "There may be a lesson hidden in this sequence (first upwards to God, then outwards to man): a corrective to static worship and shallow preaching alike."[3] The outreach of this evangelistic worship is global. We have a story to tell the nations. Every tribe, language, people, and nation deserves to hear the gospel, because that is what it means to "declare his glory among the nations, his marvelous deeds among all peoples" (v. 3).

2   Kidner, *Psalms 73–150*, 347.
3   Kidner, *Psalms 73–150*, 347.

The psalmist gives his reasons for evangelistic worship: the Lord is worthy of all praise; the Lord is greater than all gods, angels, celebrities, and leaders; all these substitute "gods" are really no "gods" at all, just idols; and since the Lord "made the heavens," "honor," "majesty," "strength," and "beauty" belong to him.[4] The sovereign Lord is not some tribal deity who sponsors an ethnic religion. The Lord reigns over all. For these reasons, worship and evangelism form a dynamic tension, each serving as an energizing and motivating catalyst for the other. Evangelism produces a powerful incentive to worship because both mission and worship are centered in God. Worship reminds us, as Wright puts it, that "mission is not ours; mission is God's." We worship the triune God who is on a mission, and when we worship, we are reminded that "it is not so much the case that God has a mission for his church in the world but that God has a church for his mission in the world. Mission was not made for the church; the church was made for mission—God's mission."[5]

The psalmist shares a vision of the Lord of glory in his sanctuary that transcends the gods—the gods we make into idols, the celebrities we treat like gods, and the rich and powerful we envy and idolize. The psalmist leads us in worship: "Splendor and majesty are before him; strength and glory are in his sanctuary" (v. 6). The psalmist envisioned the tabernacle and the temple as the testimony to God's glory. Today, believers know that the glory of God was more fully revealed in Jesus: "The Word became flesh and made his dwelling among us. We have seen his glory, the glory of the one and only Son, who came from the Father, full of grace and truth" (John 1:14).

ASCRIBE!

Ascribe to the LORD, all you families of nations,
ascribe to the LORD glory and strength.
Ascribe to the LORD the glory due his name;
bring an offering and come into his courts.
Worship the LORD in the splendor of his holiness;
tremble before him, all the earth.
Say among the nations, "The LORD reigns."

---

4   Ross, *Psalms*, 3:138–39.
5   Wright, *Mission of God*, 62.

The world is firmly established, it cannot be moved;
he will judge the peoples with equity.
—Psalm 96:7–10

Evidence builds that worship-inspired mission is successful. The inclusive gospel invites all the families of the nations to give exclusive devotion to the Lord of glory. The threefold opening imperative to "sing!" is matched by a threefold exhortation to ascribe, or give, to the Lord the glory due his name. This call to worship also appears in Psalm 29, but instead of the call going out to "all you families of nations" (v. 7), it summons "heavenly beings," or "mighty ones" (NKJV), to give God glory (Ps. 29:1). In both Psalm 96 and Psalm 29 the psalmist expands our vision of worship. The people of God are joined by angelic hosts and nations in giving God the glory due his name. The Lord is arrayed in the beauty of holiness and is worthy of all praise. To respond to this call to worship is to "tremble before him" (Ps. 96:9) at the immense scope of the Lord's reign and the largeness of his salvation.

We do well to unite the psalmist's powerful vision of worship with the apostle Paul's opening doxology in his letter to the church at Ephesus (Eph. 1:3–14). Paul leads believers in what it means to "ascribe to the LORD glory and strength" (Ps. 96:7). Everything good and right and true in our lives is wrapped up in praise to the triune God. Like the psalmist, the language Paul uses to praise God is exuberant and exalted. His praying imagination is focused on the Trinitarian pattern in creation and redemption—God the Father, Son, and Holy Spirit creates, saves, and unites everything by God's grace and for his glory. His scope is cosmic. There is nothing small or individualistic about these calls to worship. The apostle and psalmist alike call us out of our small-mindedness into the most real world of God's glory. The specificity and expanse of the apostle's doxology fills out the meaning of the psalmist's invitation to worship—"to the praise of his glory" (Eph. 1:14).

We may struggle with the largeness of their vision for worship because we are so easily tempted to reduce everything down to the small world of self-realization and self-discovery. The summons to bestow on Yahweh the honor due his name, to bow low to Yahweh in his holy majesty, and to ascribe to the Lord the glory due his name reorients our motives and trains our feelings.

186

The fervor of the psalmist's call to worship is eschatological in scope and corresponds to Jesus's Sermon on the End of the World, when he unfurled an all-encompassing picture of the end. Jesus warned that "nation will arise against nation, and kingdom against kingdom" (Matt. 24:7). He promised, "This gospel of the kingdom will be preached in the whole world as a testimony to all nations, and then the end will come" (Matt. 24:14). And angels will "gather his elect from the four winds, from one end of the heavens to the other" (Matt. 24:31). Psalm 96 points forward to the risen Lord Jesus Christ and his Great Commission: "All authority in heaven and on earth has been given to me. Therefore go and make disciples of all nations, baptizing them in the name of the Father and of the Son and of the Holy Spirit" (Matt. 28:18–19). Psalm 96 should be prayed in anticipation of the healing of the nations around the throne of God and of the Lamb (Rev. 22:2–3).

Evangelistic worship proclaims to the nations, "The Lord reigns!" The natural world of quantum physics and the moral world of justice and righteousness are under God's sovereign care and ultimate judgment. "Against the welter of raging nations and collapsing regimes," the psalmist concludes with "a new and overwhelming assertion of sovereignty. . . . The disastrous freedom of the Fall will be replaced by the only 'perfect freedom,' which is serving God."[6]

REJOICE!

Let the heavens rejoice, let the earth be glad;
let the sea resound, and all that is in it.
Let the fields be jubilant, and everything in them;
let all the trees of the forest sing for joy.
Let all creation rejoice before the LORD, for he comes,
he comes to judge the earth.
He will judge the world in righteousness
and the peoples in his faithfulness.
—Psalm 96:11–13

Psalm 96 concludes with a thrilling panorama of all creation breaking into jubilant praise. The psalmist envisions the heavens rejoicing and the

---

6   Kidner, *Psalms 73–150*, 348–49.

earth overflowing with gladness. Fields and forests are personified instruments of adoration. They sing the praises of God. In *The Lord of the Rings,* J. R. R. Tolkien imagines trees obeying the will of their Maker. His trees are sensitive to the presence of evil and righteousness, and they play an active role in protecting and defending the cause of righteousness. The psalmist's praying imagination agrees. It is as if all of creation is waiting on the edge of its seat, ready to celebrate, poised to sing "Hallelujah!" It is true "the whole creation has been groaning," but it is also true that "the creation waits in eager expectation for the children of God to be revealed." For when the Lord comes to judge the earth, creation "will be liberated from its bondage to decay and brought into the freedom and glory of the children of God" (Rom. 8:19–22).

The invitation to worship, "Come, let us sing for joy to the LORD" (Ps. 95:1), meets its ultimate climax and fulfillment in the coming of the Lord, when "he comes to judge the earth . . . in righteousness and the peoples in his faithfulness" (Ps. 96:13). These two comings—our coming to the Lord in expectation and the Lord's coming to us and to all of creation in consummation—form the nexus for exuberant, embodied worship. We worship today in anticipation "that at the name of Jesus every knee should bow, in heaven and on earth and under the earth, and every tongue acknowledge that Jesus Christ is Lord, to the glory of God the Father" (Phil. 2:10–11).

WORSHIPERS REJOICE, IDOLATERS SHAMED

Evangelistic worship celebrates the universal rule of God's justice and proclaims to the nations, "The LORD reigns" (Ps. 96:10). In this sequence of enthronement psalms, Psalm 97 explores the reality of the Lord's coming and its impact on worshipers and idolaters. That Yahweh reigns is a dynamic and universal truth that envelops the whole earth in "the splendor of his holiness" (Ps. 96:9). His powerful presence is felt from the villages of Judah to distant shores. Even the earth is glad and the upright in heart are filled with joy because the Most High rules over all the earth. The grandeur and glory of the living God is evident to all, "For since the creation of the world God's invisible qualities—his eternal power and divine nature—have been clearly seen, being understood from what has been made, so that people are without excuse" (Rom. 1:20).

THE HEAVENS PROCLAIM

The LORD reigns, let the earth be glad;
let the distant shores rejoice.
Clouds and thick darkness surround him;
righteousness and justice are the foundation of his throne.
Fire goes before him
and consumes his foes on every side.
His lightning lights up the world;
the earth sees and trembles.
The mountains melt like wax before the LORD,
before the Lord of all the earth.
The heavens proclaim his righteousness,
and all the peoples see his glory.
—Psalm 97:1–6

Psalm 97 gives worshipers a full sensory experience of the coming of the Lord that appeals to our whole being. We are meant to feel the pulsating atmosphere of the psalm as much as we are meant to understand the truths of the psalm. To break down the poetics of the psalm into indicative statements of fact is to strip the psalm of its energy and emotion. The psalmist orchestrates the message so that we feel the presence of the Lord. The coming of the Lord rolls in like the thick, dark clouds of a thunderstorm. His judgment is like fire, consuming everything in his path. His revealing light is like flashes of lightning across the sky. The coming of the Lord is escorted into our consciousness by the unleashed forces of nature. The poet psalmist knows that truth is not boring. It is vital, vibrant, and visceral. We feel it in our gut so we can feel it in our heart, so we can think it in our mind, so we can act on it in our lives. This is why the "knowing" that accompanies worship takes in everything: music, science, aesthetics, sociology, and theology.

The psalmist begins with a geographic sweep of liturgical praise. "Let the earth be glad; let the distant shores rejoice." The Bible runs with the metaphor. If the earth is glad, then the trees are clapping, the mountains and hills are singing, and the rocks are crying out in praise (Isa. 55:12; Luke 19:40). Worshipers are liturgical environmentalists, standing not apart from but within creation to praise God. They are learning the language of praise from botany and biology. Along with astrophysicists, they are dancing with the stars and with oceanographers, exploring the depths.

Natural phenomena mark the coming of the Lord. Ten plagues of nature preceded the exodus, and at Mount Sinai the Lord came "in a dense cloud," accompanied by "thunder and lightning," and the mountain shook violently (Exod. 19:9, 16, 18). Christ's coming was confirmed by "signs, wonders and various miracles" (Heb. 2:4). In the book of Revelation a fourfold repetition of thunder, rumblings, flashes of lightning, and an earthquake stand for the final and universal end of God's judgment (Rev. 4:5; 8:5; 11:19; 16:18). Psalm 97 makes a case for nature's confirmation of the gospel. "The heavens proclaim his righteousness, and all peoples see his glory" (v. 6). "News of the Lord's reign is not hidden in a secret enclave but published throughout the cosmos. The testimony of God is confirmed in creation, celebrated in community, and resonates in our conscience, so that "the 'I' that perceives is always already a 'we.'"[1] The worshiper is never alone, but always in the company of fellow worshipers. We are like the shepherds who heard the heavenly host sing, "Glory to God in the highest heaven" (Luke 2:14). We cannot help but "go tell it on the mountain." We are compelled to glorify and praise God for all the things we have heard and seen.

SACRED GAMES

> All who worship images are put to shame,
> those who boast in idols—
> worship him, all ye gods!
> —Psalm 97:7

The seemingly intrusive and glaring reference to idolaters at the center of the psalm should not be overlooked. Not everyone is convinced that the Lord reigns. Nature's phenomenal witness is brushed off by some and misinterpreted by others. What the earth perceives with jubilant joy may be rejected by the idolater with a shrug. Instead of being awed by God's righteousness and justice, the idolater is awed by images of success and reflections of himself. He is unimpressed by the consuming fire of God's judgment and unmoved by the lightning strikes of God's truth. The psalmist wastes no time on the subject of idolatry. Idolaters are dismissed with a sentence. He simply says they will be put to shame.

Nietzsche followed up his famous "God is dead" declaration with a question: "How shall we comfort ourselves . . . what festivals of atonement, what sacred games shall we have to invent?"[2] Hubert Dreyfus and Sean Kelly, two top-tier philosophers from Berkeley and Harvard, claim that living in the secular age means admitting that there are no deep and hidden truths to the universe, much less revealed truths. But that does not mean people have to live in despair, because sports offers a new form of transcendence. For Dreyfus and Kelly, "Sports may be the place in contemporary life where Americans find sacred community most easily."[3] The synapses of a brain trained to the quick visual stimulus of an NFL helmet-to-helmet hit, replayed four or five times, can hardly

---

1   Smith, *Imagining the Kingdom*, 84.
2   Nietzsche, *Gay Science*, §125, 181.
3   Dreyfus and Kelly, *All Things Shining*, 192.

cope with hearing the human voice preach the Word of God. The sensual atmosphere of heart-throbbing international soccer is hardly a level playing field for singing worship songs. True worship is bound to be a challenge for sport junkies hooked on the game's adrenaline rush. Can we watch the second-to-second, high-impact visual impressions of the NFL or NBA and learn to pray the Psalms?[4]

In the modern pantheon of American deities, sports ranks alongside money, sex, and power. It is an antidote to secular despair, a spiritual power that possesses, enthralls, and captivates the American consumer. How does the visceral experience of a ball game match up with the invisible realities grounding holy worship in the name of God the Father, the Son, and the Holy Spirit? How can the truth of our fallen human condition and God's redemptive provision compete with the throbbing excitement of a tie game in the bottom of the ninth, one man on, and the team's best hitter at the plate? Can the bread and cup compete with ballpark hot dogs? "The sports god is an enticing deity; he offers splendid moments of transcendence while never demanding that we take up our cross, forgive our enemies, or serve the poor."[5]

Most commentators skip over the reference to idolatry in this psalm and dwell on the clause "worship him, all you gods!" (Ps. 97:7). The debate centers on whether this is a reference to "false gods" or "rulers of the people" or "angels." The psalmist is either commanding "false gods" to submit to the one true and living God, or he is commanding angels to worship the Lord (see Heb. 1:6; Deut. 32:43 LXX). Ross concludes that "false gods" is the better interpretation: "Thus, even the gods that idolaters worship are inferior to God—so they are called on to submit to the Lord. The focus certainly refers to the spirit forces behind false gods."[6]

ZION REJOICES

> Zion hears and rejoices
> and the villages of Judah are glad
> because of your judgments, Lord.
> For you, Lord, are the Most High over all the earth;

---

4   Webster, "Intensity without Ultimacy."
5   Galli, "Prodigal Sports Fan," 49.
6   Ross, *Psalms*, 3:156; see Boice, *Psalms*, 2:792; Kidner, *Psalms 73–150*, 350.

you are exalted far above all gods.
Let those who love the LORD hate evil,
for he guards the lives of his faithful ones
and delivers them from the hand of the wicked.
Light shines on the righteous
and joy on the upright in heart.
Rejoice in the LORD, you who are righteous,
and praise his holy name.

—Psalm 97:8–12

Psalm 97 does not ignore evil, but neither does it dwell on it. Evil
is dealt with in justice. The fire of God's judgment consumes "his foes
on every side" (v. 3) and idolaters "are put to shame" (v. 7). Those "who
love the LORD hate evil" and are delivered "from the hand of the wicked"
(v. 10). Yet, the dominant emphasis in the psalm is on rejoicing. Joy is
the theme that runs through the psalm. The earth is glad. The distant
shores rejoice. Zion hears and rejoices. The villages of Judah are glad. The
upright in heart are filled with joy, and the righteous rejoice in the Lord.
The psalm ends on a note of praise: "Rejoice in the LORD, you who are
righteous, and praise his holy name" (v. 12).

Three fundamental attributes of the Lord account for this joy. Joy
is rooted in the Lord's judgments—"righteousness and justice are the
foundation of his throne" (v. 2; see also v. 8). Joy is based on the Lord's
authority—"For you, LORD, are the Most High over all the earth; you
are exalted far above all gods" (v. 9). Joy is secured by the Lord's faithfulness—"For he guards the lives of his faithful ones and delivers them
from the hand of the wicked" (v. 10).

Wisdom distinguishes between the joy of the Lord and the happiness
of the world. Three gut-level convictions shape the life of the believer.
We articulate these truths conceptually, we confess them doctrinally, and,
most importantly, we embrace them fully.

(1) *The Lord is exalted far above all gods* (v. 9). The Lord's command to
"have no other gods before me" (Exod. 20:3) sets the people of God free
from bondage. For "no one can serve two masters" (Matt. 6:24). We are
compelled by God's grace to "seek first his kingdom and his righteousness"
(Matt. 6:33). This exclusive truth claim (John 14:6) is not our burden, but
our blessing. For there is only "one Lord, one faith, one baptism; one God
and Father of all, who is over all and through all and in all" (Eph. 4:5–6).

(2) *To love the Lord is to hate evil* (v. 10). Amos writes, "Seek good, not evil, that you may live. . . . Hate evil, love good" (Amos 5:14–15), and the apostle Paul writes, "Love must be sincere. Hate what is evil; cling to what is good" (Rom. 12:9), and again, "Everyone who confesses the name of the Lord must turn away from wickedness" (2 Tim. 2:19).

(3) *The Lord's light dawns on the righteous, bringing them joy* (v. 11). Once we walked in darkness, but now we have seen a great light; "on those living in the land of deep darkness a light has dawned" (Isa. 9:2). We embrace this truth: "Arise, shine, for your light has come, and the glory of the LORD rises upon you" (Isa. 60:1). We look forward to a new heaven and a new earth and to the holy garden-city of God, "for the glory of God gives it light, and the Lamb is its lamp. The nations will walk by its light, and the kings of the earth will bring their splendor into it" (Rev. 21:23–24). But until that day we declare with the apostle, "God is light; in him there is no darkness at all. If we claim to have fellowship with him and yet walk in the darkness, we lie and do not live out the truth. But if we walk in the light, as he is in the light, we have fellowship with one another, and the blood of Jesus, his Son, purifies us from all sin" (1 John 1:5–7).

> Rejoice, the Lord is King;
> Your Lord and King adore!
> Rejoice, give thanks and sing
> And triumph evermore.
> Lift up your heart; lift up your voice!
> Rejoice, again I say, rejoice!
> —Charles Wesley

THE MISSION OF PRAISE

The enthronement psalms (Psalms 93–100) form an intricate mosaic of the beauty and majesty of Yahweh's reign. Christians pray these psalms today because Jesus Christ is our Savior and King. We are called to "kneel before the LORD our Maker, for he is our God and we are the people of his pasture, the flock under his care" (Ps. 95:6–7). Jesus, King of Kings and Lord of Lords (Rev. 19:16), is the sovereign Lord. He is robed in majesty (Ps. 93:1), the Judge of the earth, who avenges the righteous (Ps. 94:2). He is the Rock of our salvation, the great King above all gods (Ps. 95:1, 3). The whole earth is shouting for joy to the Lord, and the people of God are declaring "his glory among the nations, his marvelous deeds among all peoples" (Ps. 96:3). We feel the energy and passion of these psalms as they celebrate the complete salvation of the Lord.

Psalm 98 is all about praise, from beginning to end—exuberant praise. Three stanzas of equal length call the saved to celebrate, musicians to burst into jubilant song, and all of creation to resound in praise. In each stanza the psalmist emphasizes the totality of praise. The mission to praise the Lord who reigns is universal. Yahweh's faithfulness to Israel means that "all the ends of the earth have seen the salvation of our God" (v. 3). The whole earth shouts for joy to the Lord, and all creatures are invited to sing before the Lord. Psalm 98 emphasizes the Spirit-inspired synergy between worship and mission.

CELEBRATE SALVATION

Sing to the LORD a new song,
for he has done marvelous things;

his right hand and his holy arm
have worked salvation for him.
The LORD has made his salvation known
and revealed his righteousness to the nations.
He has remembered his love
and his faithfulness to Israel;
all the ends of the earth have seen
the salvation of our God.

—Psalm 98:1–3

The psalmist affirms that the leading edge of evangelism is powerful, adrenaline-triggering worship. Salvation is something we sing about, not just talk about. The meaning of salvation in Psalm 98 is the Lord's supernatural deliverance from evil and the victory of his righteousness. Salvation is entirely the work of God, and his "marvelous deeds" are judgment and justice (see Isa. 59:15–20). Yahweh's work of salvation gains specificity and "sharper definition" in the revelation of Jesus Christ, "for by one sacrifice he has made perfect forever those who are being made holy" (Heb. 10:14).[1] In his sermon on Psalm 98 Augustine leaves no doubt as to the identity of the Savior: "This very right hand, this very arm, this very salvation, is our Lord Jesus Christ of whom it is said, 'And all flesh shall see the salvation of God' (Luke 3:6)."[2]

Praise is the proclamation of salvation's most effective medium and most compelling argument. If we were merely thinking beings or believing beings, then straightforward, didactic teaching might be the way to carry out the mission of the church, but we are more than rational creatures. We are loving, feeling, emotional creatures, and it shows in how we embrace the truth and revel in the joy of salvation. "If you cannot express your joy, shout!" encourages Augustine. "Let the shout manifest your joy, if your speech cannot: yet let not joy be mute; let not your heart be silent respecting its God, let it not be mute concerning His gifts."[3]

Salvation inspires a new song; because the Lord's "holy arm" has "worked salvation," we are eager to praise him in song. Music is one of the special ways the Lord chooses to make his salvation known,

---

1   Kidner, *Psalms 73–150*, 352.
2   Augustine, *Expositions of the Psalms*, 8:481.
3   Augustine, *Expositions of the Psalms*, 8:482.

and evangelistic worship contributes to the global mission of the church. The psalmist and the apostle are in agreement on the mission of the church. Making salvation known, plus revealing the Lord's righteousness, is not a duty or a burden imposed on others, but a joyous privilege.

It is possible that Psalm 98, with its emphasis on commending the salvation of our God to all the ends of the earth, had an impact on the apostle Paul's approach to missions. Roland Allen, in his classic study of Paul's missionary methods, writes, "It seems strange to us that there should be no exhortations to missionary zeal in the Epistles of St Paul. There is one sentence of approval, 'The Lord's message rang out from you' [1 Thess. 1:8]; but there is no insistence upon the command of Christ to preach the Gospel."[4] Remarkably, this one sentence from Paul's early letter to the church at Thessalonica is consistent with the tenor and tone of Psalm 98. Missionary statesman Lesslie Newbigin agrees, when he writes,

> There has been a long tradition which sees the mission of the Church primarily as obedience to a command. It has been customary to speak of "the missionary mandate." This way of putting the matter is certainly not without justification, and yet it seems to me that it misses the point. It tends to make mission a burden rather than a joy, to make it part of the law rather than part of the gospel. If one looks at the New Testament evidence one gets another impression. Mission begins with a kind of explosion of joy. The news that the rejected and crucified Jesus is alive is something that cannot possibly be suppressed. It must be told. Who could be silent about such a fact?[5]

Not only does Paul's "explosion of joy" correspond to Psalm 98, but the largeness of his full-orbed gospel for the nations relates well to the wide-angled eschatological vision of the psalm. Paul's gospel of grace is the culmination of salvation history and the testimony of the Lord's "faithfulness to Israel" (Ps. 98:3). This is the gospel that reveals the Lord's "righteousness to the nations" and the "salvation of our God" to "all the ends of the earth" (v. 2–3).

---

4   Allen, *Missionary Methods*, 93.
5   Newbigin, *Gospel in a Pluralistic Society*, 116.

JUBILANT EVANGELISM

Shout for joy to the LORD, all the earth,
burst into jubilant song with music;
make music to the LORD with the harp,
with the harp and the sound of singing,
with trumpets and the blasts of the ram's horn—
shout for joy before the LORD, the King.

—Psalm 98:4–6

Music has been called the universal language because of its ability to transcend cultural barriers. The psalmist calls for choral music, stringed instruments like the harp and the guitar, and wind instruments like trumpets and horns to praise the Lord.[6] Music is an important medium for revealing the Lord's righteousness to the nations. Melody, harmony, rhythm, and tone are not human inventions.[7] David credited his musical ability to God. "He put a new song in my mouth, a hymn of praise to our God" (Ps. 40:3). Israel's priests gave God the credit for the song they sang. "By day the LORD directs his love, at night his song is with me—a prayer to the God of my life" (Ps. 42:8).

The Lord is the Great Composer and Chief Musician, whose acoustical world resonates with song because God designed not only the voice and ear, but the heart and spirit. Whatever creativity we express comes from God the Creator, who not only inspires the praise but gives us the gifts with which to express his praise. The prophet Zephaniah challenged the people of God to sing, "Sing, Daughter Zion; shout aloud, Israel! Be glad and rejoice with all your heart." The reason they could sing was because God rejoiced over them in song. "The LORD your God is with you, the Mighty Warrior who saves. He will take great delight in you; in his love he will no longer rebuke you, but will rejoice over you with singing" (Zeph. 3:14, 17).

The story of the people of God is not only spoken but sung. The prophet Isaiah described God's love in a love song: "I will sing for the one

---

6   Okorocha and Foulkes, "Psalms," 704. Augustine has an interesting allegorical interpretation of the brass trumpets and ram's horns. Brass trumpets are hammered out of brass to produce a "sweet sound," and courageous worshipers are hammered out of tribulation and suffering. Ram horns rise above the body of the animal, and the desires of true worshipers rise above the flesh. "He who wishes to be a horn trumpet, let him overcome the flesh" (Augustine, *Expositions on the Psalms*, 8:481–82).

7   Webster, *Living Word*, 106–7.

I love a song about his vineyard" (Isa. 5:1). Jesus sang with his disciples, such as the time he sang a hymn with them at the Last Supper (Matt. 26:30); according to the author of Hebrews, he continues to sing: "I will declare your name to my brothers and sisters; in the assembly I will sing your praises" (Heb. 2:12). To be filled with the Spirit of God is to sing and make music in our hearts to the Lord (Eph. 5:18–19).

Music tells God's great salvation history in song. The dramatic turning points and breakthroughs in God's revelation are marked by hymns of praise. Prose gives way to poetry and dialogue to doxology. Narrative becomes declarative in anthems of praise. The exodus is marked by the Song of Moses (Exod. 15). The birth of Christ is celebrated in Mary's Magnificat (Luke 1:46–55), Zechariah's Benedictus (Luke 1:67–79), and in the Song of Simeon (Luke 2:29–32). Angels offer up an exclamation of praise in the Gloria (Luke 2:14). The song of salvation was in the confession and praise of Christ in the early church. His humility and exaltation is celebrated in Paul's letter to the believers at Philippi in what is thought to be an early worship hymn (Phil. 2:6–11). Early Christians confessed in song, "He appeared in the flesh, was vindicated by the Spirit, was seen by angels, was preached among the nations, was believed on in the world, was taken up in glory" (1 Tim. 3:16).

CREATION'S ORCHESTRATED PRAISE

Let the sea resound, and everything in it,
the world, and all who live in it.
Let the rivers clap their hands,
let the mountains sing together for joy;
let them sing before the LORD,
for he comes to judge the earth.
He will judge the world in righteousness
and the peoples with equity.
—Psalm 98:7–9

All creation, from the oceans to the earth, and from the rivers to the mountains, is excited about the Lord's coming. Environmentalists take notice: the psalmist presents a picture of the whole earth, encompassing every creature and plant in the sea and on land. Nature is not alone and independent but is in fact the creative expression of God's handiwork. Truth unites what the modern experience divides. We can neither live well nor do science well without the meaning inherent in life. Worship is both devotional and scientific. It is devotional as it deepens our devotion to God, and it is scientific as it deepens our understanding of God's creation. Both theology and science are revelatory—both begin with God. Nature alone—life extracted from God—is only a figment of the modern imagination. The basic myth that postulates meaninglessness in order to do science is an irrational contradiction that deserves to be exposed as a modern heresy.

The apostles emphasized whole-earth salvation. The promise of salvation includes creation care, involving on our part the respect and regard for the environment intended by the Creator. The prophets and apostles look forward to a full restoration of creation in the new heaven and the new earth (Gen. 2:15; Isa. 65:17; Rev. 21:1). Paul writes, "For the creation waits in eager expectation for the children of God to be revealed. For the creation was subjected to frustration, not by its own choice, but by the will of the one who subjected it, in hope that the creation itself will be liberated from its bondage to decay and brought into the freedom and glory of the children of God" (Rom. 8:19–21).

Those who are saved by the strong arm of the Lord will use every available instrument to praise the Lord. They will proclaim this "new song" (Ps. 98:1) to "all the ends of the earth" (v. 3), and all of creation will "burst into jubilant song with music" (v. 4). The apostle Paul felt this all-encompassing praise when he prayed to the Father (πατέρα) "from whom every family [πατριὰ] in heaven and on earth derives its name" (Eph. 3:15). Paul prayed for everyone to come to know the grace of the Lord Jesus Christ. He emphasized the inclusiveness of the exclusive gospel of grace.

Augustine concluded his sermon on Psalm 98 by comparing two kinds of people: those who resist the Lord and those who welcome the Lord's coming to "judge the world in righteousness" (Ps. 98:9). Augustine asked his hearers to examine themselves and ask themselves whether they were hard of heart or soft of heart, whether they were resistant to the Lord's coming or receptive to his coming. To the receptive, Augustine said, "Even now rejoice that He will come. For you are a Christian!" And when you pray, "Your kingdom come," remember to "reform yourself, that you may not pray against yourself."[8]

---

8   Augustine, *Expositions of the Psalms*, 8:483.

THE KING IS HOLY

The enthronement psalms celebrate the rule of Yahweh over the nations, over all people, and over the fullness of salvation history. Christ's followers cannot pray Psalm 99 as if Jesus had not been born King of the Jews. Nor can we pretend that the magi had not come asking, "Where is the one who has been born king of the Jews? We saw his star when it rose and have come to worship him" (Matt. 2:2). The King who reigns in "the splendor of his holiness" (Ps. 96:9) has come, and he is Jesus of Nazareth, born in Bethlehem, raised in Nazareth, crucified and resurrected in Jerusalem, and seated today "at the right hand of the Majesty in heaven" (Heb. 1:3). We have no theology that makes sense of Psalm 99 apart from the history of Jesus. We are not waiting for this King to be identified; we are waiting for his return. "Therefore, since we are receiving a kingdom that cannot be shaken, let us be thankful, and so worship God acceptably with reverence and awe, for our 'God is a consuming fire'" (Heb. 12:28–29; quoting Deut. 4:24).

Three stanzas sketch the comprehensive impact of the Lord's holiness on government, justice, and redemption. The psalmist first paints a picture of the exalted King on his throne ruling over the nations. The second poetic vision is of the mighty King administering justice. Worshipers are invited to bow before him at his footstool (the ark of the covenant). The third scene pictures three famous mediators, Moses, Aaron, and Samuel, who call on the Lord for guidance and forgiveness. In all three pictures the Lord is exalted and praised because he is holy. This threefold doxology—holy, holy, holy—corresponds to the prophet Isaiah's experience when he beheld the Lord, high and exalted, seated on the throne, and the seraphim were calling to one another, "Holy, holy, holy is the LORD Almighty; the whole earth is full of his glory" (Isa. 6:3).

The holiness of the Lord is not an attribute of his character or a feature of his reign as much as the very essence of his being in relation to his creation. The Lord's holiness means that he is wholly other and radically separate from his creation. He is free from all contingencies and dependencies; he is free from all perversions, corruptions, impurities, and evils. With that said, the Lord's holy love and righteousness are essential for his creation and for human flourishing. We cannot exist for a moment without the holy otherness of God, Father, Son, and Holy Spirit. God's holiness, and there is no other kind of holiness, has made reconciliation to God possible. King Jesus holds everything together, sustains all things by his powerful word (Col. 1:17; Heb. 1:3), and reconciles to himself fallen sinful people "by making peace through his blood, shed on the cross" (Col. 1:20). His holiness sets us apart from a sin-twisted world, and sends us back into the world with the holy gospel of our Lord and Savior, with this admonition: "just as he who called you is holy, so be holy in all you do; for it is written: 'Be holy, because I am holy'" (1 Peter 1:15–16; quoting Lev. 11:44).

HOLY GOVERNMENT

The Lord reigns,
let the nations tremble;
he sits enthroned between the cherubim,
let the earth shake.
Great is the Lord in Zion;
he is exalted over all the nations.
Let them praise your great and awesome name—
he is holy.
—Psalm 99:1–3

We have a vivid sense of nation rising up against nation and kingdom against kingdom (Matt. 24:7), but no sense today of the nations trembling before the sovereign Lord. Human leaders and their peoples "plot in vain" (Ps. 2:1). The political landscape bears no resemblance to the psalmist's eschatological vision. To envision the Lord seated upon a dynamic throne of angelic power is to invite the modern reader to picture a dramatic cinematic scene in *Star Wars*. The reality of the Lord's reign is so far removed from our daily experience and political thinking that it might as well be science fiction. However, the psalmist insists here and in all the kingship psalms that this vision of the Lord's sovereignty is not wishful thinking or fake news.

Psalm 99 anticipates the power of the sovereign Lord to gather the nations under his holy government. Jesus's Sermon on the End of the World corresponds to Psalm 99. "When the Son of Man comes in his glory, and all the angels with him, he will sit on his glorious throne. All the nations will be gathered before him" (Matt. 25:31–32). In the wake of today's political chaos, the mission of the church remains constant: "go and make disciples of all nations" (Matt. 28:19), so that "the gospel of the kingdom will be preached in the whole world as a testimony to all nations, and then the end will come" (Matt. 24:14). It is important to note that the Lord is gathering the nations not by conquering them the way an ancient or modern superpower would, but by the power of the sacrificial Lamb of God. The people of God will sing a new song, saying, "Worthy is the Lamb, who was slain, to receive power and wealth and wisdom and strength and honor and glory and praise!" (Rev. 5:12). We look forward to the triumph of the Lion of the tribe of Judah, the Root of David, who is the Lamb that was slain. One day, "every creature in heaven and on earth and under the earth and on the sea, and all that is in them," will join in doxology: "To him who sits on the throne and to the Lamb be praise and honor and glory and power, for ever and ever!" (Rev. 5:13).

The political strategy of the kingdom of God does not line up with the American two-party political system or with any other political system. Psalm 99 calls Christians who feel threatened by secular culture to embrace the conviction that Jesus is King. Instead of growing bitter and resentful, we need a renewed sense of the Lord's sovereignty. If we have cherished the American dream over the kingdom of God, we are bound to be angry and fearful. The vitriolic rhetoric and slander expressed by Christians against politicians is not an indication of strength and boldness, but of fear and hate. It is wrong to place our faith and trust in political ideologies and politicians. Some Christians talk as if they had no other identity or loyalty other than to America, and when things don't go their way politically, they are filled with anger and fear. The psalmist leads us out of our ideological captivity and into the realm of Yahweh's rule. "At present we do not see everything subject to [mankind]. But we do see Jesus" (Heb. 2:8–9). Jesus was the one spoken of by the prophet when he declared that "the government will be on his shoulders. And he will be called Wonderful Counselor, Mighty God, Everlasting Father, Prince of

Peace" (Isa. 9:6). The psalmist reminds us that true worship is political. To say "Great is the Lord in Zion; he is exalted over all the nations" (Ps. 99:2) is to confess an international truth that is as true in the world as it is in the church, and is as political as it is spiritual. Holy government calls for eschatological thinking that sees today in the light of God's coming kingdom of righteousness and justice.

HOLY JUSTICE

> The King is mighty, he loves justice—
> you have established equity;
> in Jacob you have done
> what is just and right.
> Exalt the Lord our God
> and worship at his footstool;
> he is holy.
> —Psalm 99:4–5

The King's impressive strength is found in justice and righteousness. "Only in him are holiness and grace, power and justice, perfectly at one."[1] Evidence of these attributes of holiness can be found in the revelation of God's law. God "established equity" in Israel, and "in Jacob" he did "what is just and right." The law, including the sacrificial system of atonement, provided a shared moral vision and the redemptive means to overcome sin. The Lord established right and wrong (the law) and the means of grace (the sacrificial system), all of which is summed up in the Shema, or great commandment: "Hear, O Israel: The Lord our God, the Lord is one. Love the Lord your God with all your heart and with all your soul and with all your strength" (Deut. 6:4–5). Implicit in this all-encompassing command is to love our neighbor as ourselves (Lev. 19:18).

The psalmist extols the Lord's justice and righteousness, and the prophets chime in with their bold exclamation. The prophet Micah asks, "What does the Lord require of you?" He answers, "To act justly and to love mercy and to walk humbly with your God" (Mic. 6:8). On behalf of the Lord, Amos put the priority on justice. "Away with the noise of your songs! I will not listen to the music of your harps. But let justice roll on like a river, righteousness like a never-failing stream!" (Amos 5:23–24).

---

1   Kidner, *Psalms 73–150*, 354.

The psalmist calls believers to "exalt the LORD our God and worship at his footstool; he is holy" (Ps. 99:5). To lift up the Lord in praise and thanksgiving is to lower oneself and worship the Lord at his footstool. David described the ark of the covenant as God's footstool (1 Chron. 28:2). The ark of the covenant was the most important symbol of God's presence in the tabernacle. It was lined and covered with pure gold, and it was stipulated that it was not to be touched by human hands but rather moved by specially made poles. It was but a box, and not a very big box at that, measuring 3 feet, 6.5 inches long and 2 feet, 2.25 inches wide and high. Everything else in the tabernacle, from the table of the bread of presence to the altar of the burnt offering, was placed in reference to the ark of the covenant. Its lid was called the atonement cover, and its contents included a copy of the commandments. By calling the ark of the covenant the Lord's footstool, there was never any danger of confusing the object with the invisible reality of God. It pointed to the divine work of redemption and revelation necessary for the salvation of God's people, but it was never thought of as a substitute for the invisible reality of God or as an object of worship and devotion. The ark of the covenant pointed away from idolatry to the human need for redemption and to God's merciful provision.[2]

HOLY REDEMPTION

> Moses and Aaron were among his priests,
> Samuel was among those who called on his name;
> they called on the LORD
> and he answered them.
> He spoke to them from the pillar of cloud;
> they kept his statutes and the decrees he gave them.
> LORD our God,
> you answered them;
> you were to Israel a forgiving God,
> though you punished their misdeeds.

---

2   Calvin, *Psalms*, 6.4:78–79. Calvin makes two interesting observations on the ark of the covenant. (1) Calvin challenges Augustine's notion that the footstool symbolizes the Incarnate One's earthy humanity (see Augustine, *Expositions of the Psalms*, 8:485). (2) Calvin challenges "the frantic bishops of Greece," who used this passage to prove that God "was to be worshiped by images and pictures."

Exalt the LORD our God
and worship at his holy mountain,
for the LORD our God is holy.
                    —Psalm 99:6–9

In the Book of Revelation, the number three represents the triune God: God the Father, Son, and Holy Spirit. The psalmist may have written better than he knew. Besides the threefold "holy, holy, holy," we have mention of Moses, Aaron, and Samuel, and reference to the ark of the covenant (footstool), the pillar of cloud, and Zion, the holy mountain of the Lord. Three sets of three are poetically woven into the fabric of meaning, along with a constant refrain of adoration throughout the psalm: "The LORD reigns. . . . Great is the LORD in Zion. . . . The King is mighty, he loves justice. . . . Exalt the LORD our God. . . . Exalt the LORD our God . . . for the LORD our God is holy."

Three notable mediators between Yahweh and his people are identified by name and characterized as priests who called on the Lord continuously on behalf of the people. "These servants of the Lord would cry out to the Lord, and he would answer them" (see Exod. 17:11–12; 32:30–32; Num. 12:13; 1 Sam. 7:8–9; 9:12–13).[3] It may be significant that the era of salvation alluded to in the psalm took place before the people rose up and demanded a king so that they would be like the other nations (1 Sam. 8:5). The Lord's answer to Samuel's prayer is poignant: "Listen to all that the people are saying to you; it is not you they have rejected, but they have rejected me as their king" (1 Sam. 8:7). For Samuel to be the last named person in this series of enthronement psalms may suggest implicitly that Yahweh has always been Israel's one and only King.

Moses, Aaron, and Samuel called on the Lord for guidance and forgiveness. The Lord answered them first from the pillar of cloud and later from Mount Sinai, giving the people his law so that they could keep "his statutes and the decrees" (Ps. 99:7). And he answered them not only with guidance but with forgiveness. With a sense of endearment the psalmist says, "You were to Israel a forgiving God, though you punished their misdeeds" (v. 8). These key mediators in Israel's history point forward to Jesus Christ: "For there is one God and one mediator between God and mankind, the man Christ Jesus, who gave himself as a ransom for

---

3   Ross, *Psalms*, 3:181.

all people" (1 Tim. 2:5–6). Jesus became our "merciful and faithful high priest in service to God" so that "he might make atonement for the sins of the people" (Heb. 2:17). He was appointed "to offer gifts and sacrifices for sins" on our behalf (Heb. 5:1). He sacrificed for our sins "once for all when he offered himself" (Heb. 7:27), "and by his wounds we are healed" (Isa. 53:5).

Mount Sinai is not mentioned explicitly because it has been eclipsed by Mount Zion, but the author of Hebrews expands on the psalm's final emphasis: "Exalt the LORD our God and worship at his holy mountain, for the LORD our God is holy" (Ps. 99:9). The theological argument of the book of Hebrews closes with a comparison between Mount Sinai and Mount Zion. The author argues for the complete sufficiency of Christ's once-and-for-all atoning sacrifice. Everything Mount Sinai anticipated and foreshadowed has been accomplished in Christ. "You have not come to a mountain that can be touched. . . . But you have come to Mount Zion" (Heb. 12:18, 22). The religion of Mount Sinai has been replaced by something absolutely better. Instead of Sinai's awful terror, darkness, and gloom, Zion is pulsating with awe-inspiring worship, joy, and love.

> But you have come to Mount Zion, to the city of the living God, the heavenly Jerusalem. You have come to thousands upon thousands of angels in joyful assembly, to the church of the firstborn, whose names are written in heaven, You have come to God, the Judge of all, to the spirits of the righteous made perfect, to Jesus the mediator of a new covenant, and to the sprinkled blood that speaks a better word than the blood of Abel. (Heb. 12:22–24)

The psalmist's refrain "he is holy," Kidner explains, is in the end expanded "and given warmth, to read (in its actual word-order) *For holy is the Lord our God!*" Kidner adds, "The majesty is undiminished, but the last word is now given to intimacy. He is holy; He is also, against all our deserving, not ashamed to be called ours. Well may we worship."[4]

---

4   Kidner, *Psalms 73–150*, 355.

PSALM 100

JUBILATION

This tiny, five-verse, easy-to-memorize psalm explodes with meaning like a split atom.[1] Psalm 100 brings the enthronement psalms (93–100) to a resounding conclusion. "Of these royal psalms the hundredth is the doxology."[2] The pulsating rhythm of action verbs makes it impossible to sit still and say this psalm without feeling. This capstone psalm is what we would expect after celebrating the global reach of the kingdom of God. To know the Lord, who reigns in justice and righteousness and who is worshiped in the splendor of his holiness, is to express exuberant heartfelt joy. If evangelistic worship is the leading edge of the mission of the church, then Psalm 100 is its jubilant crescendo.

Two parallel stanzas call us into participatory worship. Such worship is inspired by knowing that the Lord is God, that he made us, and that we are his people. The second stanza repeats the call to worship, invoking thanksgiving and praise, for the Lord is good, his love endures forever, and his faithfulness never ends. The voice that is calling out to us is the shared voice of the worshiping community. Psalm 100 is a hymn, not a solo. Together, we share in the responsibility to encourage one another to "shout for joy to the LORD" (Ps. 100:1) and to "enter his gates with thanksgiving" (v. 4). The psalmist does not envision a pastor-dominated worship service, where we sit idly by as observers waiting to be moved and inspired. We are not an audience of spectators looking to the "professionals" to do worship to us and for us, nor are we consumers of a spiritual product; we are active participants in worship.

---

1 Augustine, *Expositions of the Psalms*, 8:487. Augustine writes, "The verses are few, but big with great subjects; may the seed bring forth within your hearts, the barn be prepared for the Lord's harvest."
2 Stott, *Favorite Psalms*, 91.

Psalm 100 is a simple call to worship that serves its purpose effectively without much interpretation. Believers grasp its powerful meaning intuitively. The poet-psalmist has arranged the rhythm of its seven verbs—"shout," "worship," "come," "know," "enter," "give thanks," and "praise"—to give the psalm a driving beat. The thrust of the psalm is assured by its positive vocabulary: "joy," "gladness," "joyful," "thanksgiving," and "praise." And most importantly, everything said and felt is centered on the Lord, who is the principal subject of everything going on in the psalm. We worship the Lord. He is God. He made us. He is our Shepherd, and we are his people. We celebrate his goodness, his enduring love, and his faithfulness through all generations.

The beauty and depth of Psalm 100 has inspired hymns and songs of praise, including "Jubilate Deo," William Kethe's "All People That on Earth Do Dwell," Isaac Watts's "Before the Lord's Eternal Throne," and Chris Tomlin's "Psalm 100." We should not be surprised that this psalm inspires musicians and artists and theologians. Its simple power should be embraced and its theological depth and pastoral implications explored.

SHOUT FOR JOY

Shout for joy to the LORD, all the earth.
Worship the LORD with gladness;
come before him with joyful songs.
Know that the LORD is God.
It is he who made us, and we are his;
we are his people, the sheep of his pasture.
—Psalm 100:1–3

The sheer joy and exuberance of Psalm 100 encourages the worshiper to shed the inhibitions rooted in pride and insecurity and come before the Lord with a freedom rooted in faith and forgiveness. This is not a call to self-expression as much as a call to self-surrender in the community of praise. We are invited into a realm of joy that brings release from being overly self-preoccupied and relief from our deeply ingrained cultural traditions and habits. Psalm 100 draws the lonely individual out of the crowd and into the joyous processional. Instead of liturgical fastidiousness or entertainment, Psalm 100 gives the believer a solid foundation for the deep meaning and joyous emotion of real, God-centered worship.

The first line of the psalm "should be thought-provoking to sing" because it "claims the world for God."[3] It harkens back to a theme running through the enthronement psalms: "Shout for joy to the LORD, all the earth, burst into jubilant song with music" (Ps. 98:4; see 96:7; 97:1). The whole earth ought to shout for joy, for we all belong to the Lord who is our maker and redeemer. Stewart Brand's 1968 Whole Earth Catalog with NASA's iconic picture of the earth on its cover celebrated two countercultural truths: the environment and the human community. Brand's intuitive grasp of creation care and human society were surely right, but what was missing was his understanding of creation's Creator and humanity's Author, Redeemer, and King. Brand thought humanity's spiritual longings could be fulfilled through technology, but only the Lord is able to bring about the new humanity for a new heaven and a new earth.

Invitation and imperative merge in the call to worship the Lord with gladness. This is not about happily attending upbeat church services. This is about finding our greatest joy and deepest meaning in serving the Lord with our whole being. Worshiping the Lord "involves a serious submission of the whole self."[4] This is body-mind-heart-and-soul worship that does not cease at the narthex, but moves out into every place and every sphere of life where we are "before him," which is to say, everywhere. There is no gap between worship and work; life is all of one piece.[5] The apostle Paul echoes this theology of worship when he urges brothers and sisters, "in view of God's mercy, to offer your bodies as a living sacrifice, holy and pleasing to God—this is your true and proper worship" (Rom. 12:1).

We worship the Lord *knowingly* because the Lord has chosen to disclose himself personally. He is the same person who promised Abraham, "All peoples on earth will be blessed through you" (Gen. 12:3). He gave his name to Moses: "I AM WHO I AM" (Exod. 3:14). He promised David an everlasting kingdom (2 Sam. 7:13) and to the prophet Jeremiah a new

---

3   Kidner, *Psalms 73–150*, 356.
4   Goldingay, *Psalms*, 3:135.
5   Kidner, *Psalms 73–150*, 356.

covenant (Jer. 31:31). We know him as our Maker; we are the work of his hands (Isa. 29:23). We say with the psalmist, "what is mankind that you are mindful of them, human beings that you care for them? You have made them a little lower than the angels and crowned them with glory and honor" (Ps. 8:4–5). We know him as our Shepherd: "we are his people, the sheep of his pasture" (Ps. 100:3). We know him as our Redeemer. Jesus said, "I am the good shepherd. The good shepherd lays down his life for the sheep" (John 10:11). To worship the Lord *knowingly* is to say with Paul, "but by the grace of God I am what I am," and to know "all are justified freely by his grace through the redemption that came by Christ Jesus" (1 Cor. 15:10; Rom. 3:24).[6] Psalm 100 celebrates the beauty of knowing God as our Creator and Redeemer with heartfelt praise and thanksgiving and without a hint of cynicism or discouragement.

ENTER WITH PRAISE

Enter his gates with thanksgiving
and his courts with praise;
give thanks to him and praise his name.
For the LORD is good and his love endures forever;
his faithfulness continues through all generations.
—Psalm 100:4–5

The universal invitation to "enter his gates" goes out to all the nations from the people of God. The reasons for God's magnanimous openness to all are clearly stated. His goodness, love, and faithfulness are forever. But the psalmist did not realize then what we know now, that "God so loved the world that he gave his one and only Son, that whoever believes in him shall not perish but have eternal life" (John 3:16). We cannot imagine Jesus praying this psalm without envisioning the universal reach

---

6   Calvin, *Psalms*, 6.4:84. In contrast to the exuberance of Psalm 100, Calvin's expo-
     sition of these verses is decidedly negative. He alludes to the papacy and the im-
     possibility of true worship of God taking place while God's glory is being profaned
     and superstition exists. Ironically, Calvin uses this psalm to address the ingratitude
     found among most people: "Scarcely one among a hundred seriously acknowledg-
     es that he holds his existence from God . . . yet every man makes a god of himself,
     and virtually worships himself, when he ascribes to his own power what God
     declares belongs to him alone."

of the gospel. The privilege and responsibility to offer this call to worship to the world belongs to the priesthood of all believers, to all those who have been commissioned by Christ to "go and make disciples of all nations" (Matt. 28:19). Our joy is to encourage and support one another in worship and service. The vision of temple worship pictured in Psalm 100 is transposed in the New Testament and applied to the church—the people of God: "But you are a chosen people, a royal priesthood, a holy nation, God's special possession, that you may declare the praises of him who called you out of darkness into his wonderful light" (1 Peter 2:9). This is why the author of Hebrews declares:

> Therefore, brothers and sisters, since we have confidence to enter the Most Holy Place by the blood of Jesus, by a new and living way opened for us through the curtain, that is, his body, and since we have a great priest over the house of God, let us draw near to God with a sincere heart and with the full assurance that faith brings, having our hearts sprinkled to cleanse us from a guilty conscience and having our bodies washed with pure water. Let us hold unswervingly to the hope we profess, for he who promised is faithful. And let us consider how we may spur one another on toward love and good deeds, not giving up meeting together, as some are in the habit of doing, but encouraging one another—and all the more as you see the Day approaching. (Heb. 10:19–25)

THE PASSION OF LEADERSHIP

The enthronement psalms (Psalms 93–100) come to a resounding conclusion with jubilant praise and thanksgiving. And in Psalm 101 the king takes responsibility for assuring righteousness and moral order in the city of God. David is credited with this psalm and Psalm 103, the only two David psalms in Book 4. Psalm 101 reflects the young king's passion for righteousness. If the jubilation expressed in Psalm 100 is going to characterize his rule, then righteousness and justice must be his number one priority. In spite of David's critical moral failures, he knew what was expected of a king who was a man after God's own heart (1 Sam. 13:14).

The gated community of Zion in the new heaven and the new earth excludes evil in all of its vile, perverse, arrogant, and deceptive forms (Rev. 22:14–15). This ideal administration concentrates first and foremost on biblical integrity and social justice. In Psalm 101 there is no division between personal morality and public justice. The king's efforts "to lead a blameless life" and to conduct his administration "with a blameless heart" (v. 2) involve surrounding himself with those "whose walk is blameless" (v. 6). The king must also be committed to separating himself and his people from "anything that is vile" (v. 3) and from those whose hearts are perverse (v. 4). The moral imperatives of this psalm leave little room for ambiguity and compromise. Against evil and its destructive ways the king is defiant: "No one who practices deceit will dwell in my house; no one who speaks falsely will stand in my presence" (v. 7).

PERSONAL COMMITMENT

> I will sing of your love [*hesed*] and justice;
> to you, LORD, I will sing praise.
> I will be careful to lead a blameless life—
> when will you come to me?
> I will conduct the affairs of my house
> with a blameless heart.
> I will not look with approval
> on anything that is vile.
> I hate what faithless people do;
> I will have no part in it.
> The perverse of heart shall be far from me;
> I will have nothing to do with what is evil.
> —Psalm 101:1–4

Worship is emphasized as a critical factor in the pursuit of justice. The psalmist pledges to chant a praise song celebrating the Lord's steadfast love and justice. David's resolve to sing about God's covenant faithfulness is fundamental to his kingdom ethic. This single verse speaks volumes, not only of the king's emotive commitment to justice, but of his theological understanding. It is the grace and holiness of God that undergirds the king's passion. Mercy and judgment originate with "the great King above all gods" (Ps. 95:3). The psalmist knows that apart from the grace of God we cannot know and obey the will of God. The king's theme song is a constant reminder that everything depends on the grace and mercy of God. This is equivalent to Jesus's beatitude-based belief or Paul's justification by faith in Romans. This is the reminder that "it is God who works in [us] to will and to act in order to fulfill his good purpose" (Phil. 2:13).

The king pledges to the Lord to lead by example. He is committed to working out his salvation "with fear and trembling" (Phil. 2:12). He longs for the imminent presence of God, for a vivid sense of God's intimate fellowship. The quest for social justice and moral order is dependent on knowing God. The rhythmic beat of Psalm 101 is set by the repetition of the psalmist's for-the-record, first-person, vowed commitments. An emphatic "I will" accentuates the determination and devotion of David's long obedience in the same direction.

By promising to "conduct the affairs of my house with a blameless heart" (v. 2), the psalmist is committed to integrity personally and publically. He melds "house" and "heart" in a unified grasp of ethical responsibility. He will rule others as he will rule himself. "House" has a range of meanings for the worshiper, from David's royal palace to the house of the Lord and the people of Israel. All believers are instructed by David's example. The pledge of moral responsibility extends from the self to the family to the household of faith and to society. In every sphere, the commitment before the Lord is the same: to "a blameless heart."

The meaning of a blameless heart is illustrated in several ways. The psalmist refuses to be influenced or enticed by anything that is vile, meaning anything that is wicked and worthless.[1] He will not tolerate what faithless people do, or put up with evil in any form. The intensity of the psalmist's repulsion is captured in the word "hate," but this is not the raw emotion of hate that is expressed in Psalm 137. It is more a matter of spiritual discernment, the wisdom necessary to distance oneself from influences that cause harm. "Hatred is an important spiritual and moral virtue (see [Ps.] 139:19–22), as Jesus affirms (Luke 14:26)."[2]

The psalmist's convictions are echoed in the apostles. The faithful have not "departed from the truth" (2 Tim. 2:18), but rather "abstain from sinful desires, which wage war against [the] soul" (1 Peter 2:11). Allusions to Psalm 101 can be found in Paul's spiritual direction to the church at Rome: "Love must be sincere. Hate what is evil; cling to what is good" (Rom. 12:9). The well-known case of incest in the church at Corinth caused Paul to distinguish between associating with sexually immoral people who claimed to be Christians and people in the world who were not Christians. Paul said, "I wrote to you in my letter not to associate with sexually immoral people—not at all meaning the people of this world who are immoral, or the greedy and swindlers, or idolaters. In that case you would have to leave the world." Paul sought to preserve ethical integrity in the household of faith and evangelistic outreach in the world. In keeping with the psalmist, Paul made it clear, "You must not associate with anyone who claims to be a brother or sister but is sexually immoral or greedy, an idolater or slanderer, a drunkard or swindler. Do not even eat with such people" (1 Cor. 5:9–11).

Some may read the urgency and intensity of the psalmist's vowed moral convictions as legalistic, but only if they fail to understand what

---

1   Ross, *Psalms*, 3:201.
2   Goldingay, *Psalms*, 3:143.

it means to seek first Christ's kingdom and his righteousness (Matt. 6:33). Jesus came not to abolish God's law, but to draw out the significance of the law and to fulfill all that God intended through the law. Jesus came to establish the law, not undermine it; to complete it, not condemn it. By reducing it to an external religious activity and legal code, the Pharisees short-circuited the intended meaning of the law. They were guilty of missing the meaning of the law by substituting external religious conformity for heart righteousness. Jesus's promise to fulfill the law and the prophets is inclusive of everything the Old Testament taught, symbolized, modeled, and looked forward to. Jesus fulfilled the covenant promises made to Abraham and David. He accomplished everything anticipated in the burnt sacrifices, Passover lamb, and tabernacle. He exemplified the perseverance of Job and the faithfulness of Abraham. He embodied the goal of the law espoused by the prophets in his own righteousness. In every way—doctrinally, ethically, and ceremonially—the law finds its completion in Jesus. All this lies behind Jesus's concise affirmation, "Do not think that I have come to abolish the Law or the Prophets; I have not come to abolish them but to fulfill them" (Matt. 5:17).[3]

PUBLIC ADMINISTRATION

> Whoever slanders their neighbor in secret,
> I will put to silence;
> whoever has haughty eyes and a proud heart,
> I will not tolerate.
> My eyes will be on the faithful in the land,
> that they may dwell with me;
> the one whose walk is blameless
> will minister to me.
> No one who practices deceit
> will dwell in my house;
> no one who speaks falsely
> will stand in my presence.
> Every morning I will put to silence
> all the wicked in the land;

---

3   Webster, *Easy Yoke*, 96.

I will cut off every evildoer
from the city of the LORD.
—Psalm 101:5–8

The pursuit of justice is the king's high calling. The challenge to root out the hidden crimes of secret slander and arrogance may impress us as nearly impossible. It is hard enough to prosecute overt evil, but the king pledges to go after "secret actions and inner attitudes."[4] He wants to remove people from public office who through their slander and arrogance cause division and discord. This level of justice in the ranks of government is unheard of, but "as head of the political machine and as the guardian of justice," the king vows to disqualify gossipers and patronizing egotists.[5] The king has his eyes on people with character who are good from the inside out. "The faithful in the land" are beatitude-based believers, with salt-and-light impact, whose heart righteousness chooses love instead of hate, purity instead of lust, fidelity instead of infidelity, honesty instead of dishonesty, reconciliation instead of retaliation, and prayer over revenge (Matt. 5:1–48).

The king's desire to root out evil in his administration is a most worthy goal. Just imagine a king who pledges to be committed every waking moment from morning to night to silencing "all the wicked in the land" and cutting "off every evildoer from the city of the LORD" (Ps. 101:8). However, this is a shared endeavor with the king taking the lead. This vow of justice and righteousness should be on the lips of every parent, official, administrator, pastor, teacher, coach, and employer. We should be able to say, "I will conduct the affairs of my house [family, office, company, class, team] with a blameless heart" (v. 2).

Psalm 101 is associated with David, but we know the king did not live up to this high calling. The psalm serves as an indictment against David's will to power over Bathsheba (2 Samuel 11–12) and his insistence on counting the fighting men (2 Sam. 24:1–17). David's confession, "I have sinned; I, the shepherd, have done wrong" (2 Sam. 24:17), is a confession that we all need to echo one way or another over the course of our lives. David's passion for righteousness and justice, along with his marked failures, serve to center our hopes and expectations on the

---

4   Goldingay, *Psalms*, 3:143.
5   Kidner, *Psalms 73–150*, 359.

one who "has been tempted in every way, just as we are—yet he did not sin" (Heb. 4:15).

Leslie Allen writes, "Ultimately the Christian will view the psalm in the light of Isaiah 11:1–5."[6] One greater than David has come, springing up "from the stump of Jesse," who has the Spirit of the Lord, the Spirit of wisdom and of understanding, the Spirit of counsel and might, the Spirit of the knowledge and fear of the Lord, and "the earth will be filled with the knowledge of the LORD as the waters cover the sea" (Isa. 11:9). In his Mars Hill sermon, the apostle Paul looked forward to the day "when [God] will judge the world with justice by the man he has appointed. He has given proof of this to everyone by raising him from the dead" (Acts 17:31).

---

6   Allen, *Psalms 101–150*, 7.

THE PRAYER OF THE DISTRESSED

This is a prayer for desperate times. The psalmist is distressed and destitute, unable to cope, and filled with despair. His life is upended, and he is barely hanging on.[1] This is not an everyday prayer. It is reserved for those times of grief, loneliness, and utter weakness that bring us to the edge of the abyss. This prayer did not originate with Job, but he may have prayed this way sitting on the ash heap after everything was taken away. The prophet Jeremiah may have prayed this very psalm, because it gave him words to articulate his pain and dismay, his agonizing desperation. Jesus's Prayer Book has several psalms that might have been prayed by our Lord in Gethsemane, and this is one of them.

What stands out about this personal lament is the worshiper's in-depth understanding and confidence in the sovereign Lord coupled with his genuine grasp of the big picture of salvation. Rarely are these two extremes, personal despair and solid theological understanding, juxtaposed in such a dynamic way. The psalmist portrays his dark desperation in tension with his unwavering belief in the Lord's sovereignty and in the future of salvation. He chooses to locate his personal trauma in the larger picture of God's eternal security. Raw emotion is freely expressed, and mature theology is beautifully articulated. We are given a psalm that melds the dark night of despair with the living hope "that is ready to be revealed in the last time" (1 Peter 1:5).

---

1   The early church classified Psalm 102 as one of the seven penitential psalms (Psalms 6, 32, 38, 51, 130, 143), but the cause of the person's suffering is not tied to a confession of sin. It is "the cry of one whose sufferings are unexplained, like Job's" (Kidner, *Psalms 73–150*, 360).

The author of Hebrews eloquently quotes seven passages at the beginning of his epistle, including Psalm 102:25–27, to prove the deity and exaltation of the Son. The Greek translation (LXX) adds "O Lord" to Psalm 102:24, so the text reads, "He [God] also says, 'In the beginning, O Lord, you laid the foundation of the earth.'" The meaning is similar to Psalm 110:1, "The LORD says to my Lord." The author of Hebrews interprets the psalm as the Father addressing the Son and crediting the Son with the creation of the cosmos. This raises the reasonable possibility that the author of Hebrews understood the whole psalm as messianic and descriptive of the life of Jesus (metalepsis). If we read Psalm 102 from the perspective of Jesus's earthly suffering and heavenly exaltation, we get the full messianic perspective. The psalmist's experience of fear and isolation correlates objectively with the Messiah's Gethsemane experience (Ps. 102:1–11). And if the psalmist felt he was "cut down in [his] prime" (v. 23 MSG), this was even more true for the Lord Jesus, whose days were cut short at the cross.

MY PRAYER, MY DAYS

Hear my prayer, LORD;
let my cry for help come to you.
Do not hide your face from me
when I am in distress.
Turn your ear to me;
when I call, answer me quickly.
For my days vanish like smoke;
my bones burn like glowing embers.
My heart is blighted and withered like grass;
I forget to eat my food.
In my distress I groan aloud
and am reduced to skin and bones.
I am like a desert owl,
like an owl among the ruins.
I lie awake; I have become
like a bird alone on a roof.
All day long my enemies taunt me;
those who rail against me use my name as a curse.
For I eat ashes as my food
and mingle my drink with tears
because of your great wrath,

for you have taken me up and thrown me aside.
My days are like the evening shadow;
I wither away like grass.
—Psalm 102:1–11

The psalmist's opening appeal is intense, personal, and ongoing. It is apparent that he has languished in fear and isolation for some time. His urgent plea is for the Lord to pay attention. He needs answers, and quickly! Those who pray the Psalms are familiar with this desperate cry for help (Pss. 39:12; 54:2; 61:1; 64:1). It is common enough that we should expect to find ourselves in similar circumstances. We can put ourselves in the psalmist's place and learn from his example. Few may experience the intensity of Job's sufferings, but all believers at some time or another find themselves in the psalmist's situation. Psalm 102 is for such times.

The psalmist flashes a series of images across the screen of our imagination to capture his suffering. He describes the horror of his unexplained suffering twelve different ways! He opens and closes his carefully crafted chiastic description with a reference to "my days" going up in smoke and "my days" fleeting like the evening shadows (Ps. 102:3, 11). He withers away like the grass (vv. 4, 11). "I forget to eat my food" parallels "I eat ashes as my food" (vv. 4, 9). He is feverish, emaciated, unable to sleep, groaning because of the pain, and weeping from despair. He feels like a lonely desert owl or a pelican far from the sea or a buzzard in the desert or a lost sparrow. Scholars cannot agree as to what kind of bird, but the meaning is clear. Added to the physical and emotional trauma is the constant barrage of taunts and slander coming from his enemies, who "use my name as a curse" (v. 8).

The source of the psalmist's unexplained suffering is found in God who is sovereign over all of life and ultimately responsible for everything that happens. We have seen this reasoning before in the Psalms where the sufferer pushes past immediate and secondary causes and brings his plight directly to the Lord. This is not an implicit admission of sin and personal wrongdoing, but rather a recognition of the psalmist's humble submission before God and a reflection of his dismay. He knows he lives in an evil and broken world.[2] The psalmist's twelvefold description of

---

2   Ross, *Psalms*, 3:217. Ross may draw a different conclusion: "When he attributes his suffering to God's wrath, he is indicating that sin is the cause of his pain (even though he does not actually say that) and that God is in collusion with the enemies."

suffering anticipates the anguish of Gethsemane, when he who was without sin contemplated being pierced for our transgressions and crushed for our iniquities (Isa. 53:5). Psalm 102 is not far removed from Jesus's Gethsemane prayer and anticipates the cry from the cross, "My God, my God why have you forsaken me?" (Mark 15:34).

BUT YOU, LORD

> But you, LORD, sit enthroned forever;
> your renown endures through all generations.
> You will arise and have compassion on Zion,
> for it is time to show favor to her;
> the appointed time has come.
> For her stones are dear to your servants;
> her very dust moves them to pity.
> The nations will fear the name of the LORD,
> all the kings of the earth will revere your glory.
> For the LORD will rebuild Zion
> and appear in his glory.
> He will respond to the prayer of the destitute;
> he will not despise their plea.
> Let this be written for a future generation,
> that a people not yet created may praise the LORD:
> "The LORD looked down from his sanctuary on high,
> from heaven he viewed the earth,
> to hear the groans of the prisoners
> and release those condemned to death."
> So the name of the LORD will be declared in Zion
> and his praise in Jerusalem
> when the peoples and the kingdoms
> assemble to worship the LORD.
> —Psalm 102:12–22

There is a decisive break and an abrupt change of tone as the psalmist moves from dark lamentation to bright hope and praise. The sharp contrast between the frailty and fleeting nature of human life and the eternal nature of the Lord's enduring throne is accentuated. The psalmist's confidence in the compassion, timing, and certainty of the Lord's deliverance catches the worshiper by surprise. We have gone from the depths of despair to the heights of praise "in a flash, in the twinkling of an eye"

(1 Cor. 15:52). The psalmist's "my days" are contrasted with the Lord's eternal renown and rule. The psalmist's time may be slipping away, but the Lord's "appointed time has come" (Ps. 102:13). One hears in Paul's statement an echo of this verse, "But when the set time had fully come, God sent his Son, born of a woman, born under the law, to redeem those under the law, that we might receive adoption to sonship" (Gal. 4:4–5).

The psalmist's weakness and powerlessness stand in sharp relief to the Lord's power to intervene, to rebuild Zion, to gather the nations, and to respond to the prayer of the destitute. The psalmist envisions a great reversal in the future so "that a people not yet created may praise the LORD" (Ps. 102:18). This hope lines up with Jesus's statement, "I am the good shepherd . . . and I lay down my life for the sheep. I have other sheep that are not of this sheep pen. I must bring them also. They too will listen to my voice, and there shall be one flock and one shepherd" (John 10:14–16). The apostle Peter said it this way: "Once you were not a people, but now you are the people of God; once you had not received mercy, but now you have received mercy" (1 Peter 2:10).

By referring to the "prayer of the destitute" and "the groans of the prisoners," the psalmist integrates the opening lament with the promise of salvation. Zechariah's prophecy captures a similar integration of promise when he describes Zion's coming king as "righteous and victorious, lowly and riding on a donkey," proclaiming peace to the nations. He adds, "As for you, because of the blood of my covenant with you, I will free your prisoners from the waterless pit. Return to your fortress, you prisoners of hope; even now I announce that I will restore twice as much to you" (Zech. 9:9–12). All of this adds up to a tremendous worship scene. The "peoples and the kingdoms" (Ps. 102:22) will gather to praise the name of the Lord in Zion. John the apostle described it this way: "The kingdom of the world has become the kingdom of our Lord and of his Messiah, and he will reign for ever and ever" (Rev. 11:15).

MY GOD, MY DAYS

> In the course of my life he broke my strength;
> he cut short my days.
> So I said:
> "Do not take me away, my God, in the midst of my days;

your years go on through all generations.
In the beginning you laid the foundations of the earth,
and the heavens are the work of your hands.
They will perish, but you remain;
they will all wear out like a garment.
Like clothing you will change them
and they will be discarded.
But you remain the same,
and your years will never end.
The children of your servants will live in your presence;
their descendants will be established before you."
                        —Psalm 102:23–28

The psalmist contrasts his few short years with the Lord's longevity: "your years go on through all generations" (v. 24). Once again the sharp contrast between personal lament and divine hope are laid bare. The author of Hebrews sees much more going on here than the dying wish of a believer who faithfully clings to the everlasting promises of God. His eyes are fixed on Jesus, "the pioneer and perfecter of faith. For the joy set before him he endured the cross, scorning its shame, and sat down at the right hand of the throne of God" (Heb. 12:2). As far as he is concerned "the whole psalm is Messianic, showing first the Messiah's sufferings and dereliction (1–11), then his eager anticipation of the kingdom in its world-wide glory (12–22)."[3]

The tension running through the psalm is a messianic tension. The one who learned obedience by the things that he suffered (Heb. 5:8) is the "heir of all things," maker of the universe, and "the radiance of God's glory and the exact representation of his being, sustaining all things by his powerful word" (Heb. 1:2–3). The author of Hebrews places polar opposite truths, absolute transcendence and deep empathy, in radical juxtaposition. In Christ, we have a high priest who is both the Son of God and the Son of Man. The Incarnate One transcends his transcendence and takes on our weakness in every respect except without sin. He became "fully human in every way, in order that he might become a merciful and faithful high priest in service to God, and that he might make atonement for the sins of the people" (Heb. 2:17). As the ascended Lord, Jesus "sat down at the right hand of the Majesty in heaven" (Heb.

---

3   Kidner, *Psalms 73–150*, 363.

1:3); as the Incarnate One, Jesus knows our needs, understands our temptations, and empathizes with our weaknesses. "Sympathy with the sinner in his trial does not depend on the experience of sin which only the sinless can know in its full intensity. He who fails yields before the last strain."[4] The promises of God keep lament and hope bound together. The psalmist concludes confidently: the world is passing away, "but you remain the same" (v. 27), and the author of Hebrews concludes, "Jesus Christ is the same yesterday and today and forever" (Heb. 13:8).

---

4   Quoted in Bruce, *Hebrews*, 116, from B. F. Westcott, *The Epistle to the Hebrews* (London: Macmillan, 1892), 108.

A SALVATION PSALM

P salm 103 is "undoubtedly, one of the best-loved psalms," observed John Stott.[1] Spurgeon called it the Song on the Mount answering Jesus's Sermon on the Mount. "Our attempt at exposition," he wrote, "is commenced under an impressive sense of utter impossibility of doing justice to so sublime a composition. . . . It is one of those all-comprehending Scriptures which is a Bible in itself, and it might alone almost suffice for the hymn book of the church."[2] Psalm 103 is the inspiration to two of our great hymns, "Praise, My Soul, the King of Heaven" and "Praise to the Lord, the Almighty"; as well as the song of praise, "Bless the Lord." "Admiring gratitude shines through every line of this hymn to the God of all grace."[3]

The psalm is pure praise, proof positive that ultimately the only true response to God's perfect grace is praise. There are no petitions, only heartfelt reflections on the mercy of God. David begins the psalm personally: "Praise the LORD, my soul." He first addresses himself, exhorting his whole being to respond to God. Next, he expands the circle of praise to include the covenant community. Then he summons the whole of creation to "praise the LORD." He finishes full circle, ending where he began, with a self-exhortation, "Praise the LORD, my soul." These three concentric circles of praise—personal, communal, and universal—encompass the scope of true worship. "Let everything that has breath praise the LORD" (Ps. 150:6).

The psalm's form and composition of praise is a testimony to the poet's skill and creativity. Worship is not a haphazard, half-hearted effort that we make up willy-nilly. George Herbert, the seventeenth-century

---

1   Stott, *Favorite Psalms*, 95.
2   Spurgeon, "Psalm 103," *Treasury of David*.
3   Kidner, *Psalms 73–150*, 363.

poet-pastor, engaged in the work of worship "by all possible art." He sought to convince his congregation of the truth of God through "earnestness of speech," a passionate attitude, and an effective delivery.[4] The Psalms share this attention to style, substance, and spirit. Psalm 103 consists of twenty-two verses, one for each letter in the Hebrew alphabet. This "alphabetizing" of the message may have symbolized the poet's desire to comprehend the essence of worship from A to Z. The psalmist is giving the ABC's of true worship without "dumbing-down" the gospel. There are three stanzas in this psalm. The first (vv. 1–5) and third stanzas (vv. 19–22) are nearly the same length bracketing the central stanza (vv. 6–18). The whole Psalm is about God's grace, which is received personally, revealed historically, and extolled universally. An intentional pattern of repetition in each stanza reinforces the theme. The eightfold repetition of "my" highlights the personal emphasis in the first stanza and the fourfold "all" underscores the totality of God's blessing. The repetition of "all" at the end further knits together the entire psalm. In the main portion of the psalm, parallel lines add special emphasis:

the LORD is compassionate and gracious,
slow to anger, abounding in love (v. 8);

He will not always accuse,
nor will he harbor his anger forever; (v. 9)

he does not treat us as our sins deserve
or repay us according to our iniquities. (v. 10)

The psalmist uses three terms for disobedience: sins, iniquities, and transgressions, and three terms for those who practice obedience, those "who do his bidding," "who obey his word," and "who do his will."

The middle stanza is knit together by a series of comparisons. Thankfully, the Lord does not treat us as our sins deserve or pay us back for what we have done. We receive what we don't deserve—God's grace. His great love is compared to the height between heaven and earth, and the distance between east and west. The Lord's compassion toward those who fear him is compared to a father's compassion for his children. The Lord knows we are weak and frail. We are likened to dust, green grass, and

---

4   Herbert, *The Country Parson*, 27.

blooming flowers, but the Lord's love is from everlasting to everlasting. His love is freely bestowed on "those who fear him," "keep his covenant," and "remember to obey his precepts."

The name of Yahweh occurs eleven times in the twenty-two verses, twice in the first stanza, four times in the second, and five in the third, as the psalm builds to a climax. This carefully crafted composition is more than a fine piece of poetry. Form and style serve a holy purpose. They inspire and reflect praise to the Lord. In the words of Henry Lyte, "Praise, my soul, the King of heaven; To His feet thy tribute bring."

SELF-EXHORTATION

> Praise the LORD, my soul;
> all my inmost being, praise his holy name.
> Praise the LORD, my soul,
> and forget not all his benefits—
> who forgives all your sins
> and heals all your diseases,
> who redeems your life from the pit
> and crowns you with love [hesed] and compassion,
> who satisfies your desires with good things
> so that your youth is renewed like the eagle's.
> —Psalm 103:1–5

Spurgeon said, "Soul music is the very soul of music. The Psalmist strikes the best keynote when he begins with stirring up his inmost self to magnify the Lord."[5] The psalmist's self-exhortation is critical for worship. Such positive and redemptive self-talk is essential for authentic worship. All real worship begins personally. We don't feel our way into worship as much as worship our way into feelings. Worship begins with the spiritual discipline of self-exhortation. "Many talk freely enough to others, but never talk to themselves," commented Spurgeon. "They are strangers to themselves—not on speaking terms with themselves—take no interest in their own souls—are dull and melancholy when alone."[6] One measurement of emotional maturity is a person's ability to reason with and exhort themselves. Of course, not all self-talk is productive. We

---

5   Spurgeon, "Psalm 103," *Treasury of David.*
6   Spurgeon, "Psalm 103," *Treasury of David.*

may be inclined to list our woes, dwell on our problems, fixate on our weaknesses, and withdraw into ourselves. This psalm leads us out of a narrow, constricted view of life and into the large world of God's salvation.

The psalmist takes responsibility for what he says to himself, even as all believers must, knowing that our self-talk has an impact on others. Cynicism among the people of God can spread like a virus through gossip and negative comments. It doesn't take much to turn "praise the LORD, my soul" into a critical spirit, but self-exhortation addressed to the soul speaks to "the inner core of the whole person" and turns murmuring into remembering.[7] The psalmist envisions the worshiper's conscience, imagination, emotions, memories, and hopes focused on praise. In a word, "soul" encompasses the breadth and depth of who we are. When David defined soul as "all my inmost being," he emphasized that our worship is derived from the inside out. To praise the Lord with our souls is to assure that our whole being worships the Lord.

The specific content of David's self-exhortation is God's amazing grace. Salvation is complete, encompassing the whole person. The first benefit of salvation is forgiveness, the foundation for our relationship with the Lord, followed by healing, redemption, empowerment, and fulfillment. The blessing of God's grace redeems every dimension of life. Holiness and health are God's blessing. "O my soul, praise him, for he is your health and salvation!"[8] Spiritual and emotional well-being are his gifts. Even in the midst of dire circumstances, we are comforted by the Lord's love and compassion. God blesses us with inner strength and outward energy. Worship begins by focusing on God and his action. The Lord forgives, heals, redeems, crowns (empowers), satisfies, and renews. It is not our activism, but God's action that inspires worship. "Yahweh is worthy of a total response of grateful worship for the totality of his blessing."[9]

Psalm 103 reflects the perfections of God's grace, beginning with the *superabundance* of *all* God's benefits.[10] For the psalmist there is no

---

7   Anderson, *On Being Human*, 177.
8   Neander, "Praise to the Lord, the Almighty."
9   Allen, *Psalms 101–150*, 22.
10   Barclay, *Paul and the Gift*, 71. John Barclay's historical and anthropological analysis distinguishes six perfections of grace: superabundance, singularity, priority, incongruity, efficacy, and non-circularity. He demonstrates how these various "perfections of grace" have shaped theological interpretation of the apostle Paul's gift of grace.

other way to begin his praise than by extolling the extravagance of God's excessive, all-encompassing benevolence. These benefits bear testimony to the *singularity* of the giver whose "sole and exclusive mode of operation is goodness." They demonstrate the *priority* of the gift because they always take place "prior to the initiative of the recipient." They show the *incongruity* of God's grace because the recipient of God's forgiveness, healing, and redemption is always unworthy and needy. They reveal the *efficacy* of God's gifts because they achieve the purpose for which they were designed. And they prove the *non-circularity* of the giving-getting exchange. There is no quid pro quo. When God crowns us with love and compassion, God is not bartering for attention or soliciting praise. True praise is never a duty or an obligation, but always the free response of gratitude and inherent response of joy for what the Lord has done.[11]

David's inner dialogue reminds us of how important it is to use our mind and our memory to "shake off apathy or gloom" and rekindle our emotions for God.[12] Self-talk that is shaped by God's grace reminds us that "we can act ourselves into a new way of feeling much quicker than we can feel ourselves into a new way of acting."[13] It is like learning to play a musical instrument. We'll never enjoy playing an instrument until we practice. The hard work of discipline and the joy of devotion go hand in hand. "Worship is an act that develops feelings for God, not a feeling for God that is expressed in an act of worship. When we obey the command to praise God in worship, our deep, essential need to be in relationship with God is nurtured."[14] We worship because we are "ransomed, healed, restored, forgiven, evermore His praises sing. Alleluia!"[15]

SALVATION'S STORY

> The LORD works righteousness
> and justice for all the oppressed.
> He made known his ways to Moses,
> his deeds to the people of Israel:
> The LORD is compassionate and gracious,

---

11 Barclay, *Paul and the Gift*, 72–73.
12 Kidner, *Psalms 73–150*, 364.
13 Peterson, *Long Obedience*, 50.
14 Peterson, *Long Obedience*, 50.
15 Lyte, "Praise, My Soul, the King of Heaven."

slow to anger, abounding in love.
He will not always accuse,
nor will he harbor his anger forever;
he does not treat us as our sins deserve
or repay us according to our iniquities.
For as high as the heavens are above the earth,
so great is his love for those who fear him;
as far as the east is from the west,
so far has he removed our transgressions from us.
As a father has compassion on his children,
so the LORD has compassion on those who fear him;
for he knows how we are formed,
he remembers that we are dust.
The life of mortals is like grass,
they flourish like a flower of the field;
the wind blows over it and it is gone,
and its place remembers it no more.
But from everlasting to everlasting
the LORD's love [*hesed*] is with those who fear him,
and his righteousness with their children's children—
with those who keep his covenant
and remember to obey his precepts.
                              —Psalm 103:6–18

The psalmist moves from the personal benefits of salvation to the big picture of the history of salvation. The people of God respond to what the Lord has done and will do. "Let the amen sound from His people again!"[16] If the first stanza is a solo call to worship, the second stanza is a powerful anthem of praise. The emphasis changes from personal salvation to the history of salvation among God's covenant people. "Praise Him for His grace and favor / To His people in distress; Praise Him still the same as ever, / Slow to chide, and swift to bless. / Alleluia!"[17]

God's unfolding plan of salvation highlights the epicenter of redemption, the exodus, the giving of the law at Mount Sinai, and the sacrificial system. Salvation history reveals the Lord's holy character, his enduring love, and our great need for salvation. In worship we take the grand themes of

---

16 Neander, "Praise to the Lord, the Almighty."
17 Lyte, "Praise, My Soul, the King of Heaven."

salvation and hold them up for praise out of joy and gratitude. We rehearse the full range of God's truth, past, present and future. We acknowledge our sinful frailty and the Lord's holiness and unfailing love (*hesed*).[18] "Father-like He tends and spares us; / Well our feeble frame He knows; / In His hands He gently bears us, / Rescues us from all our foes."[19]

The psalmist celebrates the power of God's gracious forgiveness and deliverance from sin by using spatial analogies to picture God's love: "For as high as the heavens are above the earth, so great is his love for those who fear him; as far as the east is from the west, so far has he removed our transgressions from us" (vv. 11–12). The apostle Paul echoes this spatial love language when he prays for believers "to grasp how wide and long and high and deep is the love of Christ" (Eph. 3:18).

Worship gives us a realistic and redemptive appraisal of our personal circumstances. Left to ourselves and our own opinions, we may ignore the frailty of our human condition and neglect the love and mercy of God. We struggle to hold in tension the fleeting nature of mortal life and the promise of the Lord's everlasting love and life. The brevity of life does not mean the futility of life. "The life of mortals is like grass, they flourish like a flower of the field; the wind blows over it and it is gone, and its place remembers it no more. But from everlasting to everlasting the LORD's love is with those who fear him" (Ps. 103:15–17). In worship we are reminded that God redeems us from the pit. Our mortal bodies take on immortality, as the apostle Paul says: "The body that is sown is perishable, it is raised imperishable; it is sown in dishonor, it is raised in glory; it is sown in weakness, it is raised in power" (1 Cor. 15:42–43). Corrie ten Boom, a survivor of the Nazi holocaust, offers a perspective on our mortality compatible with the psalmist:

> Often I have heard people say, "How good God is. We prayed that it would not rain for our church picnic, and look at this lovely weather!" Yes, God is good when He sends good weather. But God was also good when He allowed

---

18 DeClaissé-Walford, Jacobson, and Tanner, *Book of Psalms*, 132. Jacobson writes: "*Hesed* includes elements of love, mercy, fidelity, and kindness [occurring 130 times in the Psalms]. . . . The relational nature of the term cannot be overemphasized. It describes the duties, benefits, and commitments that one party bears to another party as a result of the relationship between them. The Lord's *hesed* is the basis on which the psalmist dares to ask for deliverance and forgiveness."

19 Lyte, "Praise, My Soul, the King of Heaven."

my sister Betsie to starve to death before my eyes in the German concentration camp. I remember one occasion when I was very discouraged there. Everything around us was dark, and there was darkness in my heart. I remember telling Betsie that I thought God had forgotten us. "No, Corrie," said Betsie, "He has not forgotten us. Remember His Word: 'For as high as the heavens are above the earth, so great is His love for those who fear Him.' There is an ocean of God's love available. . . . There is plenty for everyone. May God grant you never to doubt that victorious love, whatever the circumstances."[20]

Authentic corporate worship inspires our devotion to God, makes us more sensitive to sin (most of all our own), and deepens our passion for holiness. Worship has much more to do with being faithful than feeling good. As the psalmist emphasizes, worship and ethics belong together: "The LORD's love is with those who fear him, and his righteousness with their children's children—with those who keep his covenant and remember to obey his precepts" (Ps. 103:17–18). This emphasis on righteous acts and obedience is clearly emphasized in the New Testament as well (see Eph. 2:8–10). Goldingay writes, "Our relationship with God is wholly dependent on divine commitment, yet unless that meets with a response in the form of revering and thus obeying God, an actual relationship cannot come into being. It would be misleading to say that the divine commitment is conditional on the human response, because that would imply that the relationship was a contract. But the commitment does require the response."[21] Commenting on this psalm, Augustine took issue with those who prided themselves on memorizing the Psalms, but neglected to obey the commands of God. It is better to do them than recite them, Augustine argued. It doesn't help to sing a hymn but disobey God's will. "What good is it if your voice sings a hymn, if your life doesn't honor God?"[22] What is true of marriage can be said of worship and ethics, "What God has joined together, let no one separate" (Matt. 19:6).

COMMUNAL EXHORTATION

The LORD has established his throne in heaven,
and his kingdom rules over all.

---

20 Ten Boom, *Clippings from My Notebook*, 79.
21 Goldingay, *Psalms*, 3:177.
22 Augustine, *Expositions of the Psalms*, 8:509.

Praise the LORD, you his angels,
you mighty ones who do his bidding,
who obey his word.
Praise the LORD, all his heavenly hosts,
you his servants who do his will.
Praise the LORD all his works
everywhere in his dominion.
Praise the LORD, my soul.
                                        —Psalm 103:19–22

Psalm 103 reminds us that we bow before King Jesus. The third stanza widens the circle of praise to include all of creation. All the angels and the heavenly hosts are summoned to worship before the throne of him who rules over all. Total praise. There are no spectators. Everyone is in the choir and everything is centered around the throne of the Lord. "Praise the LORD, all his works everywhere in his dominion" (v. 22). The end of Psalm 103 reminds us of something out of Revelation: "Then I heard every creature in heaven and on earth and under the earth and on the sea, and all that is in them, saying: 'To him who sits on the throne and to the Lamb be praise and honor and glory and power, for ever and ever!'" (Rev. 5:13). This powerful, pulsating praise has practical implications for our worship. For a number of years now, churches have been designing worship according to people's preferences. Everyone, it seems, has an opinion about what kind of music and liturgy they like. However, it is important to note that whatever your perspective on worship styles, whether you like to rock out on songs of praise or sing ancient hymns, in the end we'll be worshiping together. We will not find separate worship services in heaven. Those of us who have strong opinions about what kind of worship music will be in heaven may be surprised and stretched! It is probably a good idea to begin preparing on this side of eternity for the unimaginable range of praise we will experience in heaven.

It is even more exciting to contemplate the inclusiveness of the global gospel of Jesus Christ. Everyone everywhere is called to worship the triune God, Father, Son, and Holy Spirit. There is only one Creator, Redeemer, and King, only one throne, and only one kingdom over all. Modern multiculturalism envisions a chorus of "We Are the World," but biblical universalism envisions the throne of God surrounded by angels and the heavenly hosts praising God. Worship acknowledges the rule of the Lord over every culture, tribe, nation, and people group. The key concept for the future of the human community is not ideological pluralism, but doxology.

Biblical universalism exalts "one Lord, one faith, one baptism; one God and Father of all, who is over all and through all and in all" (Eph. 4:5–6). Psalm 103 reminds us "that at the name of Jesus every knee should bow, in heaven and on earth and under the earth, and every tongue acknowledge that Jesus Christ is Lord, to the glory of God the Father" (Phil. 2:10–11). The psalm ends where it began, with personal exhortation to worship. No matter how many join the concert of praise, our soul's praise to the Lord still counts.

> Angels, help us to adore Him;
> Ye behold Him face to face;
> Sun and moon, bow down before Him,
> Dwellers all in time and space.
> Alleluia! Alleluia!
> Praise with us the God of grace.[23]

---

23 Lyte, "Praise, My Soul, the King of Heaven."

A CREATION PSALM

Psalm 104 is a fitting *response* to Psalm 103. The greatness of God in creation is best understood in the light of the goodness of God in salvation. Without the Redeemer, it is impossible to truly worship the Creator. These two psalms begin and end with doxology, "Praise the LORD, my soul" (Ps. 103:1, 22; 104:1, 35). The benefits of salvation are celebrated in Psalm 103, and the works of creation are extolled in Psalm 104. The relationship between Creator and creature depends on the redemptive relationship between Father and child—"As a father has compassion on his children, so the LORD has compassion on those who fear him" (103:13). Karl Barth claimed that we can only know the God of creation by knowing the God of redemption.

> I believe in God, the Father Almighty, Creator of heaven and earth. When we approach the truth which the Christian Church confesses in the word "Creator," then everything depends on our realizing that we find ourselves here as well, confronted by the mystery of faith, in respect of which knowledge is real solely through God's revelation. . . . We are not nearer to believing in God the Creator, than we are to believing that Jesus Christ was conceived by the Holy Spirit and born of the Virgin Mary. . . . It is impossible to separate the knowledge of God the Creator and of His work from the knowledge of God's dealings with man. Only when we keep before us what the triune God has done for us in Jesus Christ can we realize what is involved in God the Creator and His work.[1]

The salvation psalm is a necessary precursor to the creation psalm, even as Psalm 104 is an *essential* response to Psalm 103. The gospel of King Jesus is not an otherworldly spiritual ideal that separates the believer from the real world of weather and geology, biology and agriculture, water

---

1 Barth, *Dogmatics in Outline*, 50, 52.

and animal husbandry. The beauty of the gospel is its impact on all of creation from what we put up into space to the air quality coming out of our smokestacks. The psalmist makes sure we don't write off creation as a theatrical stage—a mere facade for the drama of redemption.

The notion that God created the cosmos like a well-made Swiss watch and then left it running on its own is attributed to Cambridge-educated William Paley, an English pastor and abolitionist, who in 1802 wrote *Natural Theology*. Paley made a case for the teleological argument for the existence of God. The design of the universe, he reasoned, proved that there was a Designer, an intelligent Creator. He began his apologetic discourse with an analogy: "In crossing a heath I hit my foot on a stone, and if I were asked how that stone came to be there, I might answer that for all I knew it had laid there forever. . . . But suppose I had found a watch on the ground, and I was asked how that watch happened to be in that place."[2] For Paley the watch was analogous to creation's intricate systems, such as the human eye or an animal's skeletal structure of muscles, ligaments, and bones. Paley's reasoned and reverential worship of nature's Maker is consistent with Psalm 104, even if mocked by nature-alone evolutionists. His watchmaker analogy was co-opted by nineteenth-century deists who argued that God set everything in motion and then let the forces of nature take over. Deism, they argued, was compatible with Darwinian evolution.

LORD OF THE UNIVERSE, HOPE OF THE WORLD[3]

Praise the LORD, my soul.
LORD my God, you are very great;
you are clothed with splendor and majesty.
The LORD wraps himself in light as with a garment;
he stretches out the heavens like a tent
and lays the beams of his upper chambers on their waters.
He makes the clouds his chariot
and rides on the wings of the wind.
He makes winds his messengers,
flames of fire his servants.
                    —Psalm 104:1–4

---

2   Paley, *Natural Theology*, 1.
3   Clarkson, "Lord of the Universe, Hope of the World."

The prelude to this hymn of praise establishes the greatness of the Lord God. The psalmist uses metaphor to describe the dynamic relationship between the Lord and his creation. Far from being a rival power, nature in all of its splendor and majesty is worn like a royal robe, a garment of light, thrown over the shoulders as the Lord stretches out the heavens like a tent. In a few poetic lines the psalmist may refute the Egyptian hymn to Aten, the sun god, and declares Yahweh's transcendence over the Baal myth.[4]

The imagery of dazzling light recalls the Genesis account, "And God said, 'Let there be light'" (Gen. 1:3); the description in Hebrews of the Son as "the radiance of God's glory" (Heb. 1:3); and the apostle John's vision of one like the Son of Man whose "face was like the sun shining in all its brilliance" (Rev. 1:16). The psalmist paints a picture filled with light and energy and motion. There is nothing static about this introduction to the Lord of the universe. The dynamic is captured in Walter Chalmers Smith's hymn, "Immortal, Invisible, God Only Wise."

In light inaccessible hid from our eyes (verse 1)
Unresting, unhasting, and silent as light (verse 2)
'Tis only the splendor of light hideth Thee! (verse 4)[5]

The author of Hebrews sets the Son apart from angels when he quotes from the Greek translation (LXX) of Psalm 104:4: "He makes his angels spirits, and his servants flames of fire" (Heb. 1:7). Whether the Lord is using wind and fire or angels to carry out his purposes, it is the Son who "is the radiance of God's glory and the exact representation of his being" (Heb. 1:3).[6] "His sovereignty is unfathomable: he is surrounded by his servants, for everything he has made in the heavens and on earth stands ready to do his will, to be his messengers and the agents of carrying out

---

4   Allen, *Psalms 101–150*, 28–29; Allen observes that Psalm 104 may borrow features from the Egyptian hymn to Aten to stress Yahweh's transcendence over the sun and Ugaritic material concerning the temple of Baal to express the cosmic meaning of Solomon's temple (cf. 1 Kings 8:13). Ross concludes that there is insufficient evidence to show direct borrowing, adding, "Israel's theology of creation was unique in the ancient world; for example, the sun was merely a creation of Yahweh God, and not a god, and all the glory belongs to the Lord who is over all creation, not part of it." *Psalms*, 3:245.
5   Smith, "Immortal, Invisible, God Only Wise."
6   Okorocha, "Psalms," 708.

his will."[7] The second stanza of Robert Grant's "O Worship the King"
draws from Psalm 104: "O tell of his might and sing of his grace / Whose
robe is the light, whose canopy space. / His chariots of wrath the deep
thunderclouds form, / And dark is His path on the wings of the storm.[8]

CREATION'S MAKER AND SUSTAINER

He set the earth on its foundations;
it can never be moved.
You covered it with the watery depths as with a garment;
the waters stood above the mountains.
But at your rebuke the waters fled,
at the sound of your thunder they took to flight;
they flowed over the mountains,
they went down into the valleys,
to the place you assigned for them.
You set a boundary they cannot cross;
never again will they cover the earth.
He makes springs pour water into the ravines;
it flows between the mountains.
They give water to all the beasts of the field;
the wild donkeys quench their thirst.
The birds of the sky nest by the waters;
they sing among the branches.
He waters the mountains from the upper chambers;
the land is satisfied by the fruit of his work.
He makes grass grow for the cattle,
and plants for people to cultivate—
bringing forth food from the earth:
wine that gladdens human hearts,
oil to make their faces shine,
and bread that sustains their hearts.
The trees of the Lord are well watered,
the cedars of Lebanon that he planted.
There the birds make their nests;
the stork has its home in the junipers.
The high mountains belong to the wild goats;

---

7   Ross, *Psalms*, 3:249.
8   Grant, "O Worship the King."

the crags are a refuge for the hyrax.
He made the moon to mark the seasons,
and the sun knows when to go down.
You bring darkness, it becomes night,
and all the beasts of the forest prowl.
The lions roar for their prey
and seek their food from God.
The sun rises, and they steal away;
they return and lie down in their dens.
Then people go out to their work,
to their labor until evening.
—Psalm 104:5–23

The poet leaves plenty of room for the scientist to explore and explain. His aim is worship. He is more interested in showing the character of the one who creates and sustains nature than he is in the science behind natural phenomena. Yet, far from discouraging the scientist, the psalmist's artistic and emotive metaphors serve to inspire. Like a builder, God sets the earth on its foundations. Like a mother covering her children with a blanket, God spreads out the oceans. Like a farmer, he provides grass for cattle. God is at the center of how the universe works, not as *deus ex machina* or God at the point of our ignorance, but the Lord whose character is found in nature's order, in the wild donkey's quenched thirst, and in the mountain goat's craggy castle.

The rhyme and reason behind all of this is divine providence, not blind chance and fate. The Creator's wisdom and beauty is manifest everywhere. Springs of water, singing birds, and seasons marked by the journey of the moon are all evidence of God's sustaining grace. Like a good host God has thought of everything, wine and bread to gladden human hearts and the balm of Gilead for health. From sun up to sun down the Lord shows he cares for his creation. Nocturnal animals hunt for food, and at daybreak people go out to work. The order and rhythm of creation inspires the psalmist's commentary on Genesis. He agrees: "God saw all that he had made, and it was very good" (Gen. 1:31).

Echoes of Psalm 104 occur throughout Jesus's ministry. God's large-scale handiwork is made manifest on an intimate scale when Jesus "rebuked the wind and said to the waves, 'Quiet! Be still!'" (Mark 4:39; see Ps. 104:7). It is evident at the wedding feast in Cana of Galilee, when Jesus changed the water to wine, and then again on the far side of the sea of Galilee, when he fed the more than five thousand (John 2:1–12; 6:1–13; see Ps. 104:15). In the Sermon on the Mount, when Jesus said, "Look at the birds of the air; they do not sow or reap or store away in barns, and yet your heavenly Father feeds them," we are reminded of this psalm (Matt. 6:26; cf. Ps. 104:12). Psalm 104 is reflected in the life and ministry of Jesus and prepares us for the apostle's Christology (Col. 1:15–17).

GOD'S CREATION CARE

How many are your works, LORD!
In wisdom you made them all;
the earth is full of your creatures.
There is the sea, vast and spacious,
teeming with creatures beyond number—
living things both large and small.
There the ships go to and fro,
and Leviathan, which you formed to frolic there.
All creatures look to you
to give them their food at the proper time.
When you give it to them,
they gather it up;
when you open your hand,
they are satisfied with good things.
When you hide your face,
they are terrified;
when you take away their breath,
they die and return to the dust.
When you send your Spirit,
they are created,
and you renew the face of the ground.
                        —Psalm 104:24–30

The sea is often described in the Bible as a threat that inspires fear, but in Psalm 104 it is a picture of the Lord's vast and amazing creativity. The earth and sea are teeming with life. Leviathan, the mythic sea monster, is pictured as a playful whale frolicking in the ocean. Cargo-laden ships are navigating sea routes. And over it all—earth and sea and every living creature—God is sovereign. The author of Hebrews echoes this conviction: "By faith we understand that the universe was created by the word of God, so that what is seen was not made out of things that are visible" (Heb. 11:3 ESV).

All of creation is dependent on the Lord's care and provision. The complex food chain is pictured in God's open-handed provision, and the gift of life and breath depends upon the Lord turning his face toward his creatures. Life is sustained at every point by the active and personal involvement of the Lord. "To our modern ears it all sounds very naive," writes Stott. "But the truth behind the figures stands. . . . No Christian can have a mechanistic view of nature. The universe is not a gigantic machine that operates by inflexible laws, nor has God made laws to which he is himself now a slave."[9]

"Every living thing is an elaboration on a single original plan," writes Bryson. "It cannot be said too often: all life is one. That is, and I suspect will forever prove to be, the most profound true statement there is."[10] The unity of nature is miraculous. We are awed that human beings are so closely related to fruits and vegetables and that over 60 percent of human genes are the same as those in fruit flies. The scientific view of the human person is inevitably and understandably reductionistic, breaking down the person into component parts, reading DNA, mapping genomes, and discovering proteomes. But all evidence in this vast universe bears the fingerprint of its Creator and Sustainer. All things are sustained moment by moment by this powerful word (Heb. 1:3).

LIFE IS SACRAMENTAL

> May the glory of the LORD endure forever;
> may the LORD rejoice in his works—
> he who looks at the earth, and it trembles,
> who touches the mountains, and they smoke.
> I will sing to the LORD all my life;
> I will sing praise to my God as long as I live.
> May my meditation be pleasing to him,
> as I rejoice in the LORD.
> But may sinners vanish from the earth
> and the wicked be no more.

---

9   Stott, *Favorite Psalms*, 101.
10 Bryson, *Short History of Nearly Everything*, 415.

Praise the LORD, my soul.
Praise the LORD.
                    —Psalm 104:31–35

The psalmist ends where he began, by extolling the glory of God. His poetic meditation on creation has only served to enhance our grasp of the transcendence and majesty of God. Our reverential fear for the awesome power of God has only deepened. The psalmist vows to glorify God as long as he lives, and he prays that his meditation and reflection on life will be pleasing to God. There is a sacramental cast to life. The psalmist is life affirming, rather than life rejecting. He is focused on "life's positive richness-es," reveling in the beauty, truth, and love derived from the divine nature.[11]

The psalmist's focus is on the dynamic beauty and energy of God's creation, but he is not naive when it comes to "nature red in tooth and claw." Lions roar for the prey and earthquakes happen (vv. 21, 32), but the psalmist prefers in this moment to marvel and embrace the wonders of creation.[12] Only one short, sober sentence brings us back to Psalm 104 and our great need for redemption: "But may sinners vanish from the earth and the wicked be no more" (v. 35). The psalmist acknowledges our fallen human condition: "for all have sinned and fall short of the glory of God" (Rom. 3:23).

A deeply disturbing, apocalyptic narrative streams live across our imag-ination and threatens to compete with the inspiration of Psalm 104. The psalmist's ratio of positive to negative is instructive, but with the realities of nuclear proliferation, global warming, internet-deception campaigns, and terrorism, the competition is menacing. The Bulletin of Atomic Sci-entists has set the Doomsday Clock, the marker of how close humanity is to a civilization-threatening catastrophe, at one hundred seconds to midnight.[13] Jesus's Prayer Book is honest with what threatens ourselves and our planet. To pray the Psalms is to become well acquainted with human frailty, depravity, and mortality. But in the midst of all of that hard news, the ratio of grace supersedes doom and gloom. The psalmist inspires our self-exhortation, "Praise the LORD, my soul. Praise the LORD" (Ps. 104:35).

---

11   Blamires, *Christian Mind*, 173.
12   Allen, *Psalms 101–150*, 34.
13   Bulletin of the Atomic Scientists, "At Doom's Doorstep: It Is 100 Seconds to Mid-
     night," January 20, 2022, https://thebulletin.org/doomsday-clock/current-time.

A COVENANT-KEEPING GOD

B ook 4 concludes with a four-movement symphony of praise arousing the people of God to worship the Lord for his saving grace (Psalm 103), his sovereign care (Psalm 104), his covenant faithfulness (Psalm 105), and his steadfast love and mercy (Psalm 106). Psalm 105 begins with a vigorous call to action. The servants of God are summoned to do the work of worship by a blitz of action verbs. All of the singing, glorying, telling, seeking, and rejoicing revolve around remembering God's wonderful works. The work of remembering recalls a history of the Lord's covenant promises beginning with Abraham and ending with Joshua. In this psalm, Israel's rebellious and wayward ways are forgotten for the moment, and only the Lord's great faithfulness is remembered. Psalm 106 tells the other side of the story.

REMEMBER HIS WONDERFUL ACTS

Give praise to the LORD, proclaim his name;
make known among the nations what he has done.
Sing to him, sing praise to him;
tell of all his wonderful acts.
Glory in his holy name;
let the hearts of those who seek the LORD rejoice.
Look to the LORD and his strength;
seek his face always.
Remember the wonders he has done,
his miracles, and the judgments he pronounced,
you his servants, the descendants of Abraham,
his chosen ones, the children of Jacob.
—Psalm 105:1–6

The psalmist knows we are primarily lovers. Real worship, the kind of worship envisioned by the psalmist, shapes and transforms our identities "by forming our most fundamental desires and our most basic attunement to the world. . . . What defines us is what we love."[1] The call to worship given in Psalm 105 calls for action, body, mind, and soul. A string of lively imperatives calls for praise and proclamation. An intense intentionality coupled with a keen sense of ultimacy lies behind this worship. The global outreach of praise is united with heartfelt worship. The narrow-minded spectator is out of place in this assembly of globally minded worshipers bent on energetic and thoughtful praise.

The psalmist's first concern is for God-centered worship. It is the Lord whose name is proclaimed, whose deeds are made known, and whose wonderful acts are celebrated. Worship is centering because the people of God proclaim his name, sing to him, tell of his acts, glory in his holy name, and remember his wonders, his miracles, and his judgments. "In worship God gathers his people to himself as center: 'The Lord reigns' (Ps. 93:1). Worship is a meeting at the center so that our lives are centered in God and not lived eccentrically. We worship so that we live in response to and from this center, the living God."[2]

The psalmist's second concern is for worship to "make known among the nations what he has done" (v. 1). The goal of worship is consistent with Yahweh's promise to Abraham: "all peoples on earth will be blessed through you" (Gen. 12:3), and with Jesus's Great Commission (Matt. 28:19). Paul's emphasis on intelligible worship fits the psalmist's concern: "Unless you speak intelligible words with your tongue, how will anyone know what you are saying? You will just be speaking into the air" (1 Cor. 14:9). This second concern is inseparable from the first and is essential if the nations are going to hear of the Lord's wonderful acts. Worship and mission form a positive, dynamic tension, each serving as an energizing and motivating catalyst for the other. Both sides of the equation work equally well. We can worship our way into mission and mission our way into worship.

The psalmist identifies the worshipers as the Lord's "servants, the descendants of Abraham, his chosen ones, the children of Jacob" (v. 6).

---

1   Smith, *Desiring the Kingdom*, 25.
2   Peterson, *Reversed Thunder*, 60.

This description is good news for all those who have accepted Jesus as the Messiah. In the past the Jewish identity was tied to circumcision, but now it is rooted in faith. As the apostle Paul explains, "Scripture foresaw that God would justify the Gentiles by faith, and announced the gospel in advance to Abraham: 'All nations will be blessed through you.' So those who rely on faith are blessed along with Abraham, the man of faith" (Gal. 3:8–9). "A person is not a Jew who is one only outwardly, nor is circumcision merely outward and physical. No, a person is a Jew who is one inwardly; and circumcision is circumcision of the heart, by the Spirit, not by the written code. Such a person's praise is not from other people, but from God" (Rom. 2:28–29). The true children of Abraham receive Christ, the Messiah to the Jews and the Savior of the world.

> So in Christ Jesus you are all children of God through faith, for all of you who were baptized into Christ have clothed yourselves with Christ. There is neither Jew nor Gentile, neither slave nor free, nor is there male and female, for you are all one in Christ Jesus. If you belong to Christ, then you are Abraham's seed, and heirs according to the promise. (Gal. 3:26–29)

Psalm 105 covers the early chapters of our family history. For all those who are in Christ, this is our story, too. We are servants of the Lord, descendants of Abraham, chosen by God, and children of Jacob. Everybody has a story, but only one story redeems our story. It is the story of the one who came who was greater than Abraham, greater than Joseph, and greater than Moses.

When the psalmist told the story of salvation history, only half of it could be told. Much more was yet to come. But now we have a fuller story to tell to the nations to turn their hearts to the Lord. The call of Abraham and the patriarchal journey, the story of Joseph and Egyptian bondage, the exodus and the conquest of the Promised Land are all wonderful acts of protection, provision, deliverance, guidance, and redemption. These miracles and wonders—these redemptive analogies—need to be remembered, along with all that has happened since. In the coming of Jesus Christ, in answer to all the promises and prophecies, the salvation story reached its fulfillment—not yet its culmination, but its climax—in the death, resurrection, and ascension of Jesus Christ. If the people of God had a wonderful story to tell more than a thousand years before Jesus was born, how much more do the people of God today have a story to tell? Today, we await the King with even greater reasons to worship and even greater news to share.

HIS EVERLASTING COVENANT

He is the LORD our God;
his judgments are in all the earth.
He remembers his covenant forever,
the promise he made, for a thousand generations,
the covenant he made with Abraham,
the oath he swore to Isaac.
He confirmed it to Jacob as a decree,
to Israel as an everlasting covenant:
"To you I will give the land of Canaan
as the portion you will inherit."
                                        —Psalm 105:7–11

The psalmist declares, "He is Yahweh our God!" This is the truth around which every promise, prophecy, and purpose is centered. The Lord is no tribal deity, no ethnic god, no regional myth. His judgments are in all the earth. The psalmist emphasizes the Lord's *everlasting* covenant with Abraham, Isaac, and Jacob in two parallel lines. In verse 8, "forever" is equal to "a thousand generations." Augustine explains that one thousand is a symbolic number, "because the solid square of the number ten, ten times ten, and this taken ten times amounts to a thousand" signifies the eternal inheritance of those who live by faith in the covenant promises of God.[3] For the Lord to remember his covenant with Abraham, Isaac, and

---

3   Augustine, *Expositions of the Psalms*, 8:521. In the book of Revelation there is
     a threefold reference to the one thousand years of protection for the people of
     God (Rev. 20:1–7). One thousand (10 x 10 x 10) is a figurative number for the
     ideal church age extending from Christ's life, death, resurrection, and ascension to
     Christ's second coming. During that time Satan's influence persists but his power
     is limited. Beale summarizes his argument: "That this is not a literal chronological
     number is apparent from: (1) the consistently figurative use of numbers elsewhere
     in the book, (2) the figurative nature of much of the immediate context ('chain,'
     'abyss,' 'dragon,' 'serpent,' 'locked,' 'sealed,' 'beast'), (3) the predominantly figu-
     rative tone of the entire book (1:1), (4) the figurative use of '1,000' in the OT
     [and the NT, see Deut. 32:30; Josh. 23:10; Job 9:3; 33:23; Eccl. 7:28; Isa. 30:17;
     2 Peter 3:8], and (5) the use in Jewish and early Christian writings of '1,000' years
     as a figure for the eternal blessing of the redeemed" (Beale, *Revelation*, 995).

Jacob means that he acts on the promise to give the land "as the portion you will inherit" (v. 11). All three dimensions of the covenant—its everlastingness, its patriarchal principals, and its pledge of the land—converge when Jesus responds to the faith of the centurion: "Truly I tell you, I have not found anyone in Israel with such great faith. I say to you that many will come from the east and the west, and will take their places at the feast with Abraham, Isaac and Jacob in the kingdom of heaven" (Matt. 8:10–11). The promise of the land is fulfilled and transcended in the global reach of the gospel.[4] For Augustine, "This is the everlasting inheritance."[5] Christ's followers have an inheritance that is imperishable, undefiled, and unfading. This inheritance fulfills and transcends the covenant promises given to Israel. It is no longer tied to the land or to political autonomy.[6] "The notion of a holy land is superseded by that of a holy community (1 Peter 2:4–10)."[7] This is the inheritance Jesus promised when he said:

> Truly I tell you . . . no one who has left home or brothers or sisters or mother or father or children or fields for me and the gospel will fail to receive a hundred times as much in this present age: homes, brothers, sisters, mothers, children and fields—along with persecutions—and in the age to come eternal life. But many who are first will be last, and the last first. (Mark 10:29–31)

The promise of a homeland (Gen. 12:1–5) is "central to understanding the plan of redemption." Tim Keller explains,

---

4   The dispensational template interprets the Bible dualistically. Instead of seeing the promises to Israel fulfilled in the church and in the one new humanity created in Christ Jesus, dispensationalists argue that God has a separate destiny for Israel that involves reconstituting the nation, repatriating the land, and restoring the temple. God's promises to ethnic Jews will be fulfilled after the church is raptured, when Israel turns to her Messiah during the great tribulation. This interpretive template calls for two new covenants, one for Israel and one for the church; and two different last days, one for Israel and one for the church. Christ's return comes in two stages, the rapture and the second coming; and there are two final judgments, the judgment seat of Christ and the final great white throne judgment. This dualism depends on a template imposed on the Bible, rather than a straightforward reading of the biblical text.

5   Augustine, *Expositions of the Psalms,* 8:522.

6   Webster, *Outposts of Hope,* 29.

7   Elliott, *1 Peter,* 336.

We long for a home, a place of security, comfort, and love. We were made for a world without death or parting from love, a world in which we walked with God and knew him face to face. The world has been marred by sin and is no longer home, and we are restless exiles since our expulsion from Eden. So when the Son of God came he had no place to lay his head (Luke 9:58) and was crucified outside the city. He took the great exile we deserved so we could be brought into God's household (Eph. 2:17–19). And someday he will turn the world back into home indeed (Rev. 21:1–8).[8]

HIS PROTECTION

When they were but few in number,
few indeed, and strangers in it,
they wandered from nation to nation,
from one kingdom to another.
He allowed no one to oppress them;
for their sake he rebuked kings:
"Do not touch my anointed ones;
do my prophets no harm."
He called down famine on the land
and destroyed all their supplies of food;
and he sent a man before them—
Joseph, sold as a slave.
They bruised his feet with shackles,
his neck was put in irons,
till what he foretold came to pass,
till the word of the LORD proved him true.
The king sent and released him,
the ruler of peoples set him free.
He made him master of his household,
ruler over all he possessed,
To instruct his princes as he pleased
and teach his elders wisdom.
            —Psalm 105:12–22

The psalmist sketches the story of Genesis from Abraham to Joseph. He compresses half of the book of Genesis and several hundred years into eleven poetic verses. But he does not fail to stress the homeless vulnerability

---

8   Keller, *Songs of Jesus*, 265.

of the patriarchs, their divine protection, and the Lord's sovereign direction. The Lord secured the people of God with a protective warning: "Do not touch my anointed ones" (v. 15). He guarded these resident aliens as they wandered from nation to nation. The world called them nomads and strangers, but the Lord called them his anointed ones, his prophets. He saw them as his chosen ones. They were his embodied testimony to the nations.

In tandem with calling down a famine, the Lord sends a man before them—Joseph, sold as a slave. The psalmist provides additional commentary to the Genesis account of Joseph's journey from Canaan to Egypt. His feet and neck are shackled, and he is caged like an animal until "the word of the LORD proved him true" (v. 19). The sending and the suffering of Joseph, a person defined by the word of God, makes him a type pointing forward to Jesus Christ. One who the world despised became a ruler of peoples, a master of the king's household, and an instructor of princes. And all of this was the Lord's doing!

HIS DELIVERANCE

Then Israel entered Egypt;
Jacob resided as a foreigner in the land of Ham.
The LORD made his people very fruitful;
he made them too numerous for their foes,
whose hearts he turned to hate his people,
to conspire against his servants.
He sent Moses his servant,
and Aaron, whom he had chosen.
They performed his signs among them,
his wonders in the land of Ham.
He sent darkness and made the land dark—
for had they not rebelled against his words?
He turned their waters into blood,
causing their fish to die.
Their land teemed with frogs,
which went up into the bedrooms of their rulers.
He spoke, and there came swarms of flies,
and gnats throughout their country.
He turned their rain into hail,
with lightning throughout their land;
he struck down their vines and fig trees

and shattered the trees of their country.
He spoke, and the locusts came,
grasshoppers without number;
they ate up every green thing in their land,
ate up the produce of their soil.
Then he struck down all the firstborn in their land,
the firstfruits of all their manhood.
He brought out Israel, laden with silver and gold,
and from among their tribes no one faltered.
Egypt was glad they left,
because dread of Israel had fallen on them.
                                        —Psalm 105:23–38

Israel's resident alien status continues with Joseph's family fleeing to Egypt because of the famine. The psalmist's line "Jacob resided as a foreigner in the land of Ham" (v. 23) underscores Israel's refugee status. They came in search of food. Their future looked hopeless, but "the Lord made his people very fruitful" (v. 24). At first they were pitied by the Egyptians because they were weak and vulnerable, but over time their families grew and flourished. Then they were perceived as a threat and hated by the Egyptians. The worshiper may be surprised that the psalmist credits the sovereign Lord with both the famine and the Egyptian change of heart. The Lord turned their hearts to hate his people! The covenant people of God do not have the luxury of secondary causes and second-guessing. The Lord is sovereign over all. "In Israel's historiography," writes Reardon, ". . . all was theology."[9] For "we know that in all things God works for the good of those who love him, who have been called according to his purpose" (Rom. 8:28).

Like Joseph, Moses, the Lord's servant, was *sent* along with Aaron to perform the Lord's "signs among them" (Ps. 105:27). The initiative and the action belong to the Lord. It is his *sending* that sets these two representatives apart as types foreshadowing the coming of the sent One (John 3:34; 1 John 4:9–10). And with the sending of Moses, the Lord sent "signs" and "wonders" (plagues) among the Egyptians. The psalmist describes eight of the ten plagues, leaving out the fifth plague against the livestock and the sixth plague of boils. He begins the sequence with the ninth plague of darkness and offers this reason

---

9   Reardon, *Christ in the Psalms*, 207.

for the judgment: "For had they not rebelled against his [the Lord's] words?" (Ps. 105:28). The psalmist ends with the tenth plague, the death of the firstborn sons. "These two frame all of the other plagues with their significance for judgment, first on the sun god and then on Pharaoh."[10]

Israel did not escape Egypt through the people's own courage and wisdom. The Lord delivered them. The Lord "brought out Israel, laden with silver and gold, and from among their tribes no one faltered" (v. 37). The psalmist illustrates the completeness of the deliverance in three ways: Israel did not leave Egypt empty handed, the solidarity of Israel remained unbroken, and the "dread of Israel" fell on Egypt. The Lord's victory was material, spiritual, and emotional.

HIS FAITHFULNESS

> He spread out a cloud as a covering,
> and a fire to give light at night.
> They asked, and he brought them quail;
> he fed them well with the bread of heaven.
> He opened the rock, and water gushed out;
> it flowed like a river in the desert.
> For he remembered his holy promise
> given to his servant Abraham.
> He brought out his people with rejoicing,
> his chosen ones with shouts of joy;
> he gave them the lands of the nations,
> and they fell heir to what others had toiled for—
> that they might keep his precepts
> and observe his laws.
> Praise the LORD.
> —Psalm 105:39–45

The psalmist has made his point; the Lord has honored his everlasting covenant with Israel, and he is worthy of all praise. His protection, deliverance, and faithfulness are everywhere evident in the specific details and in the grand sweep of Israel's history. His sketch of Israel's trek through the wilderness and the conquest of the Promised Land are only briefly

---

10 Ross, *Psalms*, 3:269.

mentioned. The psalmist credits the Lord's provision of food, water, and guidance to his commitment to honor his promise to Abraham. "For he remembered his holy promise given to his servant Abraham" (v. 42). The psalmist doesn't actually come out and say, "And what more shall I say? I do not have time to tell about . . ." (Heb. 11:32), but he leaves that impression. He closes with a spirited description of joyful deliverance, abundant blessing, and renewed obedience to the will of God.

> Remember this! He led his people out singing for joy;
> his chosen people marched, singing their hearts out!
> He made them a gift of the country they entered,
> helped them seize the wealth of the nations
> So they could do everything he told them—
> could follow his instructions to the letter.
> Hallelujah!
> —Psalm 105:43–45 MSG

A COVENANT-BREAKING PEOPLE

Psalms 105 and 106 form a diptych, a two-paneled work of art that is meant to hang together. These two long psalms are dedicated to the great faithfulness of the Lord and his covenant love. Salvation history bears witness to God's sustaining grace from the call of Abraham to the conquest of the Promised Land. Yahweh is worthy of all praise for remembering and acting on his holy promise to his servant Abraham (Ps. 105:42). In Psalm 105 there is an intentional omission: little is said about human ingratitude and rebellion. The focus is entirely on external threats to the patriarchs and the Israelites in Egypt and the Lord's protection, provision, and deliverance. The inspiration for praise is the Lord's steadfast love overcoming insurmountable obstacles to sustain his people in spite of outside opposition.

Psalm 106 retraces this same history, but this time the focus is on the many ways the people of God resisted the will of the Lord and rejected his love and mercy. Psalm 105 is a eulogy, recounting the blessings of God; Psalm 106 is a confession, recounting the waywardness of Israel. But the theme and purpose of both psalms leads the worshiper to praise the Lord for his great faithfulness. The apostle Paul made reference to "a trustworthy saying" in the early church: "If we died with him, we will also live with him; if we endure, we will also reign with him. If we disown him, he will also disown us; if we are faithless, he remains faithful, for he cannot disown himself" (2 Tim. 2:11–13). Both Psalm 106 and the early church's saying emphasize the Lord's faithfulness in the midst of our willfulness and weakness.

The opening and closing sections (vv. 1–5; 47–48) are critical for defining this final psalm of Book 4 as a psalm of praise and placing the long middle section (vv. 6–46) in perspective. It is important to take in the movement of the whole psalm so as not to turn Psalm 106 into simply a survey of the Old Testament. A verse-by-verse exposition of the psalm, which references all the Old Testament texts alluded to in the psalm, may be valuable in explaining the text, but such a method does not necessarily bring out the purpose and the power of the psalm. It is easy to get lost in historical detail if we give the same weight to each verse and do not allow the momentum of the psalm to carry us along. The lengthy confession describes seven incidents, all of which are woeful acts of disobedience (vv. 6–33), followed by an eighth case study in evil with a sevenfold description of outrageous paganization (vv. 34–39). The psalmist orchestrates a dark crescendo that leaves the people of God without excuse and presents in bold relief the Lord's faithfulness to his holy promises—his everlasting covenant.

SHARED JOY

> Praise the LORD. [Hallelujah!]
> Give thanks to the LORD, for he is good;
> his love endures forever.
> Who can proclaim the mighty acts of the LORD
> or fully declare his praise?
> Blessed are those who act justly,
> who always do what is right.
> Remember me, LORD, when you show favor to your people,
> come to my aid when you save them,
> that I may enjoy the prosperity of your chosen ones,
> that I may share in the joy of your nation
> and join your inheritance in giving praise.
> —Psalm 106:1–5

The psalmist's personal passion for praise is evident from the outset. These opening verses reflect Asaph's prayer when the ark of the covenant was brought into Jerusalem (1 Chronicles 16) as well as Jeremiah's hopeful prophecy for the return of the exiles to the land of Judah (Jer. 33:10–11). The psalmist draws from and contributes to a rich tradition of worship that combines praise, thanksgiving, and humility. This invitation to praise recalls the "liturgy at the gate" of Psalm 15—the worship protocol of personal preparation and self-examination. No one is adequate to do justice to "the mighty acts of the LORD or fully declare his praise" (Ps. 106:2). But beatitude-based belief delights in God's justice and always seeks his righteousness. Miserable sinners we most certainly are (1 John 1:9–10), but the passion for praise means nothing if it is not joined with a passion for justice and righteousness (Mic. 6:8).

"Remember me" is voiced without a hint of self-centeredness. Kidner writes, "This little prayer beautifully relates the one to the many, refusing to lose the individual in the crowd, yet retreating into no private corner of enjoyment."[1] Implied in this remembrance is the inclusiveness of the "body-and-soul-in-community."[2] The individual's blessing is all wrapped up in the blessing of "your people," "your chosen ones," "your nation," and "your inheritance." There are no independent proprietors, only "fellow citizens with God's people and also members of his household, built on the foundation of the apostles and prophets, with Christ Jesus himself as the chief cornerstone" (Eph. 2:19–20). It is difficult to imagine the apostles praying Psalm 106 any other way. In the light of Christ, is there any other way to receive the invitation to praise than through the Lord Jesus Christ?

CONFESSION OF INDIFFERENCE

We have sinned, even as our ancestors did;
we have done wrong and acted wickedly.
When our ancestors were in Egypt,
they gave no thought to your miracles;
they did not remember your many kindnesses,
and they rebelled by the sea, the Red Sea.
Yet he saved them for his name's sake,
to make his mighty power known.
He rebuked the Red Sea, and it dried up;
he led them through the depths as through a desert.
He saved them from the hand of the foe;
from the hand of the enemy he redeemed them.

---

1   Kidner, *Psalms 73–150*, 378.
2   Stott, *Christian Mission*, 29–30.

The waters covered their adversaries;
not one of them survived.
Then they believed his promises
and sang his praise.

                                                    —Psalm 106:6–12

To say "we have sinned" is a necessary confession, and to say we
have sinned "even as our ancestors did" is a necessary acknowledgment.
We are no different from other generations. "For all have sinned and fall
short of the glory of God" (Rom. 3:23). The fallen human condition is
our shared solidarity. We are dead in our transgressions and sins. All of
us have gratified the cravings of our flesh and followed our own desires
and thoughts (Eph. 2:1–3). To hear the psalmist confess the sins of someone else and not our own is to be guilty of sin. We cannot pray Psalm
106 and forget this. If we do, we begin to think that our big problems
are fear, insecurity, loneliness, frustration, and anxiety, but these are
only symptoms of a far deeper problem. We need to trace the roots of
despair back to their source. Any illusion that a convenient marriage of
sentimental piety and self-help will free our souls is sadly mistaken. The
power of sin has us in its grip, and no amount of money, success, weight
loss, adventure, sex, plastic surgery, or power can free us from bondage.
There is no workout routine or cool set of friends that saves the soul.[3]

These seven case studies in evil, beginning with the apathy of the Israelites in Egypt over God's miraculous plagues, do not require exhaustive
exegetical analysis as much as corresponding reflection on how these sins
are manifest today. We do not need to look far in the New Testament
for examples of sinful indifference to God's saving acts. The preacher in
Hebrews exhorted believers, "We must pay the most careful attention,
therefore, to what we have heard, so that we do not drift away," adding,
"how shall we escape if we ignore so great a salvation?" (Heb. 2:1, 3).
Calvin acknowledged that "we will easily find that we have equal need"
to confess our sins, even as we all find it easier to excuse our sins rather
than confess our sins.[4]

In most of these confessions the Lord responds in a unique way to
judge and to save, but in this first one there is only redemption. The

---

3   Webster, *Christ Letter*, 29.
4   Calvin, *Psalms*, 6.4:211.

257

psalmist marvels that the Lord saved the Israelites from their Egyptian enemies in spite of their indifference. He saved them "for his name's sake" (Ps. 106:8). It was only after the fact that they came to believe in the promises and sing his praise.

CONFESSION OF CRAVING

> But they soon forgot what he had done
> and did not wait for his plan to unfold.
> In the desert they gave in to their craving;
> in the wilderness they put God to the test.
> So he gave them what they asked for,
> but sent a wasting disease among them.
> —Psalm 106:13–15

The epicenter of redemption prior to the cross of Jesus was the exodus. Ten plagues led up to the event, along with the Passover meal, the crossing of the Red Sea, and the annihilation of the Egyptian army. There is a lot there to forget! How could so much good news be so quickly forgotten? Added to their forgetfulness was their refusal to wait for God's unfolding plan, their craving for their Egyptian diet, and their insistence on putting God to the test.

Jesus in the wilderness stands in sharp contrast to the exodus Israelites in the wilderness (Luke 4:1–13). His disciplined commitment to the Father's will despite physical and spiritual hardships, plus his refusal to put the Lord to the test even though he was under extreme testing, demonstrated the power of faithfulness. Jesus embodied in himself what Israel was meant to do: "Worship the Lord your God and serve him only" (Luke 4:8; see Deut. 6:13).

The Lord's measured reaction to their discontent was to give them what they asked for. As with a willful child, the Lord used their own sinful attitudes and actions against them to prove the value of trusting in him. You want food? Here's food! (Num. 11:18–20), and "they gorged themselves so greedily that in the process many of them became ill and died."[5] When we read in Romans of God giving people up to their sinful desires (Rom. 1:24, 26, 28), it is not difficult to identify

---

5   Ross, *Psalms*, 3:288.

with the psalmist's statement, "So he gave them what they asked for" (Ps. 106:15).

CONFESSION OF ENVY

> In the camp they grew envious of Moses
> and of Aaron, who was consecrated to the LORD.
> The earth opened up and swallowed Dathan;
> it buried the company of Abiram.
> Fire blazed among their followers;
> A flame consumed the wicked.
> —Psalm 106:16–18

Envy and jealousy are added to the litany of evil coming between the Lord and his people. Instead of acknowledging the authority of God vested in Moses and Aaron, a small group of men "rose up against Moses" (Num. 16:2) and convinced two hundred and fifty leading Israelites to oppose Moses and Aaron and accuse them of pride and arrogance.

Did Psalm 106 inspire Stephen's speech before the Sanhedrin in Acts 7? There appears to be definite parallels between Israel's sins outlined in Psalm 106 and the pattern of stiff-necked, hard-hearted rebellion exposed by Stephen. He twice refers to the people's rejection of Moses. "This is the same Moses they had rejected with the words, 'Who made you ruler and judge?'" and again, "But our ancestors refused to obey him. Instead, they rejected him and in their hearts turned back to Egypt" (Acts 7:35, 39). This pattern of rebellious behavior cited by the psalmist and Stephen continues to plague the people of God today. Only, in the case of Moses and Aaron, the Lord intervened and saw fit to open up the earth and swallow the likes of Dathan and Abiram. But in the case of Jesus, the stiff-necked people who were just like their ancestors, always resisting the Holy Spirit, betrayed and murdered the Righteous One (Acts 7:51–52).

CONFESSION OF IDOLATRY

> At Horeb they made a calf
> and worshiped an idol cast from metal.
> They exchanged their glorious God
> for an image of a bull, which eats grass.

> They forgot the God who saved them,
> who had done great things in Egypt,
> miracles in the land of Ham
> and awesome deeds by the Red Sea.
> So he said he would destroy them—
> had not Moses, his chosen one,
> stood in the breach before him
> to keep his wrath from destroying them.
> —Psalm 106:19–23

The further we go into the confessions, the more dire the situation becomes until the Lord's patience seems at a breaking point. The idolatry of the golden calf and Aaron's "festival to the Lord" represents a new low for the people of God (Exodus 32–34). Undoubtedly, Aaron reasoned that a bull suggested Yahweh's "strength and liveliness."[6] But the psalmist sees an image of an ox that eats grass. "Although the idolaters feign to serve God with great zeal," wrote Calvin, "yet when, at the same time, they represent to themselves a God visible, they abandon the true God, and impiously make for themselves an idol."[7] To bow before an image "involves abandoning Yahweh for another deity."[8]

Moses, the Lord's chosen one, performed a startling redemptive act. He stood "in the breach" before God, "to keep his wrath from destroying them" (Ps. 106:23). It is not difficult to see that this act points forward to God's own Son. How can Christians pray this psalm without seeing this? Moses pled with God: "Oh, what a great sin these people have committed! They have made themselves gods of gold. But now, please forgive their sin—but if not, then blot me out of the book you have written" (Exod. 32:31–32). Jesus, the one greater than Moses, "was sacrificed once to take away the sins of many" (Heb. 9:28). "God made him who had no sin to be sin for us, so that in him we might become the righteousness of God" (2 Cor. 5:21). Psalm 106 gave the apostle Paul

---

6   Goldingay, *Psalms*, 3:230.
7   Calvin, *Psalms*, 6.4:223. Calvin distinguishes here the metal calf from the ark of the covenant: "Should any one be disposed to say that the ark of the covenant was a representation of God, my answer is, that that symbol was given to the children of Israel, not to engross the whole of their attention, but only for the purpose of assisting and directing them in the spiritual worship of God."
8   Goldingay, *Psalms*, 3:230.

the words he used in Romans 1 to describe human depravity. The line "Although they claimed to be wise, they became fools and exchanged the glory of the immortal God for images made to look like a mortal human being and birds and animals and reptiles" (Rom. 1:22–23) comes right out of Psalm 106:20.

CONFESSION OF DISOBEDIENCE

> Then they despised the pleasant land;
> they did not believe his promise.
> They grumbled in their tents
> and did not obey the LORD.
> So he swore to them with uplifted hand
> that he would make them fall in the wilderness,
> make their descendants fall among the nations
> and scatter them throughout the lands.
> —Psalm 106:24–27

The confession continues with a description of Israel's refusal to enter the Promised Land. This rebellion involved a cluster of related sins. The majority despised the gift of God, rejected his promise, grumbled against the Lord, and disobeyed him (Num. 13:26–14:45). Their refusal to go into the Promised Land summed up their chronic contempt for God. "Kadesh became the symbol of Israel's disobedience, the place where God's past redemption was forgotten and where divine promise no longer impelled the people to obedience."[9] There was a persistent pattern of stubborn rebellion and hard-hearted resistance to the will of God. Their constant waywardness is captured in the Lord's verdict: "Their hearts are always going astray, and they have not known my ways" (Heb. 3:10; cf. Ps. 95:10).[10]

We are more like the Israelites in the wilderness than we care to admit. We are guilty of turning "away from the living God" (Heb. 3:12) in self-justifying ways that impress us as preeminently reasonable. Like the majority report of the twelve spies, we are ready to capitulate

---

9   Lane, *Hebrews*, 1:85.
10 See Psalm 95. The author of Hebrews saw a close parallel between the wilderness generation and the recipients of his letter.

to the perceived strength of the prevailing culture. The culture before us is stronger than we are, and we lack the faith and resolve to boldly proclaim and live the gospel. We have chimed in with the "bad report" and concluded, "We seemed like grasshoppers in our own eyes, and we looked the same to them" (Num. 13:33).[11]

CONFESSION OF APOSTASY

> They yoked themselves to the Baal of Peor
> and ate sacrifices offered to lifeless gods;
> they aroused the LORD's anger by their wicked deeds,
> and a plague broke out among them.
> But Phinehas stood up and intervened,
> and the plague was checked.
> This was credited to him as righteousness
> for endless generations to come.
> —Psalm 106:28–31

With the speed of a fast-paced movie trailer, the psalmist races through Israel's wilderness history, highlighting in graphic detail the people's faithlessness. Instead of being yoked to Yahweh, many were seduced to worship Baal of Peor (Num. 25:3). They openly engaged in sexual immorality with Moabite women, participated in the sacrificial meals to Baal, and bowed before their inert, dead gods. The anger of the Lord is not a temperamental outburst but a meted-out, measured punishment designed to stop the apostasy in its tracks. Phinehas receives special commendation by the Lord because "he was as zealous for my honor among them as I am" (Num. 25:11).

CONFESSION OF REBELLION

> By the waters of Meribah they angered the Lord,
> and trouble came to Moses because of them;
> for they rebelled against the Spirit of God,
> and rash words came from Moses' lips.
> —Psalm 106:32–33

---

11 Webster, *Preaching Hebrews*, 78.

The psalmist's closing illustration of the Israelites in the wilderness goes back to the incident at Meribah so as to explain why Moses was unable to enter the Promised Land (Numbers 20). Up until now Moses had always acted as Yahweh's representative, a mediator on behalf of God and the people. But at Meribah, Moses took the people's rebellion personally as an act of defiance, not only against Yahweh, but against himself. When he struck the rock in anger, instead of speaking to the rock as the Lord had commanded, and said, "Listen, you rebels, must we bring you water out of this rock?" (Num. 20:10), he put himself on the same level as the Lord. In that instance he was no longer representing the Lord, but himself.

CONFESSION OF PAGAN ASSIMILATION

> They did not destroy the peoples
> as the LORD commanded them,
> but they mingled with the nations
> and adopted their customs.
> They worshiped their idols,
> which became a snare to them.
> They sacrificed their sons
> and their daughters to false gods.
> They shed innocent blood,
> the blood of their sons and daughters,
> whom they sacrificed to the idols of Canaan,
> and the land was desecrated by their blood.
> They defiled themselves by what they did;
> by their deeds they prostituted themselves.
> —Psalm 106:34–39

Israel was meant to be a light to the nations (Isa. 49:6). The Lord intended them to be his treasured possession, a kingdom of priests, and a holy nation, all for the sake of the salvation of the nations (Exod. 19:5–6). The Lord mandated Israel to be an instrument of judgment, because of the evil perversity and violent intensity of the Canaanite inhabitants. But instead of living into their identity as the people of God, they became just like all the other surrounding nations. Israel's integrity and survival as the people of God depended upon obeying God's specific command to destroy the nations occupying the Promised

Land. Israel and the church were *set apart* and *set above* for the holy purpose of revealing the one and only God to all the nations, but their respective strategies are polar opposites. The church is commanded to "go and make disciples of all nations, baptizing them in the name of the Father and of the Son and of the Holy Spirit, and teaching them to obey everything I have commanded you" (Matt. 28:19–20). Joshua's conquest strategy was necessary in his day, and Jesus's Great Commission strategy is necessary in our day. The power of the cross, which refuses to rely on violence and coercion, replaces political and military aggression. Under no circumstances were the Israelites to accommodate themselves to the surrounding cultures. These idolatrous and degenerate cultures were judged by God to be a serious threat to the identity of the people of God. The message of Moses left little doubt as to how Israel was to operate in the culture (Deut. 7:2–6).

The eighth confession is focused on the danger of paganization. This sin involves seven charges: disobedience to the Lord's command, rapid cultural accommodation and assimilation through intermarriage, blatant idolatry, pagan religious syncretism, child sacrifice, violence against innocent people, and sexual immorality. The litany of evil ends with a depressing array of personal and social evils. These acts are antithetical to the will of God yet consistent with human depravity.

The danger of pagan assimilation remains, but the strategy of cultural impact has changed. The apostle Peter understood this dynamic, believing that a positive Christian identity would prove not only resilient but persuasive in the face of evil. He exhorted believers, "Live such good lives among the pagans that, though they accuse you of doing wrong, they may see your good deeds and glorify God on the day he visits us" (1 Peter 2:12). Peter's Christ-*for*-culture strategy includes what Christ opposes in our sinful, broken, and fallen human culture, not for the sake of opposition, but for the sake of redemption and reconciliation.

THE LORD'S JUDGMENT AND MERCY

Therefore the LORD was angry with his people
and abhorred his inheritance.
He gave them into the hands of the nations,

and their foes ruled over them.
Their enemies oppressed them
and subjected them to their power.
Many times he delivered them,
but they were bent on rebellion
and they wasted away in their sin.
Yet he took note of their distress
when he heard their cry;
for their sake he remembered his covenant
and out of his great love he relented.
He caused all who held them captive
to show them mercy.
                    —Psalm 106:40–46

The psalmist sums up the dark side of salvation history with an all-encompassing description that ranges from the period of the Judges to the Babylonian exile. In spite of chronic rebellion and persistent sin, the good news of God's great love prevails. The Lord remembers his covenant and acts to save his people. The psalmist's sober confession remains true today, "We have sinned, even as our ancestors did; we have done wrong and acted wickedly" (v. 6). Faithful believers do not stand over ancient Israel in judgment; we stand with them in solidarity. At every turn the Lord's grace prevails and persists in spite of great sin, both their sin and ours. The extension of God's grace to the Israelites made God's grace in Christ possible. This is why when Augustine came to the end of Psalm 106 he exclaimed, "Come then, whoever reads this, and recognize the grace of God, by which we are redeemed unto eternal life through our Lord Jesus Christ."[12]

The apostles frequently turned to the dark side of Israel's rebellious history as a warning against apathy and apostasy. They drew a direct line from Israel to the church and made a case for learning from Israel's mistakes. "Now these things occurred as examples to keep us from setting our hearts on evil things as they did" (1 Cor. 10:6). The author of Hebrews wrote, "Let us, therefore, make every effort to enter that rest, so that no one will perish by following their example of disobedience" (Heb. 4:11). Psalm 106 is a good reminder to the followers of Christ to check any idealistic and triumphalist notions of the church. We ought

---

12   Augustine, *Expositions of the Psalms*, 8:531.

to pray like the psalmist, "Remember me, LORD, when you show favor to your people, come to my aid when you save them" (Ps. 106:4).

"SAVE US!"

Save us, LORD our God,
and gather us from the nations,
that we may give thanks to your holy name
and glory in your praise.
Praise be to the LORD, the God of Israel,
from everlasting to everlasting.
Let all the people say, "Amen!"
Praise the LORD.
—Psalm 106:47–48

The first believers who prayed this psalm envisioned the Lord gathering the exiled children of Abraham back to the Promised Land. Believers today envision the global church, made possible by the mercy of God, gathering disciples from "every nation, tribe, people and language" (Rev. 7:9). Meanwhile, we await the coming King in a posture of humility and in an attitude of praise. Psalm 106 prompts us to "work out [our] salvation with fear and trembling, for it is God who works in [us] to will and to act in order to fulfill his good purpose" (Phil. 2:12–13). Book 4 ends with an enthusiastic declaration of praise. The tragedy of human depravity will not prevail, but the triumph of the Lord's steadfast love and faithfulness will. Praise the Lord. Hallelujah!

BIBLIOGRAPHY

Allen, Leslie C. *Psalms 101–150*. Word Biblical Commentary 21. Grand Rapids: Zondervan, 2015.

Allen, Roland. *Missionary Methods: St. Paul's or Ours?* Grand Rapids: Eerdmans, 1962.

Alter, Robert. *The Art of Biblical Poetry*. New York: Basic Books, 1986.

Andersen, Francis I. *Job*. Tyndale Old Testament Commentaries. Downers Grove, IL: InterVarsity, 2008.

Anderson, A. A. *Psalms*. 2 vols. The New Century Bible Commentary. Grand Rapids: Eerdmans, 1972.

Anderson, Leith. *Dying for Change*. Minneapolis: Bethany House, 1990.

Anderson, Ray Sherman. *On Being Human: Essays in Theological Anthropology*. Grand Rapids: Eerdmans, 1982.

Athanasius. "The Letter of St. Athanasius to Marcellinus on the Interpretation of the Psalms." In *On the Incarnation*, 97–119. Crestwood, NY: St. Vladimir's Seminary Press, 1977.

Augustine. *Confessions*. Translated by Henry Chadwick. Oxford University Press. 1992.

———. *Expositions of the Psalms*. Edited by John E. Rotelle. Translated by Maria Boulding. Vol. 3, bks. 15–20 of *The Works of Saint Augustine: A Translation for the 21st Century*. New York: New City, 2000.

———. *Expositions on the Book of Psalms*. Translated by A. Cleveland Coxe. First Series, Vol. 8 of *Nicene and Post-Nicene Fathers*, edited by Philip Schaff. Peabody, MA: Hendrickson, 1995.

Barclay, John M. G. *Paul and the Gift*. Grand Rapids: Eerdmans, 2015.

Barclay, William. *Beatitudes and the Lord's Prayer for Everyman*. New York: Harper Collins, 1975.

Barrett, Lisa Feldman. "When Is Speech Violence?" *The New York Times*, July 15, 2017. https://www.nytimes.com/2017/07/14/opinion/sunday/when-is-speech-violence.html.

Barth, Karl. *The Christian Life: Church Dogmatics*, IV/4. *Lecture Fragments*. Translated by Geoffrey W. Bromiley. Grand Rapids: Eerdmans, 1981.

_____. *Dogmatics in Outline*. Translated by G. T. Thomson. New York, Harper & Row, 1959.

Barth, Markus. *Ephesians 1–3*. Vol. 34 of *The Anchor Bible*. New York: Doubleday, 1974.

Bauckham, Richard. *The Climax of Prophecy: Studies on the Book of Revelation*. London: T&T Clark, 1993.

Beale, G. K. *The Book of Revelation*. Grand Rapids: Eerdmans, 1999.

Beale, G. K., and D. A. Carson, eds. *Commentary on the New Testament Use of the Old Testament*. Grand Rapids: Baker, 2007.

Becker, Ernest. *The Denial of Death*. New York: Simon & Schuster, 1973.

Belcher, Richard P. *The Messiah and the Psalms: Preaching Christ from All the Psalms*. Geanies House, Fearn, Ross-shire, Scotland: Mentor, 2006.

Blaiklock, E. M. "Caesarea Philippi." In *Zondervan Pictorial Encyclopedia of the Bible*, edited by Merrill Tenney, 1:682–83. Grand Rapids: Zondervan, 1975.

Blamires, Harry. *The Christian Mind*. London: SPCK, 1978.

Boice, James Montgomery. *Psalms*. 3 vols.. Grand Rapids: Baker, 1996.

Bonhoeffer, Dietrich. *The Cost of Discipleship*. Translated by R. H. Fuller. New York: Macmillan, 1963.

_____. *Life Together*. Translated by John W. Doberstein. San Francisco: Harper Collins, 1954.

_____. *Meditating on the Word*. Translated by David McI. Gracie. New York: Ballantine, 1986.

_____. *Psalms: The Prayer Book of the Bible*. Minneapolis: Augsburg, 1970.

Bray, Gerald. *God Is Love: A Biblical and Systematic Theology*. Wheaton, IL: Crossway, 2012.

Brown, H. Jackson, Jr. *Life's Little Instruction Book*. Nashville: Rutledge Hill, 1991.

Bruce, F. F. *The Epistle to the Hebrews*. Grand Rapids: Eerdmans, 1990.

Brueggemann, Walter. *The Message of the Psalms*. Minneapolis: Augsburg, 1984.

_____. "The Psalms as Prayer," "Bounded by Obedience and Praise" In *The Psalms and the Life of Faith*, edited by Patrick Miller, 33–66, 189–216. Minneapolis: Fortress, 1995.

Brueggemann, Walter, and William H. Bellinger Jr. *Psalms*. New Cambridge Bible Commentary. New York: Cambridge University Press, 2014.

Bruner, Frederick Dale. *The Gospel of John: A Commentary*. Grand Rapids: Eerdmans, 2012.

_____. *Matthew: A Commentary*. 2 vols. Grand Rapids: Eerdmans, 2004.

Bryson, Bill. *A Short History of Nearly Everything*. New York: Broadway, 2004.

Buechner, Frederick. *Telling Secrets*. New York: HarperCollins, 1991.

Burch, George Bosworth. *Alternative Goals in Religion*. Montreal: McGill-Queen's University Press, 1973.

Calvin, John. Calvin's Commentaries: *The Book of Psalms, vol. 4: Psalms 1–35*, translated by Henry Beveridge; *vol. 5: Psalms 36–92*, and *vol. 6: Psalms 93–150*, translated by James Anderson, Grand Rapids: Baker, 1981.

Carson, D. A. *The Gospel according to John*. Grand Rapids: Eerdmans, 1991.

Chambers, Oswald. *So Send I You*. 1939. Reprint, London: Marshall, Morgan & Scott, 1964.

Chesterton, G. K. *Orthodoxy*. New York: Image, 1959.

Chrysostom, John. *Homilies on the Gospel of John*. Homilies 81–82. Vol. 14, first series of *Nicene and Post-Nicene Fathers*, edited by Philip Schaff, 299–306. Peabody, MA: Hendrickson, 1995.

_____. *Six Books on the Priesthood*. Translated by Graham Neville. Crestwood, NY: St. Vladimir's Seminary Press, 2003.

Clapp, Rodney L. "Shame Crucified." *Christianity Today*, March 11, 1991, 26–28.

Clarkson, Margaret. *A Singing Heart*. Carol Stream, IL: Hope Publishing Company, 1987.

Clifford, Richard J. *Psalms 73–150*. Nashville: Abingdon, 2003.

Colquhoun, Frank. *Hymns That Live*. Hadette, UK: Hodder & Stoughton, 1980.

Craigie, Peter. *Psalms 1–50*. Word Biblical Commentary 19. Waco, TX: Word, 1983.

Crick, Francis. *The Astonishing Hypothesis: The Scientific Search for the Soul*. New York: Simon & Schuster, 1994.

Cundall, A. E. "Baal." In *Zondervan Pictorial Encyclopedia of the Bible*, edited by Merrill Tenney, 1:431–33. Grand Rapids: Zondervan, 1975.

Cushman, Robert. *The Cry of a Stone*. Edited by Michael R. Paulick. Transcribed by James W. Baker. Plymouth, MA: General Society of Mayflower Descendants, 2016.

Davidson, Robert. *The Vitality of Worship: A Commentary on the Book of Psalms*. Grand Rapids: Eerdmans, 1998.

Dawkins, Richard. *The God Delusion*. Boston: Houghton Mifflin, 2006.

DeClaissé-Walford, Nancy, Rolf A. Jacobson, and Beth LaNeel Tanner. *The Book of Psalms*. The New International Commentary on the Old Testament. Grand Rapids: Eerdmans, 2014.

Delitzsch, Franz. *Biblical Commentary on the Psalms*. Vols. 1–3. Translated by Francis Bolton. Grand Rapids: Eerdmans, 1971.

Denham, Michael. *Reverberating Word: Powerful Worship*. Eugene, OR: Wipf & Stock, 2018.

Dillard, Annie. *Teaching a Stone to Talk: Expeditions and Encounters*. New York: Harper & Row, 1982.

Dinwiddie, Richard D. "The God Who Sings." *Christianity Today*, July 15, 1983, 21–24.

Dreher, Rod. *The Benedict Option: A Strategy for Christians in a Post-Christian Nation*. New York: Random House, 2017.

Dreyfus, Hubert, and Sean Dorrance Kelly. *All Things Shining: Reading the Western Classics to Find Meaning in a Secular Age*. New York: Free Press, 2011.

Dyrness, William. "Aesthetics in the Old Testament: Beauty in Context." *JETS* 28, no. 4 (December 1985): 421–32.

Eaton, John. *The Psalms*. New York: Continuum, 2005.

Elliot, Elizabeth. *Shadow of the Almighty: The Life and Testament of Jim Elliot*. New York: Harper & Row, 1958.

Elliott, John H. *1 Peter*. The Anchor Yale Bible. New Haven, CT: Yale University Press, 2000.

Ellul, Jacques. *The Political Illusion*. New York: Vintage, 1972.

Feinberg, C. L. "Asaph." In *Zondervan Pictorial Encyclopedia of the Bible*, edited by Merrill Tenney, 1:345. Grand Rapids: Zondervan, 1975.

Feinberg, John S. *Deceived by God? A Journey through the Experience of Suffering*. Wheaton, IL: Crossway, 1997.

France, R. T. *The Gospel of Matthew*. The New International Commentary on the New Testament. Grand Rapids: Eerdmans, 2007.

Futato, Mark D. *Interpreting the Psalms: An Exegetical Handbook*. Grand Rapids: Kregel, 2007.

Galli, Mark. "The Prodigal Sports Fan." *Christianity Today*, April 8, 2005, 49–50.

Gardiner, John Eliot. *Bach: Music in the Castle of Heaven*. New York: Knopf, 2014.

George, Timothy. *Theology of the Reformers*. Rev. ed. Nashville: Broadman & Holman, 2013.

Gillquist, Peter. "The Christian Life: A Marathon We Mean to Win?" *Christianity Today*, October 23, 1981, 22–23.

Goetz, David. *Death by Suburb*. San Francisco: HarperCollins, 2006.

Goldingay, John. *Psalms*. Vols. 1–3. Grand Rapids: Baker, 2006–2008.

Grant, Jamie A. *The King as Exemplar: The Function of Deuteronomy's Kingship Law in the Shaping of the Book of Psalms*. Atlanta: Society of Biblical Literature, 2004.

Grant, Robert. "O Worship the King." In *The Celebration Hymnal*, 104. Dallas: Word Music, 1997.

Griedanus, Sidney. *Preaching Christ from the Psalms: Foundations for Expository Sermons in the Christian Year*. Grand Rapids: Eerdmans, 2016.

Groothius, Doug. "The Church in Danger." *Moody Magazine*, February 2003, 36–37.

Guelich, Robert A. *The Sermon on the Mount: A Foundation for Understanding*. Waco, TX: Word, 1982.

Guthrie, George H. "Hebrews." In *Commentary on the New Testament Use of the Old Testament*, edited by G. K. Beale and D. A. Carson, 919–95. Grand Rapids: Baker, 2007.

Harink, Douglas. *1–2 Peter*. Brazos Theological Commentary on the Bible. Grand Rapids: Brazos, 2009.

Harrington, Samuel, MD. *At Peace: Choosing a Good Death after a Long Life*. New York: Grand Central Life and Style, 2018.

Hays, Richard B. *Echoes of Scripture in the Gospels*. Waco, TX: Baylor University Press, 2016.

———. *Echoes of Scripture in the Letters of Paul*. New Haven, CT: Yale University Press, 1989.

_____. *First Corinthians.* Interpretation: A Bible Commentary for Teaching and Preaching. Louisville, KY: Westminster John Knox, 1997.

Heine, Ronald, E. *Gregory of Nyssa's Treatise on the Inscriptions of the Psalms.* Oxford: Clarendon, 1995.

Henry, Carl F. H. *God, Revelation, and Authority.* Vol. 1. Dallas: Word, 1976.

Henry, Matthew. *Psalms.* Lexington, KY: n.p., 2016.

Herbert, George. *The Country Parson, The Temple.* Edited by John Wall. New York: Paulist, 1981.

Hess, Richard S. *The Old Testament: A Historical, Theological, and Critical Introduction.* Grand Rapids: Baker Academic, 2016.

Hestenes, Roberta. "Personal Renewal: Reflections on 'Brokenness.'" *TSF Bulletin* (November–December 1984): 23–24.

Hicks, Zac. *The Worship Pastor.* Grand Rapids: Zondervan, 2016.

Holmes, Catherine. *Annotations to William Faulkner's* The Hamlet. Oxford: Taylor & Francis, 1996.

Horton, Michael S. "How the Kingdom Comes." *Christianity Today*, January 1, 2006, 46.

Hunter, George. *Radical Outreach: The Recovery of Apostolic Ministry and Evangelism.* Nashville: Abingdon, 2003.

Hunter, James Davison. *To Change the World: The Irony, Tragedy, and Possibility of Christianity in the Late Modern World.* New York: Oxford University Press, 2010.

Jobes, Karen H. *1 Peter.* Baker Exegetical Commentary on the New Testament. Grand Rapids: Baker, 2005.

Kapolyo, Joe. "Matthew." In *Africa Bible Commentary*, edited by Tokunboh Adeyemo, 1105–170. Grand Rapids: Zondervan, 2006.

Keller, Phillip. *A Shepherd Looks at Psalm 23.* Grand Rapids: Zondervan, 1974.

Keller, Timothy, with Kathy Keller. *The Songs of Jesus: A Year of Daily Devotions in the Psalms.* New York: Viking, 2015.

Kidner, Derek. *Psalms 1–72.* Downers Grove, IL: InterVarsity, 1973.

Kierkegaard, Søren. *Attack upon "Christendom."* Translated by Walter Lowrie. Princeton, NJ: Princeton University Press, 1968.

———. *Either/Or: A Fragment of Life*. In *A Kierkegaard Anthology*, edited by Robert Bretall, 19–108. Princeton, NJ: Princeton University Press, 1946.

———. *Provocations: Spiritual Writings of Kierkegaard*. Edited by Charles E. Moore. Farmington, PA: The Plough Publishing House, 1999.

———. *Purity of Heart Is to Will One Thing*. Translated by Douglas V. Steere. New York: Harper & Row, 1956.

———. *The Sickness unto Death*. Princeton, NJ: Princeton University Press, 1974.

Kreeft, Peter. *Three Philosophies of Life: Ecclesiastes, Job, Song of Songs*. San Francisco: Ignatius, 2016.

Kuhn, H. B. "Names of God." In *Zondervan Pictorial Encyclopedia of the Bible*, edited by Merrill Tenney, 2:760–66. Grand Rapids: Zondervan, 1975.

Labberton, Mark. *Called: The Crisis and Promise of Following Jesus Today*. Downers Grove, IL: InterVarsity, 2014.

———. *The Dangerous Act of Worship: Living God's Call to Justice*. Downers Grove, IL: InterVarsity, 2007.

Lane, William L. *Hebrews*. 2 vols. Word Biblical Commentary 47a–b. Dallas: Word, 1991.

Leupold, Herbert C. *Exposition of the Psalms*. Grand Rapids: Baker, 1989.

Lewis, C. S. *The Four Loves*. New York: Harcourt Brace, 1960.

———. *A Grief Observed*. New York: Bantam Books, 1961

———. *Mere Christianity*. New York: Collier, 1960.

———. *Miracles*. London: Fontana, 1972.

———. *The Problem of Pain*. New York: Macmillan, 1962.

———. *Reflections on the Psalms*. New York: Harcourt Brace Jovanovich, 1958.

———. *Surprised by Joy*. London: Fontana, 1972.

———. *The Weight of Glory*. New York: Collier, 1965.

Lincoln, Andrew T. *Ephesians*. Word Biblical Commentary 42. Dallas: Word, 1990.

Longman, Tremper, III. *How to Read the Psalms*. Downers Grove, IL: InterVarsity, 1988.

Luther, Martin. *First Lectures on the Psalms: Psalms 1–75*. Luther's Works 10. Edited by Hilton C. Oswald. Saint Louis: Concordia, 1974.

Lyte, Henry F. "Praise, My Soul, the King of Heaven." *The Celebration Hymnal*, 1. Dallas: Word Music, 1997.

Mangina, Jospeh L. *Revelation*. Brazos Theological Commentary on the Bible. Grand Rapids: Brazos, 2010.

Martens, Elmer. *God's Design: A Focus on Old Testament Theology*. 3rd ed. North Richland Hills, TX: BIBAL, 1998.

McEwan, Ian. *Saturday*. New York: Knopf, 2006.

McKnight, Scot. *Kingdom Conspiracy*. Grand Rapids: Brazos, 2016.

Mounce, Robert. *Revelation*. New International Commentary. Grand Rapids: Eerdmans, 1994.

Mouw, Richard. "The Life of Bondage in the Light of Grace." *Christianity Today*, December 9, 1988, 41–44.

Muir, John. "A Wind-Storm in the Forests." Chap. 10 in *The Mountains of California*. New York: Century, 1894. https://vault.sierraclub.org/john_muir_exhibit/writings/the_mountains_of_california/chapter_10.aspx.

Neander, Joachim. "Praise to the Lord, the Almighty." *Psalter Hymnal*, 253. Grand Rapids: CRC, 1987.

Nehrbass, Daniel Michael. *Praying Curses: The Therapeutic and Preaching Value of the Imprecatory Psalms*. Eugene, OR: Pickwick, 2013.

Newbigin, Lesslie. *The Gospel in a Pluralistic Society*. Grand Rapids: Eerdmans, 1989.

———. *The Light Has Come: An Exposition of the Fourth Gospel*. Grand Rapids: Eerdmans, 1982.

Nicholi, Armand M., Jr. *The Question of God: C. S. Lewis and Sigmund Freud Debate God, Love, Sex, and the Meaning of Life*. New York: Free Press, 2002.

Nietzsche, Friedrich. *Beyond Good and Evil*. In *Basic Writings of Nietzsche*. Translated and edited by Walter Kaufmann. New York: Modern Library, 2000.

———. *The Gay Science*. Translated and edited by Walter Kaufmann. New York: Vintage, 1974.

Norris, Kathleen. "Why the Psalms Scare Us." *Christianity Today*, July 15, 1996, 21–23.

O'Brien, Peter T. *The Letter to the Hebrews*. Grand Rapids: Eerdmans, 2010.

Okorocha, Cyril, and Francis Foulkes. "Psalms." In *Africa Bible Commentary*, edited by Tokunboh Adeyemo, 605–746. Grand Rapids: Zondervan, 2006.

Old, Hughes Oliphant. *The Reaching and Preaching of the Scriptures in the Worship of the Christian Church: Moderatism, Pietism, and Awakening*. Vol. 5. Grand Rapids: Eerdmans, 2004.

Packer, J. I. *Keep in Step with the Spirit*. Old Tappan, NJ: Revell, 1984.

Paley, William. *Natural Theology: Evidences of the Existence and Attributes of the Deity Collected from the Appearances of Nature*. 1802.

Palmer, Parker, J. *The Courage to Teach: Exploring the Inner Landscape of a Teacher's Life*. San Francisco: Jossey-Bass, 1998.

Payne, Philip B. "Jesus's Implicit Claim to Deity in His Parables." *Trinity Journal* 2 (Spring 1981): 3–23.

Peterson, Eugene H. *Answering God: The Psalms as Tools for Prayer*. New York: Harper & Row, 1989.

———. *As Kingfishers Catch Fire: A Conversation on the Ways of God Formed by the Words of God*. Grand Rapids: Eerdmans, 2017.

———. *Christ Plays in Ten Thousand Places: A Conversation in Spiritual Theology*. Grand Rapids: Eerdmans, 2005.

———. *Earth and Altar: The Community of Prayer in a Self-Bound Society*. Downers Grove, IL: InterVarsity, 1985.

———. "Growth: An Act of the Will." *Leadership* (Fall 1988): 40–42.

———. *Leap Over a Wall: Earthy Spirituality for Everyday Christians*. San Francisco: Harper, 1997.

———. *A Long Obedience in the Same Direction: Discipleship in an Instant Society*. Downers Grove, IL: InterVarsity, 1980.

———. *The Message Remix*. Colorado Springs: NavPress, 2003.

———. *The Pastor: A Memoir*. New York: HarperOne, 2011.

———. *Reversed Thunder: The Revelation of John and the Praying Imagination*. San Francisco: Harper & Row, 1988.

———. *Working the Angles: The Shape of Pastoral Integrity*. Grand Rapids: Eerdmans, 1987.

Pollan, Michael. *In Defense of Food: An Eater's Manifesto*. New York: Penguin Books, 2009.

Reardon, Patrick Henry. *Christ in the Psalms*. Chesterton, IN: Ancient Faith, 2011.

Redman, Matt. "The Otherness of God." *Christianity Today*, September 7, 2004.

Robertson, O. Palmer. *The Flow of the Psalms: Discovering Their Structure and Theology*. Phillipsburg, NJ: P&R, 2015.

Ross, Allen P. *A Commentary on the Psalms*. 3 vols. Grand Rapids: Kregel, 2011, 2013, 2016.

_____. "Living and Worshiping with the Psalms." Sermon delivered at Beeson Divinity School, Birmingham, Alabama, September 7, 2006.

Rutledge, Fleming. *The Crucifixion: Understanding the Death of Jesus Christ*. Grand Rapids: Eerdmans, 2015.

Seifred, Mark. "Romans." In *Commentary on the New Testament Use of the Old Testament*, edited by D. A. Carson and G. K. Beale. Grand Rapids: Baker, 2007.

Sire, James W. *Praying the Psalms of Jesus*. Downers Grove, IL: InterVarsity, 2007.

Sittser, Gerald L. *A Grace Disguised*. Grand Rapids: Zondervan, 1996.

Smith, James K. A. *Desiring the Kingdom*. Grand Rapids: Baker, 2009.

_____. *Imagining the Kingdom: How Worship Works*. Grand Rapids: Baker, 2013.

Smith, Robert, Jr. *The Oasis of God: From Mourning to Morning—Biblical Insights from Psalms 42 and 43*. Mountain Home, AR: BorderStone, 2014.

Smith, Walter Chalmers. "Immortal, Invisible, God Only Wise." *The Celebration Hymnal*, 33. Dallas: Word Music, 1997.

Spurgeon, Charles H. *Christ's Words from the Cross*. Grand Rapids: Baker, 1997.

_____. *Spurgeon's Sermons on the Psalms*. Edited by Charles Cook. London: Marshall, Morgan & Scott, 1960.

_____. *The Treasury of David*. 1885. The Spurgeon Archive. https://archive.spurgeon.org/treasury.

Steyn, Mark. *America Alone: The End of the World as We Know It*. Washington, DC: Regnery, 2006.

Stott, John R. W. *Christian Counter-Culture: The Message of the Sermon on the Mount*. Downers Grover, IL: InterVarsity, 1978.

_____. *Christian Mission in the Modern World*. Downers Grove, IL: InterVarsity, 1975.

_____. *Favorite Psalms*. Chicago, IL: Moody, 1988.

_____. *God's New Society: The Message of Ephesians*. Downers Grove, IL: InterVarsity, 1979.

_____. "Meditation on Psalm 8." *Wheaton Alumni Magazine*, November 1975, 5–6.

Strawn, Brent A., and Roger E. Van Harn, eds. *Psalms for Preaching and Worship: A Lectionary Commentary*. Grand Rapids: Eerdmans, 2009.

Sullivan, Andrew. "Andrew Sullivan on the Opioid Epidemic in America." *New York Magazine*, February 2018. https://nymag.com/daily/intelligencer/2018/02/americas-opioid-epidemic.html.

Tada, Joni Eareckson. *Anger: Aim It in the Right Direction*. Torrance, CA: Rose, 2012.

Taylor, Charles. *A Secular Age*. Cambridge, MA: Harvard University Press, 2007.

Taylor, LaTonya. "The Church of O." *Christianity Today*, April 1, 2002, 43–45.

Temple, William. *Readings in St. John's Gospel*. London: Macmillan, 1959.

ten Boom, Corrie. *Clippings from My Notebook*. Nashville: Thomas Nelson, 1982.

Thielicke, Helmut. *Life Can Begin Again: Sermons on the Sermon on the Mount*. Eugene, OR: Wipf & Stock, 2003.

Turner, Steve. *Amazing Grace: The Story of America's Most Beloved Song*. New York: HarperCollins, 2002.

Volf, Miroslav. *Exclusion and Embrace: A Theological Exploration of Identity, Otherness, and Reconciliation*. Nashville: Abingdon, 1996.

von Balthasar, Hans Urs. *Unless You Become Like This Child*. San Francisco: Ignatius, 1991.

Waltke, Bruce K. *An Old Testament Theology*. Grand Rapids: Zondervan, 2007.

Waters, Larry J., and Roy B. Zuck, eds. *Why O God? Suffering and Disability in the Bible and Church*. Wheaton, IL: Crossway, 2011.

Webster, Brian L., and David R. Beach. *The Essential Bible Companion to the Psalms*. Grand Rapids: Zondervan, 2010.

Webster, Douglas D. *The Christ Letter: A Christological Approach to Preaching and Practicing Ephesians*. Eugene, OR: Cascade, 2012.

_____. *The Easy Yoke*. Colorado Springs: NavPress, 1995.

_____. *Finding Spiritual Direction*. Downers Grove, IL: InterVarsity, 1991.

_____. *Follow the Lamb: A Pastoral Approach to the Revelation*. Eugene, OR: Cascade Books, 2014.

_____. *The God Who Comforts*. Eugene, OR: Cascade, 2016.

_____. *The God Who Kneels*. Eugene, OR: Cascade, 2015.

_____. *The God Who Prays*. Eugene, OR: Cascade, 2017.

_____. "Intensity without Ultimacy: A Christian Perspective on Sports." *The Other Journal*, March 21, 2016. https://theotherjournal.com/2016/03/21/intensity-without-ultimacy-christian-perspective-sports.

_____. *Living in Tension: A Theology of Ministry*. 2 vols.. Eugene, OR: Cascade, 2012.

_____. *The Living Word: Ten Life-Changing Ways to Experience the Bible*. Chicago: Moody, 2003.

_____. "Oppression." In *Evangelical Dictionary of Theology*, edited by Walter A. Elwell, 799–801. Grand Rapids: Baker, 1984.

_____. *Outposts of Hope: First Peter's Christ for Culture Strategy*. Eugene, OR: Cascade, 2015.

_____. *A Passion for Christ: An Evangelical Christology*. Grand Rapids: Zondervan, 1987.

_____. *Preaching Hebrews: The End of Religion and Faithfulness to the End*. Eugene, OR: Cascade, 2017.

_____. *Second Thoughts for Skeptics*. Vancouver, BC: Regent College, 2010.

_____. *Soulcraft: How God Shapes Us through Relationships*. Downers Grove, IL: InterVarsity, 1999.

_____. *Soundtrack of the Soul: The Beatitudes of Jesus*. Toronto: Clements, 2009.

_____. *Text Messaging: A Conversation on Preaching*. Toronto: Clements, 2010.

Webster, Jeremiah. *A Rumor of Soul: The Poetry of W. B. Yeats*. Milwaukee: Wiseblood Books, 2015.

Weil, Simone. *Gravity and Grace*. New York: Routledge, 2002.

Weinberg, Steven. *The First Three Minutes: A Modern View of the Origin of the Universe*. New York: Basic Books, 1977.

Wells, David F. *No Place for Truth*. Grand Rapids: Eerdmans, 1993.

Wesley, John. "Serious Thoughts Occasioned by the Late Earthquake at Lisbon." In *The Works of John Wesley*, 11:1–13. New York: J. Emory & Waugh, 1818.

White, R. E. O. *A Christian Handbook to the Psalms*. Grand Rapids: Eerdmans, 1984.

———. "Salvation." In *Evangelical Dictionary of Theology*, edited by Walter Elwell, 967–69. Grand Rapids: Baker, 1984.

Wilberforce, William. *Real Christianity*. Edited by James M. Houston. Bloomington, MN: Bethany House, 1997.

Wilcock, Michael. *The Message of Psalms*. 2 vols. Downers Grove, IL: InterVarsity, 2001.

Wilson, Gerald H. *Psalms*. Vol. 1. NIV Application Commentary. Grand Rapids: Zondervan, 2002.

Wiman, Christian. *My Bright Abyss: Meditations of a Modern Believer*. New York: Farrar, Straus & Giroux, 2013.

Witvliet, John. *The Biblical Psalms in Christian Worship: A Brief Introduction and Guide to Resources*. Grand Rapids: Eerdmans, 2007.

Wolf, Katherine, and Jay Wolf. *Hope Heals: A True Story of Overwhelming Loss and an Overcoming Love*. Grand Rapids: Zondervan, 2016.

Wright, Christopher J. H. *An Eye for an Eye: The Place of Old Testament Ethics Today*. Downers Grove, IL: InterVarsity, 1983.

———. *The Mission of God: Unlocking the Bible's Grand Narrative*. Downers Grove, IL: InterVarsity, 2006.

Yancey, Philip. *The Bible Jesus Read*. Grand Rapids: Zondervan, 1999.

Yankelovich, Daniel. *New Rules: Searching for Self-Fulfillment in a World Turned Upside Down*. New York: Bantam, 1981.